신경향

핵심 영문독해

토익 · 토플 · 텝스 · 공무원시험 등
각종 시험을 위한 영문독해전략!

신규철 지음

신아사

머리말

인터넷 시대를 살아가는 우리에게 세계어로서 영어에 관한 관심과 그 영향이 점점 커가는 가운데, 영어 학습 방법에 대한 관심과 연구도 계속 깊이를 더 해가고 있다. 특히 영문독해는 영어학습의 제 영역 중 그 비중과 중요성이 매우 중요한 분야임을 아무도 부인하지 않는다. 그러나 영문독해에 대한 우리의 학습 방법을 돌이켜 보면, 대부분 짧은 지문과 어려운 내용의 단문독해를 통하여 어려운 문제를 풀고 어려운 단어를 사전에 의존하여 번역해 보는 과정을 계속해 왔다.

이에 필자는 이러한 부정적인 영문독해 방법에서 탈피하여 좀 더 흥미 있고 내용중심의 읽기가 되도록 독해유형별로 나누어 독해전략을 소개하고 주요 구문 설명과 어휘를 심층적으로 설명하여 보다 효율적인 학습이 되도록 하였다. 또한 독해문제를 풀어가는 과정을 자세한 풀이과정과 함께 소개하여 독해문제를 쉽게 이해하도록 만들었다.

이 책은 토익、토플、텝스、공무원 시험 및 대입 영어시험에 필요한 독해전략을 아울러 소개하고 있다. 아무쪼록 이 책을 통해 공부하는 학생들에게 영문독해에 대한 새로운 관심과 행운이 항상 함께 하기를 기원한다.

끝으로 이 책이 나오기까지 많은 도움을 주신 신아사 사장님과 편집진에게 감사의 말씀을 보낸다.

2008. 3.

지 은 이

Contents

CHAPTER 1

문맥속의 어휘

Vocabulary

Tips for Fluent Reading

영어 공부에 있어서 단어는 총알과도 같습니다. 군인이 전쟁에 나갈 때 총알이 많아야 유리하듯이, 단어는 많이 알면 알수록 영어 사용에 큰 도움이 됩니다. 많은 친구들이 외우는 것이 귀찮아 단어 공부를 게을리 합니다. 단어는 무작정 외우는 것이 아니라, 본문의 내용을 이해해가면서 문맥에 맞는 의미를 찾아가는 훈련을 통해 익히도록 해야 합니다.

Key Structure

I have **a dream** this afternoon **that the brotherhood of man will become a reality in this day**.(동격, 즉 **a dream=that the brotherhood of man ~day**.)

예제 1

I have a dream this afternoon, that the brotherhood of man will become a reality in this day. With this faith, I will go out and carve a tunnel of hope through the mountain of despair. With this faith, I will go out with you and transform dark yesterdays into bright tomorrows. With this faith, we will be able to achieve this new day when all of God's children, black men and white men, Jews and Gentiles, Protestants and Catholics will be able to join hands and sing with the negroes in the spiritual of all. Free at last! Free at Last! Thank God Almighty! (Martin Luther King Jr.)

1. Which of the following is closest in meaning to the word "despair"?

(a) insult (b) slaughter
(c) hopelessness (d) rapture

기초어휘

brotherhood 형제간, 형제의 연분 carve 베다, 새기다 Gentile 이방인, 이교도

심화어휘

1. brotherhood; 형제간, 형제의 우애[사랑], 조합, 협회

sisterhood; 자매임, 자매 관계, 자매의 도리[의리], 여성 단체[전도회, 자선회]
childhood; 어린 시절, 유년
neighborhood; 근처, 인근(隣近), 이웃, [집합적] 이웃 사람들(neighbors), (어떤 지역의) 주민

2. transform; 변형시키다, 〈성질 · 기능 · 용도 등을〉 바꾸다, 전환하다

transform a face 얼굴을 바꾸다
transform character 성격을 바꾸다
transform heat into energy 열을 에너지로 바꾸다
transform an area(a scene) 지역(장면)을 바꾸다

Key Structure

The energy the faith the devotion which we **bring** to this endeavor **will light** our country and all who serve it–and the glow from that fire can truly light the world.

하나의 문장 속에 두 개의 동사가 있을 때 첫 동사와 두 번째 동사 사이에 접속사/관계사가 없으면, 언제나 두 번째가 문장의 동사임–bring과 will light 사이에 접속사/관계사가 없으므로 will light이 문장 동사, 문장 주어는 The energy, the faith, the devotion.

예제 2~3

In the long history of the world, only a few generations have been granted the role of defending freedom in its hour of maximum danger. I do not shrink from this responsibility–I welcome it. I do not believe that any of us would exchange places with any other people or any other generation. The energy, the faith, the devotion which we bring to this endeavor will light our country and all who serve it–and the glow from that fire can truly light the world.

And so, my fellow Americans Ask not what your country can do for you–ask what you can do for your country.

My fellow citizens of the world: Ask not what America will do for you, but what together we can do for the freedom of man.

Finally, whether you are citizens of America or of the world, ask of us the same high standards of strength and sacrifice that we shall ask of you.

(John F. Kennedy: Inaugural Address)

2. The expression "shrink from" of closest in meaning to ____________.

(a) receive (b) hold up
(c) give out (d) evade

3. Which of the following is closest in meaning to the word "endeavor"?

(a) effort (b) negligence
(c) inattention (d) procrastination

기초어휘

shrink 오그라들다, 줄다 shrink from 움츠러들다 devotion 헌신, 전념
endeavor 노력 exchange places with 자리(입장)를 바꾸다

심화어휘

1. grant; (인정하여 정식으로) 주다, 수여하다, 〈탄원 · 간청 등을〉 승인하다, 허가하다

grant an exception 예외를 인정하다 grant holidays 휴가를 주다
grant money 돈을 주다

2. defend; 방어하다, 지키다, (언론 등에서)옹호하다

defend freedom 자유를 수호하다 defend a title 타이틀을 방어하다
defend the country 국가를 지키다

Key Structure

There are two factors **causing** this decrease in students seeking an MBA degree.
≪주어 바로 뒤에 오는 "동사원형ing"는 언제나 현재분사로 바로 앞의 주어를 수식한다.≫

예제 4~6

Business schools in the United states have Started to face harder times than ever. In recent years, only Harvard's MBA School has shown a substantial increase in enrollment. Both Princeton and Yale have seen decreases in their enrollments. Since 1990, the number of people receiving MBA degrees has dropped about 5 percent to 85000, and the trend of lower enrollment is expected to continue.

There are two factors causing this decrease in students seeking an MBA degree. The first one is that many graduates of four-year colleges are finding that an MBA degree does not guarantee a plush job on Wall Street, or in other financial districts of major American cities. Many of the entry-level management jobs are going to need students graduating with Master of Arts degrees in English and the humanities as well as those holding MBA degrees. Students have asked the question, "Is an MBA degree reallywhat I need to be best prepared for getting a good job?" The second factor has been the cutting of American payrolls and the lower number of entry-level jobs being offered. Business needs are changing, and MBA schools are struggling to meet the new demands.

4. The phrase 'trend of' is closest in meaning to ___________.
(a) reluctance of (b) drawback to
(c) movement toward (d) extraction

5. The word 'plush' most probably means _____________.
(a) legal (b) satisfactory
(c) fancy (d) reliable

6. The word 'struggling' is closest in meaning to which of the following?
(a) evolving (b) plunging
(c) starting (d) striving

기초어휘

enrollment 등록 guarantee 보장하다 plush 호화로운, 편안한

심화어휘

1. face; 〈사람 · 건물이〉 향하다, …에 면하다, 〈위험 · 재난 등에〉 정면으로 대하다, 대항하다, 〈사실 등에〉 직면하다, 직시하다

face the light 밝은 곳을 향하다　　face the future 미래에 맞서다
face a crisis 위기에 대처하다

2. offer; 〈물건 · 원조 등을〉 제공하다, 제출하다, 〈의견 등을〉 제의[제안]하다, 〈손 등을〉 내밀다

offer an opinion 의견을 제공하다　　offer a benefit 혜택을 제공하다
offer a course 과정을 제공하다

Key Structure

He **<u>is reported</u> <u>to be</u>** able to rally around him up to 3,000 fighters.

≪to+동사원형(능동형 단순 부정사)/to be+p.p(수동형 단순 부정사)의 시제는 문장 동사의 시제와 같다. 따라서 이 문장에서 to be의 시제는 문장 동사가 현재이므로 역시 같은 현재시제이다.≫

예제 7~8

Osama Bin Laden is both one of the CIA's most wanted men and a hero to many young people in the Arab world. He and his associates were already being sought by the US on charges of international terrorism, including in connection with the 1998 bombing of American embassies in Africa and last year's attack on the US Cole in Yemen.

Bin Laden, an <u>immensely</u> wealthy and private man, has been granted a safe haven by Afghanistan's ruling Taleban government. During his time in hiding, he has called for a holy war against the US, and for the killing of Americans and Jews. He is reported to be able to rally around him up to 3,000 fighters. He is also suspected of helping to set up Islamic training centres to prepare soldiers to fight in Chechnya and other parts of the former Soviet Union. (BBC report)

7. The word "immensely" is closest in meaning to ____________.

(a) narrowly　　(b) greatly
(c) imitatively　　(d) mysteriously

8. The word 'rally' most probably means ______________.

(a) reassemble (b) recoil

(c) rebel (d) rebound

기초어휘

associate 동료 on charge of ~의 혐의로 private 비밀스러운 haven 은신처 suspect 의심하다

심화어휘

1. charge; 〈지불을〉 부담시키다, 〈대가 · 요금을〉 청구하다, 비난하다, 고발하다, 책망하다 [종종 수동형으로] 〈의무 · 책임 등을〉 지우다, 과하다
charge for the shipping〈fueling/admission/handling〉 배송비〈연료비/입장료/취급료〉를 청구하다

2. set up; (1) 세우다, 똑바로 놓다 (2) 짜맞추다, 박제(剝製) 표본 등으로 만들다;장황(粧潢)하다(mount) (3) 시작하다, 창설[설정]하다 (4) 출발시키다 (5) (충분히) 지급하다, 제공하다, 갖추다
set up an alibi 알리바이를 증명하다 set up a business 사업체를 세우다
set up the standard 표준을 정하다

Key Structure

<u>It is</u> a very vulgar mind <u>that</u> would wish to command where he can have the service for the asking and have it with willingness and good feeling instead of resentment.

≪It is(was)~that 강조구문으로, a very vulgar mind를 강조하며, 여기서 that은 주격 관계대명사이다.≫

예제 9~10

While it is true that there is no law that compels us to say "Please" there is a social practice much older and more sacred than any law which enjoin us to be civil. And the first requirement of <u>civility</u> is that we should acknowledge a service. "Please" and "Thank you" are the small change with which we pay our way as social begins. They are the little courtesies by which we keep the machine of life oiled and running sweetly. They put our intercourse upon the basis of a friendly cooperation, an easy give-and-take, instead of on the basis of superiors dictating to inferiors. It is a very vulgar mind that would wish to command where he can have the service for the asking, and have it with willingness and good feeling instead of <u>resentment.</u> (Alfred Gardiner: *Many Furrows*)

9. The word 'civility' most probably means ___________.

(a) honesty (b) integrity

(c) politeness (d) fidelity

10. The word 'resentment' most probably means ___________.

(a) grief (b) madness

(c) delight (d)grudge

기초어휘

compel 강요하다 sacred 신성한 requirement 필요조건 change 잔돈 courtesy 예의 intercourse 교제 dictate 지시하다 vulgar 저속한 civility 정중, 예의바름

심화어휘

1.friendly; 친한, 정다운, 자기편의, (…에게) 호의 있는, (…에) 도움이 되는

friendly wind 순풍 friendly shower 단비

friendly game(match) 친선경기

2.command; 명령하다, 지휘하다, 〈감정 등을〉 지배하다, 억누르다

command silence 침묵을 명하다 command a ship 배를 지휘하다

command a fine view 경치가 좋다

Key Structure

Droplets and ice crystals behave somewhat like dust <u>**in the air made**</u> visible in a shaft of sunlight.

≪전치사 뒤에는 주어+동사가 올 수 없다. 따라서 the air made에서 the air는 주어가 아니고, made는 동사가 아닌 과거분사-dust를 수식-이다.≫

예제 11~13

What makes it rain? Rain falls from clouds for the same reason anything falls to earth.

The Earth's gravity pulls it. But every cloud is made of water droplets or ice crystals. Why doesn't rain or snow fall constantly from all clouds? The droplets or ice crystals in clouds are exceedingly small. The effect of gravity on them is <u>minute.</u> Air currents move and lift droplets so that net downward displacement is zero, even though the droplets are in constant <u>motion</u>.

Droplets and ice crystals behave somewhat like dust in the air made visible in a shaft of sunlight. To the casual observer, dust seems to act in a totally random fashion, moving about chaotically without fixed direction. But in fact dust particles are much larger than water droplets and they finally fall. The average size of a cloud droplets is only 0.0004 inches in diameter. It is so small that it would take sixteen droplets to grow to a diameter of 0.008 inches or large enough to it fall from the cloud. The average raindrop contains a million times as much water as a tiny cloud droplet. The growth of a cloud droplet to a size large enough to fall out is the cause of rain and other forms of precipitation. This important growth process is called "coalescence."

11. The word "minute" is closest in meaning to which of the following?

(a) second (b) tiny

(c) slow (d) steady

12. The word "motion" is closest in meaning to ____________.

(a) wind (b) change

(c) movement (d) humidity

13. The word "random" is closest in meaning to ______________.

(a) unpredictable (b) perplexing

(c) independent (d) abnormal

기초어휘

droplet 작은 물방울 displacement 치환 shaft 한 줄기 광선 coalescence 연합, 합체

심화어휘

1. visible; 눈에 보이는, (육안으로) 볼 수 있는, 명백한

visible rays 가시광선
visible increase(decrease) 눈에 두드러진 증가(감소)
visible impatience 눈에 보이는 초조함

2. random; 닥치는 대로의, 되는 대로의, 임의의

random guess 어림짐작 / random remark 두서없는 말
random sampling 무작위 표본추출

Key Structure

<u>It was</u> in the United States therefore <u>that</u> the great advances in nineteenth-century agricultural machinery first came.

≪It is(was)~that 강조구문이고 "in the United States"가 강조되고 있으며, 여기서 that은 관계부사 where와 같다.≫

예제 14~16

Agriculture in the nineteenth century involved two things: the invention of labor-saving machinery and the development of scientific agriculture. Labor-saving machinery <u>naturally</u> appeared first where labor was scarce. "In Europe," said Thomas Jefferson, "the object is to <u>make the most of</u> their land, labor being abundant; here it is to make the most of our labor, land being abundant." It was in the United States, therefore, that the great advances in nineteenth-century agricultural machinery first came.

At the opening of the century, with the exception of a crude plow, farmers could have carried practically all of the existing agricultural implements on their backs; by 1860, most of the machinery in use had been designed in an early form. The most important of the early inventions was the iron plow. As early as 1790 Charles Newbold of New jersey had been working in the idea of a cast-iron plow and spent his entire fortune in introducing his invention.

The farmers, however, were not interested in it, claiming that the iron poisoned the soil and made the weeds grow. Nevertheless, many people devoted their attention to the plow, until in 1869 James Oliver of South Bend, Indiana, turned out the first chilled-steel plow.

14. The word "naturally" is closest in meaning to ___________.

(a) unsurprisingly (b) gradually
(c) apparently (d) safely

15. The expression "make the most of" of closest in meaning to ___________.

(a) get the best yield from (b) raise the price of
(c) exaggerate the worth of (d) earn a living on

16. The word "here" refers to ________________.

(a) Europe
(b) the United States
(c) New Jersey
(d) Indiana

기초어휘

abundant 풍족한 yield 산출 implement 도구 crude 투박한, 조잡한
turn out 생산하다, 만들어내다

심화어휘

1. abundant; 풍부한, 많은

abundant resources 풍부한 자원 abundant supply 풍부한 공급
abundant harvest 풍작

2. carry; 나르다, 〈소식 · 소리 등을〉 전하다, 〈병을〉 옮기다, 휴대하다, 〈무게를〉 지탱하다

carry a message 메시지를 전하다
carry a driver's license 운전면허증을 휴대하다
carry an important meaning 중요한 의미를 지니다

Key Structure

The charming personality that his loving followers knew much more intimately than I **did made** his impression on one through one's meeting him face to face.
≪"did"는 knew를 대신하는 대동사이고, "made"가 문장 주어 The charming personality에 대한 동사이다.≫

예제 17~18

It seems to be certain that, for many centuries to come, Grant will be remembered as a heroic figure, but what is the future portrait of his going to be? The charming personality that his loving followers knew much more intimately than I did made his impression on one through one's meeting him face to face. At second or tenth hand, much of this vividness of personal impression will be lost, and, in time, may be all but gone. Will he be remembered as a great soldier? Without question he was one. But I suggest and I believe I am right, that his excellence in military affairs was not the foremost quality that distinguishes him from other national heroes.

17. The word "intimately" of closest in meaning to ____________.

(a) friendly (b) famously
(c) fatally (d) stately

18. The expression "Without question" of closest in meaning to __________.

(a) utterly (b) certainly
(c) deceitfully (d) exaggeratingly

기초어휘

vividness 생생함

심화어휘

1. figure; (아라비아) 숫자, (숫자) 계산, (윤곽이 뚜렷한) 꼴(shape), 형태 (사람의) 모습, (회화 · 조각 등의) 인물상, [보통 수식어와 함께] (중요한) 인물

double figures 두 자리 수 slender figure 날씬한 모습(몸매)
a prominent figure 거물

2. personal; 개인의, 사적인, 개인에 대한, 본인이 직접 하는

personal opinion 개인 의견 personal remarks 인신 공격
personal interview 직접 면접

Key Structure

The democratic doctrine of freedom of speech and of the press whether we regard it as a natural and inalienable right or not rests upon certain assumptions.
≪"whether we regard it as a natural and inalienable right or not"은 삽입절로 부사절(양보의 의미)이다.≫

예제 19~20

The democratic doctrine of freedom of speech and of the press, whether we regard it as a natural and inalienable right or not, <u>rests upon</u> certain assumptions. One of these is that men desire to know the truth and will be disposed to be guided by it. Another is that the sole method of arriving at the truth <u>in the long run</u> is by the free competition of opinion in the open market. Another is that, men will inevitably differ in their opinion, provided they accord to others the same right. And the final assumption is that from this mutual tolerance and comparison of diverse opinions the one that seems the most rational will emerge and be generally accepted.

(Carl L. Becker: *Freedom of speech and press*)

19. The phrase 'rest upon' is closest in meaning to ______________.

(a) base on　(b) depend on
(c) hold on　(d) keep on

20. The expression "in the long run" of closest in meaning to ___________.

(a) in large quantities　(b) frequently
(c) in the end　(d) for a long time

기초어휘

assumption 가설　competition 경쟁　inevitable 피할 수 없는　tolerance 관용
doctrine 원리　inalienable 양도할 수 없는　be disposed to ~하고 싶은 기분이다
the open market 공개 시장, 공개 토론장　urge 주장하다, 권하다　strenuously 열렬하게
accord 주다, 허용하다　diverse 다양한　rational 이성적인

심화어휘

1. mutual; 서로의, 상호의, 서로 관계있는, 공동의, 공통의

mutual friend 서로간의 친구/mutual respect 상호 존중/mutual distrust 상호 불신

2. accept; 〈선물 등을 기꺼이〉 받아들이다, 〈여자가 남자의〉 구혼에 응하다, 〈초대 · 신청 · 임명 등을〉 수락하다, 받아들이다, 〈설명 · 학설 등을〉 인정하다, 용인하다, 믿다

accept an offer 제안을 받아들이다
accept a low salary 낮은 월급을 받아들이다
accept the job(position) 일자리(직책)를 받아들이다

Key Structure

Sometimes these efforts have only partial success so that the result is an individual whose heart continues to beat **but** whose brain is irreversibly damaged.

≪whose heart continues to beat과 whose brain is irreversely damaged는 등위접속사 but에 의해 병렬되며 공통의 선행사인 an individual을 수식함.≫

예제 21~22

Our primary purpose of transplantation is to define irreversible coma as a new criterion for death. There are two reasons why there is need for a definition: Improvements in <u>resuscitative</u> and supportive measures have led to increased efforts to save those who are desperately injured. Sometimes these efforts have only partial success so that the result is an individual whose heart continues to beat but whose brain is irreversibly damaged. The burden is great in patients who suffer permanent loss of intellect, on their families or, on the hospital beds already occupied by these comatose patients. <u>Obsolete</u> criteria for the definition of death can lead to controversy in obtaining organs for transplantation.

21. Which of the following is closest in meaning to the word "resuscitative" ?

(a) rewarding (b) retaliatory
(c) reviving (d) retroactive

22. The meaning of the word "Obsolete" is ____________.

(a) Outmoded (b) Operatic
(c) Resultant (d) Sordid

기초어휘

irreversible 변경할 수 없는, 회복할 수 없는 resuscitative 소생시키는
obsolete 진부한, 시대에 뒤진 criterion 기준, 표준 transplantation 이식

심화어휘

1. permanent; 영속하는, (반)영구적인, 상설의, 〈물건이〉 오래 가는;변색[퇴색]하지 않는

permanent residence 영주 permanent employment 종신 고용
permanent damage 영구적인 손상

2. occupy; 〈장소를〉 차지하다, 〈시일을〉 소비하다, …의 마음[주의]을 끌다, 점유하다, 〈군대 등이〉 점령[점거]하다, 〈지위 · 일자리를〉차지하다

occupy too much space 너무 많은 공간을 차지하다
occupy an important position 중요한 자리를 차지하다
occupy the fortress 요새를 점령하다

CHAPTER 2

직접 정보 찾기

Directly answered questions

Tips for Fluent Reading

글에서 직접적인 정보를 찾아 답을 하는 형식은 독해에서 비교적 쉬운 영역에 속한다. 글을 전체적으로 파악한 다음, 문제를 잘 이해하고, 문제에서 요구하는 정보를 글 가운데에서 찾아 답을 하면 된다. 이 때, 본문의 문장과 보기에 주어진 문장을 살펴보면 뜻은 같지만 모양이 다른 단어를 사용하는 경우가 많으므로 뜻이 같은 여러 단어를 알아두면 문제를 푸는 데 많은 도움이 될 것이다.

Key Structure

As for the preferred occupation of their future spouses civil servants topped the list among female students **while** the majority of male students preferred their spouses to be teachers.

≪종속접속사 while 앞 뒤에 상반되는 어구가 올 경우, while의 뜻은 "반면에"로 해석하면 된다.≫

예제 1

As for the preferred occupation of their future spouses, civil servants topped the list among female students while the majority of male students preferred their spouses to be teachers. A representative at the survey firm said that the findings suggest the growing preference among students for stable jobs amid the current economic slump.

1. Recent students want their spouses to have ____________.

(a) active jobs (b) creative jobs

(c) firm jobs (d) exciting jobs

기초어휘

preferred 우선의, 더 좋아하다 occupation 직업 spouses 배우자 civil servant 공무원
stable 안정된(= firm) amid ~이 한창일 때

심화어휘

1. stable; 안정된, 견실한, 동요하지 않는

stable job 안정적인 일자리 stable supply 안정적인 공급
stable economy 안정적인 경제

2. current; 지금의, 현재의, 현행의, 통용하는, 유통[유포]되고 있는, 현재 유행하는, 초서체의(running)

current issue 최근호(잡지 등) current news 현재의 뉴스(시사뉴스)
current writing 초서체

Key Structure

The Commerce Department report **set for release Tuesday** found that 143 million Americans, or 54 percent of the country, were using the internet as of September.
–"**set for release Tuesday**"는 컴마와 컴마 사이에 낀 삽입구로 분사구문이며, 이는 which was set for release Tuesday의 의미이다–

예제 2

Internet use continued to grow rapidly last year in the U.S., with new government data showing that the number of Americans using the Web in 2001 passed 50 percent of the population for the first time. The Commerce Department report, set for release Tuesday, found that 143 million Americans, or 54 percent of the country, were using the internet as of September. The number was up 26 percent from a year earlier.

2. According to the passage, what percent the number of Americans using web in 2001 was?

(a) 54% (b) 50%

(c) 26% (d) 25%

기초어휘

Commerce Department 통상부 as of 현재의 (as of May; 5월 1일 현재)

심화어휘

1. release(v); 〈사람 · 동물을〉 석방[방면]하다, 해방시키다, 〈폭탄을〉 투하하다, 면하게 하다, 〈영화 등을〉 개봉하다, 〈레코드 등을〉 발매하다, 〈뉴스 등을〉 발표하다, 공개하다

release prisoners 죄수들을 석방하다
release a report(information) 보고서(정보)를 발표하다
release a new product(film) 신제품(새 영화)을 발표하다

Key Structure

The airline has launched **a month-long in-flight music festival** in which musicians will play guitars and lively violin melodies as well as **taking requests from passengers.**

-상관접속사 "as well as"는 a month-long in-flight music festival"과 "taking requests from passengers"를 병렬로 연결하고 있다.-

예제 3

Want to escape the streets of the daily life? Indian domestic carrier Air Sahara began serenading its passengers to live music. The airline has launched a month-long in-flight music festival in which musicians will play guitars and lively violin melodies, as well as taking requests from passengers.

3. What service do Air Sahara prepare?

(a) Indian food
(b) De-stress program
(c) Live music
(d) In-flight movie

기초어휘

domestic 가정의, 국내의 carrier 운송회사 serenade 세레나데(를 연주하다)
launch 착수하다, 시작하다

심화어휘

1. domestic; 가정의, 가사의, 가정적인, 살림이 알뜰한, 〈동물이〉 길든, 국내의

domestic chores 집안 허드렛일
domestic flights 국내항공
domestic appliances 가정용품
domestic animal 가축

2. launch; 〈새로 만든 배를〉 진수(進水)시키다, 〈사람을〉 (세상 등에) 내보내다, 진출시키다, 〈기업 · 계획 등을〉 착수하다, 〈신제품 · 상품 따위를〉 시장에 내다, 〈책을〉 출판하다, 〈화살 · 창 등을〉 쏘다, 던지다; 〈어뢰 · 유도탄 · 로켓 등을〉 발사하다

launch a ship or a boat 배를 진수시키다
launch an investigation 조사를 시작하다
launch a new film, disc, or book 새로운 영화, 디스크, 책을 출시하다
launch a rocket, missile, or satellite 로켓, 미사일, 위성을 발사하다

Key Structure

When nicotine leaves the body, weight may return to where **it would have been if you hadn't smoked** especially if you continue the same eating and exercise habits.

≪it would have been if you hadn't smoked는 가정법 과거완료로 과거 사실에 대한 반대를 가정하고, if you continue the same eating and exercise habit은 직설법 현재의 조건절≫

예제 4

Nicotine does seem able to make the body burn more calories than might happen in normal circumstances. When nicotine leaves the body, weight may return to where it would have been if you hadn't smoked, especially if you continue the same eating and exercise habits. But you can counter that effect by either eating smaller portions to reduce the number of calories accumulated or getting more exercise to increase the amount of calories burned.

4. Choose the one which is NOT mentioned in the above passage.
(a) Nicotine make the body burn more calories.
(b) To stop smoking can make the weight return.
(c) Getting exercises can reduce the weight.
(d) Smoking can't reduce the weight.

기초어휘

portion 일부, 부분 accumulated 쌓이다, 축적되다

심화어휘

1. reduce; 〈양 · 액수 · 정도 따위를〉 줄이다, 〈신분 · 지위를〉 낮추다, 격하시키다, 영락[몰락]하게 하다

reduce consumption(spendings) 소비를 줄이다
reduce risks 위험을 줄이다 reduce demand 수요를 줄이다

Key Structure

When he **stopped working** he spent time on his other interests.
≪"stop+동사원형ing"~을 더 이상하지 않다/ "stop+to+동사원형"~하기 위해 걸음을 멈추다.≫

예제 5

Franklin retired from the printing business when he was in his forties. When he stopped working, he spent time on his other interests: science, inventions, and politics. Franklin was curious about everything. He was especially interested in electricity. He had a theory: his idea was that lightning was really electricity. To prove this, he performed his famous kite experiment: he attached a piece of metal to the top of the kite, a key to a kite string, and flew the kite during a storm. When lightning hit the piece of metal on the kite, Franklin touched the key. When he got a shock, he knew that this theory was correct.

5. Which of the following is NOT true of the passage?
   (a) Franklin is interested in invention.
   (b) Franklin believed lightning was really electricity.
   (c) Franklin enjoyed to fly a kite.
   (d) Franklin had gotten a shock by lightning.

기초어휘

retire 퇴직하다 electricity 전기 theory 이론 experiment 실험 attach 붙이다, 달다

심화어휘

1. perform; 〈임무 · 일 · 약속 · 명령 등을〉 이행하다, 실행하다, 〈의식 등을〉 집행[거행]하다, 〈극을〉 상연하다, 〈역(役)을〉 연기하다, 〈음악을〉 연주하다
   perform surgery 수술을 시행하다 perform a contract 계약을 이행하다
   perform analysis 분석을 시행하다
2. attach; 붙이다, [흔히 attach oneself로] 〈…을〉 (단체 등에) 소속시키다, 가입시키다 〈자격 · 조건 등을〉 (…에) 첨부하다, 첨가하다
   attach a price tag 가격표를 붙이다 attach an identification tag 이름표를 붙이다
   attach a condition 조건을 붙이다

Key Structure

Sometimes however the kings would pay the Vikings in order to persuade them **not** to attack.

≪부정사/분사/동명사를 부정하는 "not/never"는 이들 앞에 위치한다≫

예제 6

The Vikings made their attacks very quickly and without any warning. They were very cruel to the people of the towns they attacked, and they sometimes destroyed the towns by burning down the buildings. In some parts of Europe, the local kings would often fight against the Vikings. Sometimes, however, the kings would pay the Vikings in order to persuade them not to attack.

Although the Vikings were known as fierce warriors, they also built excellent ships.

The wooden Viking ships, called longboats, were able to sail even in very bad weather. Many Viking longboats were about 20 meters long, but some were nearly 90 meters long. The Viking sailors used both sails and oars to move their ships.

6. Which is the following is NOT true of the passage?
   (a) The vikings are fierce.
   (b) The vikings built excellent ships.
   (c) The vikings sometimes built their houses.
   (d) The viking ships are made of woods.

기초어휘

cruel 잔인한 persuade 설득하다 fierce 사나운 / oar 노

심화어휘

1. destroy; 파괴하다, 〈문서 등을〉 파기하다, 괴멸[박멸]하다, 무효로 하다, 〈계획 · 희망 등을〉 망치다
   destroy many lives 많은 사람을 죽이다 destroy hopes 희망을 말살시키다
   destroy credit cards 신용카드를 파기하다
2. fierce; 사나운, 흉포한, 〈열 · 감정 등이〉 격렬한, 〈비 · 바람 등이〉 거센, 〈경쟁이〉 치열한, 지독한, 불쾌한
   fierce heat[cold] 혹서[혹한] fierce pain 격통
   a fierce cold 지독한 감기

Key Structure

Many Chinese men died in accidents while constructing the railroads.(=while they constructed the railroads)

≪"while constructing the railroads"는 분사구문이고, 시간적 의미인 것을 명확히 보여주기 위해 접속사 "while"을 생략하지 않고 쓴 것이다.≫

예제 7

Thousands of Chinese men were brought to North America to work on the railroads. They did good work, but their employers treated them badly. The work day was very long, and working conditions were very unsafe. Many Chinese men died in accidents while constructing the railroads. Some Chinese women also came to North America, but there were many more men than women.

After the railroads were completed, by about the year 1900, very few Chinese people were allowed to come to North America. Most people in Canada and the United States were not familiar with Chinese people and did not want strangers to come to their countries. Any Chinese person who came to North America had to pay an expensive tax. This made it difficult for Chinese men to bring their wives and families to join them in North America. Later, the governments of Canada and the United States made Chinese immigration illegal.

7. The underlined This refers to ______________________.

(a) Any Chinese person who came to North America had to pay an expensive tax.

(b) North America

(c) Chinese person

(d) strangers

기초어휘

be familiar with~ ~에 익숙하다 immigration 이주, 이민 illegal 불법의

심화어휘

1. treat; 대우하다, 다루다, 취급하다, 치료하다, (따뜻하게) 대접하다, …에게 한턱을 내다

treat fairly 공평하게 대우하다 treat alike 똑같이 취급하다
treat hypertension 고혈압을 치료하다
treat ~ to an ice cream[a movie]. ~에게 아이스크림을 사 주다[영화를 구경시켜 주다]

2. construct; 건설[건조]하다, 세우다, (부품 등을) 조립하다, 〈문장 · 논문 등을〉 구성하다

construct a house 집을 짓다
construct a road(dam/railway/canal) 도로(댐/철도/운하)를 건설하다

Key Structure

One of the most recognized and widely debated **terms** in recent times is "globalization."

≪전치사 뒤에는 동사가 올 수 없으므로 "recognized"는 동사가 아닌 과거분사이고, 등위접속사 and 뒤의 debated 또한 과거분사로 둘 다 명사 "terms"를 꾸민다.≫

예제 8

One of the most recognized and widely debated terms in recent times is "globalization." While there is little consensus as to what it actually is, there is little doubt that the world has in one way or another become more inter-connected. Mass communications and transportation technology, in addition to the rise of transnational corporate culture, have combined to produce a new global culture.

8. The phrase "a new global culture" in line 6 refers to ______________.

(a) world
(b) globalization
(c) communications
(d) transportation technology

기초어휘

debate 논쟁하다 obalization 세계화 consensus 일치, 여론 to~ ~에 관하여
transnational 초국적의, 다국적의 combine 결합시키다

심화어휘

1. term; (일정한) 기간, 기한, 임기, [pl.] 교제 관계, (친한) 사이, [pl.] (지불 · 요금 등의) 조건, 조항, 용어

a term of service 복무기간
be on good terms with -와 좋은 사이이다
financial terms 경제적 조건
in terms of -의 의미로

Key Structure

Unfortunately, some women **are** concerned about being very thin, but some women **have** different concerns <u>related</u> to the appearance of their body.

≪but 앞의 동사는 "are", 뒤의 동사는 "have"로 모두 현재 시제이며, 목적어인 "concerns" 뒤에는 또 동사가 오지 않으므로, "related"는 과거분사로 바로 앞 명사인 "concerns"를 수식함.≫

⊃ 예제 9

Unfortunately, some women are concerned about being very thin, but some women have different concerns related to the appearance of their body. For example, some women believe that their breasts are not large enough, and undergo surgery to enlarge their breasts. In this surgery, some artificial substance is implanted inside the breast to make it larger. Many women have had this surgery, but many of them have suffered serious health problems as a result.

9. What is the reason Many women have had plastic surgery?

(a) to gain weight (b) to lose weight

(c) to look better (d) to get healthy

기초어휘

be concerned about~ ~에 관심을 가지다, ~을 걱정하다 undergo (수술을) 받다
artificial 인조의, 인공적인 implant 주입하다, 박다

심화어휘

1. thin; 얇은, 가는, 여윈, 〈털이〉 드문드문한, 〈공급 등이〉 부족한, 〈액체 · 기체 등이〉 엷은, 묽은, 〈음성 등이〉 가는, 힘없는

thin ice 얇은 얼음
a thin finger 가는 손가락
thin hair 성긴 머리칼
a thin argument 설득력 없는 의논
a thin voice 가냘픈 목소리

2. thick; 두꺼운, 뚱뚱한, 빽빽한, 〈목소리가〉 불명료한, 탁한, 〈안개 · 연기 등이〉 짙은, 〈액체 등이〉 진한

a thick book 두꺼운 책
a thick line 굵은 선
thick cloud 짙은 구름
thick soup 진한 국

Key Structure

But **what is even more impressive about these plays** is Shakespeare's use of the English language.

≪관계대명사 "what"이 전체 문장의 주어(what is even more impressive about these plays)가 되는 명사절을 이끌고 있다. 명사구(절)은 언제나 3인칭 단수 취급한다≫

⊃ 예제 10

In his plays, Shakespeare revealed a very wide knowledge of many areas of life. The characters in his plays discuss many different topics, often with the knowledge of experts. But what is even more impressive about these plays is Shakespeare's use of the English language. His vocabulary was very large, and Shakespeare seems to have introduced many words to the language! Also, many of the phrases that are said by Shakespeare's characters are now used in everyday conversation. Today, writers often use quotations from Shakespeare's plays in their own works.

But perhaps even the most impressive features of Shakespeare's plays are the characters within <u>them.</u> The many characters in his plays seem very different from each other, but they seem very realistic. The emotions they feel, the words they say, and the actions they perform are all easily understood. Many people who watch one of Shakespeare's plays will find that they know people who remind them somewhat of the characters in those plays.

10. The pronoun <u>them</u> refers to ________________________.

(a) impressive features (b) Shakespeare's plays
(c) Shakespeare (d) real story

기초어휘

expert 전문가 impressive 인상적인, 감명을 주는 quotation 인용

심화어휘

1. impressive; 〈의식 · 경관 등이〉 강한 인상을 주는, 감명을 주는
   impressive result 인상적인 결과 impressive resume 인상적인 이력서
   impressive movie 인상적인 영화
2. character; 성격, 기질, (물건의) 특성, 인격, (소설 등의) 등장인물, (연극의) 역(役), 기호(mark), 문자
   a national character 국민성/a man of character 인격자/a public character 공인

Key Structure

In fact, **it** was said **that the people of France did not stop celebrating the New Year until the first day of April!**

≪가주어 it, 진주어 "that~April!"구문이고 여기서 that은 접속사이다.≫

예제 11

While April fool's day is not an official holiday, it is celebrated by many people, especially the young. Its start is explained in more than one way. The most popular belief is probably the one where it originated way back sometime in the 16th century in France. At that time, the first day of the new calender year, or, New Year's day, was celebrated on the 25th day of March. This date also coincided with the spring equinox. It was not only the beginning of a new year, but it was also the beginning of a new year of life and renewal of the earth. As it is now, celebrating the New Year in the earlier times meant parties and much revelry. In fact, it was said that the people of France did not stop celebrating the New Year until the first day of April!

11. How long did the people of France celebrate the New Year?

(a) one day
(b) for a week
(c) for a month
(d) They didn't celebrate the New Year

기초어휘

April fool's day 만우절 originate 시작하다 incide with~ ~과 일치하다
equinox 춘분 renewal 소생, 부활 revelry 환락, 흥청거림

심화어휘

1. popular; 인기 있는, 대중의, 대중적인, 민간 전승의

a popular preacher 인기 있는 목사
popular opinion 여론
popular suffrage 보통 선거권
popular support 대중의 지지
popular superstitions 민간의 미신

2. party; (사교상의) 파티, (목적 · 임무 등을 위해 함께 행동하는) 일행, (논쟁 · 분쟁 등에서의) 지지 단체, 자기편[쪽], 정당, (계약 · 소송 등의) 당사자, 상대방

a sightseeing party 관광단
a rescue party 구조대
a search party 수색대
a political party 정당
join[leave] a party 입당[탈당]하다

Key Structure

Paying by check over the phone almost always costs money.

≪"Paying by check over the phone"는 동명사구(=명사구)이며, 명사구(절)는 언제나 3인칭 단수이기에, 단수동사 "costs"가 왔다.≫

➲ 예제 12

Having a credit card is a tricky thing. You can take advantage of a zero percent card, but you have to follow lots of rules that are in the fine print. If you are even one day late on a monthly payment, your 0% interest will go up as high as 22% and you will have to pay as much as a $30 fee. The best thing to do is to pay online. The company can debit your bank account and it's usually free. Paying by check over the phone almost always costs money. It's ideal to pay the full balance right away early in the month.

12. It is implied in the passage that having a credit card is ______________.

(a) safe
(b) beneficial
(c) complicated
(d) convenient

기초어휘

tricky 교묘한, 까다로운 / take advantage of~ ~을 이용하다
payment 지불 / debit 차변에 기입하다

심화어휘

1. tricky; 〈사람 · 행위 등이〉 교활한, 교묘한, 〈역할 · 일 등이〉 하기 까다로운, 신중을 요하는, 〈의견 등이〉 남을 속이는, 고장이 잘 나는

a tricky guy 교활한 친구
a tricky customer 까다로운 고객
a tricky car 고장이 잦은 차

2. account; (사건 등에 대한) 설명, 기술(記述), (금전 · 책임의 처리에 관한) 보고, (은행 등과의) 거래, (예금) 계좌

demand an account 설명을 요구하다
bank account 은행 계좌
user account 사용자 계정

Key Structure

This state-of-the-art formula also contains royal jelly, which scientists and fitness experts alike know to be a super concentrate of high potency vitamins and minerals.

≪여기서 관계대명사 "which"의 격은 목적격(know의 목적어)선행사는 "royal jelly"이고, 관계사절 전체는 선행사에 대한 추가적인 정보를 제공한다.≫

예제 13

Introducing GinsEnergy, with 500mg of the most powerful combination of standardized ginseng extracts from around the world. GinsEnergy delivers a consistent, powerful punch of stabilized energy that helps to improve physical endurance and performance and strengthen your immune system. And what's more, it's capsule formula. That means it doesn't have any adverse odors characteristic of similar products.

GinsEnergy contains the equivalent of 500mg of high-powered American, Chinese and Korean ginseng extracts, plus seven other high-energy herbs, providing an instant energy burst. This state-of-the-art formula also contains royal jelly, which scientists and fitness experts alike know to be a super concentrate of high potency vitamins and minerals.

13. It can be inferred from the passage that GinsEnergy is ________.

(a) herbal tea
(b) fitness equipment
(c) vitamins
(d) a dietary supplement

기초어휘

extract 추출물, 엑기스 immune 면역의 formula 방식, 공식 adverse 거스르는 potency 효능

심화어휘

1. deliver; 〈물건 · 편지를〉 배달하다, 인도하다, 〈연설 · 설교를〉 하다, 구해내다, 분만[해산]시키다
deliver a package 소포를 배달하다 deliver a speech(lecture) 연설하다(강의하다)
deliver a verdict of guilty 유죄 평결을 선포하다 deliver a baby 아기를 낳다

2. improve; 개선[개량]하다, 진보[향상]시키다, 〈시간 · 기회 등을〉 이용하다, (경작 · 건설 등으로) 〈토지 · 부동산의〉 가치를 높이다
improve one's health 건강을 증진하다
improve one's leisure by reading 여가를 이용하여 독서하다
improved farmland 개량 농지

Key Structure

Kennywood is located between the beautiful Monga river and the towering Kanah Mountain range.

≪위치나 장소를 표시할 때는 수동태를 쓴다.≫

예제 14

Kennywood is located between the beautiful Monga river and the towering Kanah Mountain range. It is the finest traditional amusement park in the west. The park features 25 major rides, including roller coasters, two water rides, and 20 kinds of land rides. There are also 35 games, two video arcades, and four souvenir shops through out the park. And there is a Park Terrace that is a cafe style restaurant. Advanced reservations are available online. Parking is free.

14. How can tickets be purchased in advance?

(a) at the ticket box (b) at the amusement park
(c) by phone (d) via internet

기초어휘

locate 위치하다 towering 높이 치솟은 souvenir 기념품, 선물

심화어휘

1. locate; 〈상점 · 사무소 등을〉 (어떤 장소에) 정하다, (…에) 차리다[두다], 〈물건의 위치 등을〉 알아내다, 밝혀내다, 발견하다

locate a research center in Busan 부산에 연구소를 정하다
locate missing children 실종된 아이들을 찾다
locate a house on the map 지도상에서 집을 찾다

2. available; 이용할 수 있는, 소용이 되는, 쓸모 있는, (면회[일]에 응할 수 있는) 시간이 있는, 여가가 있는, (정해진 상대가 없어서) 사귈 수 있는, (결혼 · 교제 등의) 상대가 될 수 있는

available positions 이용가능한 자리
available memory 사용가능한 메모리
seats available 사용가능한 좌석

Key Structure

Owners started wondering how they'd motivate workers <u>if they couldn't reward them in the style</u> (that) they were used to.

≪"how they'd motivate workers~"는 wonder의 목적절이다.≫

예제 15

When the economy went south, morale went with it. Owners started wondering how they'd motivate workers if they couldn't reward them in the style they were used to. But every owner has resources to provide the reward employees want most– appreciation.

In a survey conducted when perks were theirs for the asking, workers said what they really wanted was for their owner or manager to: personally congratulate or thank them for doing a good job, write a personal note praising their performance, publicly recognize their efforts, gather the staff together to celebrate success.

15. According to the passage, what do workers want the most from their owner or manager?

(a) wage increase

(b) getting proper compliments for what they've done

(c) a chance to get promoted

(d) a great retirement plan

기초어휘

morale 사기, 의욕 / motivate ~에게 동기를 주다 / reward 보상, 보수
appreciation 감사, 존중 / perks(= perquisite) 임시수입, 부수입
for the asking 청구만 하면, 거저

심화어휘

conduct; 행동하다, 처신하다(behave), 지휘하다, 〈업무 등을〉 수행하다, 〈열 · 전기 · 소리 등을〉 전도하다
conduct oneself well 처신을 잘하다 conduct survey(test) 조사(실험)를 하다
conduct an orchestra 오케스트라를 지휘하다

Key Structure

After the American Civil War ended in 1865 <u>disbanded soldiers</u> who were former black slaves, and young men seeking adventure <u>headed</u> west.

≪"who~adventure"는 관계대명사절로서, 선행사이자 문장 주어인 "disbanded soldiers"에 대한 추가적인 정보를 제공하고, 문장 동사는 "headed"이다.≫

➲ 예제 16~18

The Golden Age of the American cowboy was short lived. It began in the 1860s with the great cattle drives from Texas north to Kansas. By 1890, when railroads had reached remote areas, there was no more need for large-scale cattle drives.

Of course, cowboys have a history before 1860. In fact, there were Mexican cowboys long before that. The Spanish conqueror of Mexico, Hernan Cortes, brought cattle with him in 1521. Cortes also branded his cattle with a three cross design. The Spanish sharp-horned cattle roamed the deserts and prairies freely. Eventually, they found their way to Texas. American settlers in Texas interbred their animals with the Spanish breed – the Texas longhorn cow was the result! It was famous for its bad temper and aggressiveness. The Longhorn was a dangerous animal, with each of its horns measuring up to three and one-half feet long.

After the American Civil War ended in 1865, disbanded soldiers, who were former black slaves, and young men seeking adventure headed west. At that time, there were about five million cattle in Texas. Back in the East, there was a big demand for beef. By this time, railways from the east extended as far west as Kansas. It was still more than 600 miles from South Texas to the railway. Between the two places there were rivers to cross, Indian tribes, badlands and other problems. A fur trader named Jesse Chisholm had driven his wagon north in 1865. Cowboys and cattle followed the Chisholm Trail north to Abilene, Kansas. This cattle trail became the most famous route for driving cattle, until it was barred with barbed wire in 1884.

16. What is the best title for the passage?

(a) American cowboy's history (b) Long horn cow

(c) American civil war (d) The cattle train

17. Who brought cattle in Mexico?

(a) soldiers (b) American settlers

(c) Jesse Chisholm (d) Hernan cortes

18. The author mentions all of the following except ________________.

(a) Cowboys have a history after 1884.

(b) The Longhorn is a dangerous animal.

(c) After American civil war, there was a big demand for beef.

(d) A fur trader had driven his wagon north in 1865.

기초어휘

cattle 소 / remote 먼, 외딴 / brand 소인을 찍다 / prairie 초원, 목초지
interbreed 이종 교배하다 / aggressiveness 공격성 / disband 군대를 해체하다
badland 황무지 / bar 줄을 긋다, 방해하다 / barbed wire 가시철사

심화어휘

1. extend; 〈손 · 발 등을〉 뻗다, 내밀다, 〈철도 · 도로 등을〉 연장하다, 〈기간을〉 늘이다, 〈범위 · 영토 등을〉 넓히다, 확장하다, 〈은혜 · 친절 등을〉 베풀다, 제공하다

extend a helping hand 구원의 손길을 뻗치다
extend visa 비자를 연장하다
extend sympathy to a person …에게 동정을 베풀다

2. drive; 몰다, 쫓다, 〈차 등을〉 몰다, 운전[조종]하다, …하게 내몰다

drive a mad dog away 미친 개를 쫓다
drive one's son to school 아들을 학교까지 차로 태워주다
drive a person mad(angry/crazy/insane) -를 화나게(미치게)내몰다
drive a person hard …을 혹사시키다

3. follow; (순서로서) …의 뒤를 따라가다[오다], …의 가르침[주의, 학설]을 받들다, 추종하다, 〈선례 · 풍습 등에〉 따르다, 본받다, 〈길 등을〉 따라가다, 〈사람 등을〉 쫓다, 뒤쫓아가다, 추구하다, 〈직업에〉 종사하다

follow example본보기를 따르다
follow ideal 이상을 추구하다
follow the law 법률에 종사하다, 변호사 노릇을 하다
follow the sea 선원 노릇을 하다

Key Structure

- There are several different branches of psychology <u>each of which studies a different aspect of behaviour.</u>
  ≪목적격 관계대명사(전치사 of의 목적어) which의 선행사는 "several different branches of psychology"이고 관계대명사절 동사(studies)의 주어는 "each"이다.≫
- These psychologists try to figure out <u>why it is that some animals have "instincts" for various behaviors such as parenting, mating, or fighting</u>.
  ≪"it is(was)~that~"강조구문이고, 여기서 강조되는 말은 "why"이다.≫-

예제 19~23

Are you interested in the behaviour of people and animals? If you are, then you might enjoy the study of psychology. Psychology is the study of behaviour, but this is a very large area of study. There are several different <u>branches</u> of psychology, each of which studies a different aspect of behaviour.

Social psychologists study interactions among people. For example, a social psychologist might try to learn about the situations that cause people to behave aggressively. Another question studied by social psychologists is why certain people become attracted to each other. One of the interesting problems in social psychology is conformity: what causes people to behave in the same way, and to follow what others do and say?

Cognitive psychologists study thinking, memory, and language. One problem studied by cognitive psychologists is how people remember numbers. For example, what is the best way to memorize some numbers? Is it better to repeat the numbers to oneself, or to try to attach some meaning to these numbers? A cognitive psychologist might also study language. For example, why can young children learn a second language so quickly and easily? Cognitive psychologists are also interested in the ways that people learn to solve problems, such as finding a new place.

Clinical psychologists study mental illnesses. For example, a clinical psychologist might try to find out the causes of depression and to figure out ways of helping people who are depressed. Other clinical psychologists might study the behaviour of people who suffer from addiction to drugs, so that this problem can be prevented and treated. Another topic of interest to clinical psychologists is violent behaviour. It is very important to find ways of preventing violence and to change the behaviour of persons who act violently.

Some psychologists are interested in the measurement of psychological characteristics. For example, psychologists might develop tests to assess a person's intelligence, personality traits, or interests. These tests can be used to help people make decisions about education, occupation, and clinical treatment.

Psychologists who study the behaviour of animals are called ethologists. Ethologists often go into wilderness areas to watch the activity of birds, fish, or other animals. These psychologists try to figure out why it is that some animals have "instincts" for various behaviours such as parenting, mating, or fighting. Some ethologists have learned very much about the unusual behaviours observed in many animals.

<u>These</u> are only a few of the many areas of psychology. Truly, psychology is one of the most interesting areas of knowledge!

19. What is the main idea of the passage?
   (a) There are several different kinds of psychology.
   (b) People enjoy the study of psychology.
   (c) People like to behave in the same way.
   (d) Psychology is the interesting study.

20. The word branches could best be replaced by __________.
   (a) stick (b) part
   (c) study (d) behaviour

21. Which of the following is NOT mentioned in the passage?
   (a) Psychology is the study of people and animals.
   (b) Social psychologists study interactions among people.
   (c) Cognitive psychologists don't study languages.
   (d) Clinical psychologists study mental illnesses.

22. What is the tone of the passage?
   (a) ironic (b) informative
   (c) comparative (d) negative

23. Ethologists are ______________________.

(a) psychologists who study the behaviour of people

(b) psychologists who study the behaviour of animals

(c) animal protector

(d) people who study language

기초어휘

psychology 심리학 / branch 분야(= field) / aspect 측면 / interaction 상호작용
aggressively 공격적으로 / conformity 일치 / addiction 중독 / prevent 예방하다
trait 특성 / ethologist 동물행동학 / instinct 본능 / mating 교미, 교배

심화어휘

1. attract; (자력 등으로) 끌어당기다, 〈주의 · 흥미 등을〉 끌다, 끌어당기다

attract interest/attention 관심/주의를 끌다
attract customers 고객을 끌다
attract millions of dollars 수 백만 달러를 유치하다

2. solve; …을 풀다, 해명하다; [어려움 따위]를 해결하다; [수학 문제 따위]를 풀다 [채 따위]를 갚다

solve problems/puzzles 문제/수수께끼를 풀다
solve the mystery 미스테리를 풀다
solve environmental crisis 환경위기를 해결하다

3. develop; [산업 · 능력 따위]를 발달시키다, 발전시키다, …을 계발(啓發)하다, [자원 따위]를 개발하다

develop business 사업을 발전시키다
develop a theory 이론을 전개하다
develop resources 자원을 개발하다
develop foreign markets 해외시장을 개척하다

4. assess; [재산 · 수입 따위]를 평가[산정]하다; [손해 · 세금 · 벌금 따위]를 사정하다

assess an apartment 아파트를 평가(산정)하다
assess students 학생들을 평가하다
assess suitability 적절성을 평가하다
assess a tax(fine) on a person –에게 세금(벌금)을 사정하다

Key Structure

These beverages are made by allowing a process called fermentation to occur.
≪원래는 "which is called fermentation"인데, "which is"가 생략된 것이다.≫

예제 24~27

Alcohol is the oldest drug that is used in Western countries. For thousands of years, people have made alcoholic beverages. These beverages are made by allowing a process called fermentation to occur. Alcoholic fermentation happens when yeasts or bacteria break down the sugars that occur in some liquids, and convert some of those sugars into alcohol. Many liquids, such as fruit juices, can ferment.

Thousands of years ago, alcoholic drinks were common in the Middle East. However, the Islamic religion forbids alcohol, so very little alcohol is consumed in this part of the world. In European countries, and in other parts of the world, many different kinds of alcoholic beverages are produced and consumed.

In warmer areas of Europe, people make wine by allowing grape juice to ferment. In cooler areas of Europe, people make beer by fermenting liquids made from water and various grains. The process of fermentation is also used to make stronger drinks known as "spirits." These drinks include vodka, whiskey, and rum. The techniques for making good wine, beer, and spirits have been developed over hundreds of years, and require scientific precision. Some people have developed a great appreciation for well-made wine, beer, or spirits, and have become experts about the many different varieties of these beverages.

Many people appreciate the taste of alcoholic beverages, but many also enjoy the feelings that alcohol causes. Alcohol belongs to a category of drugs called "depressants" because it "depresses" the central nervous system, causing a person to feel less inhibited or restrained. Many people enjoy this feeling, but when a person drinks a lot of alcohol, he or she loses co-ordination, balance, and judgment. Speech may become unclear, and the person may speak too much.

Some people become aggressive or depressed. When a person is under the influence of alcohol, the person is said to be drunk.

One of the problems that can result from alcohol consumption is known as "drunk driving." Some people try to drive a car after having consumed alcohol, but this is extremely dangerous. Each year, thousands of people are killed by drunk drivers who lose control of their cars. In recent years, attempts have been made to reduce this problem by public education campaigns and by strict laws and punishments. If you drink, don't drive!

Another problem associated with alcohol is addiction, known as alcoholism. Some people drink so frequently that they develop a physiological addiction to alcohol. This problem can have terrible consequences for a person's health, personal relationships, and career.

Alcoholic beverages are firmly a part of Western culture, and of many other cultures also. On the one hand, drinks provide many people with much enjoyment and appreciation. On the other hand, alcohol is a drug that can be abused, leading to accidents and addiction.

24. Which of the following could be best title?

(a) Alcoholic beverages
(b) Fermentation
(c) Drunk driving
(d) Techniques for making alcoholic beverages

25. According to the passage, which is NOT mentioned?

(a) Ways of making alcoholic beverages
(b) Problems of alcoholic beverages
(c) History of alcohol
(d) Price of alcoholic beverages

26. The author's attitude in paragraph 4 can be best described ________.

(a) positive
(b) careful
(c) negative
(d) angry

27. According to the passage, when a person drinks a lot of alcohol, he or she ____________.

(a) wakes up
(b) sleeps
(c) happy
(d) loses balance

기초어휘

fermentation 발효 / yeast 효모, 곰팡이 / convert into 전환하다 / forbid 금하다
appreciation 감상, 식별 / depressant 진정제 / inhibited 억제된(=restrained)
co-ordination 조정 / alcoholism 알코올 중독

심화어휘

1. produce; …을 (재료에서) 제조하다, 생산하다, [농산물]을 생산하다

produce food 식품을 생산하다
produce fruits 열매를 낳다(생산하다)
produce a sensation 센세이션을 일으키다

2. consume; …을 다 써버리다, 소모하다, [시간 · 금전 따위]를 낭비하다,

consume fuel 연료를 소비하다
consume time 시간을 소모하다
consume money 돈을 소비하다

Key Structure

That way, people <u>who work at night</u> **or** <u>who have trouble sleeping</u> can drop in at any time.

≪등위접속사 "or"는 문장 주어 "people"을 수식하는 두 개의 관계대명사 "who"절을 병렬하고, 문장동사는 "can drop"이다.≫

➲ 예제 28~32

"Let's go for coffee!" All over North America friends like to meet at the coffee shop. Here people sit and talk about the day's business, news and sports, personal concerns, shop talk, or simply gossip. Coffee shops have an informal atmosphere that encourages conversation. You don't have to dress up either! Students drop in wearing T-shirts and blue jeans, and sit beside businessmen wearing suits and ties. Many coffee shops are open 24 hours a day, including Sundays and holidays. That way, people who work at night or who have trouble sleeping can drop in at any time.

Because coffee and donuts are relatively inexpensive, people feel comfortable sitting for a while, knowing that they are not spending a lot of money. Although coffee and donuts are the main items sold at coffee shops, many also serve other beverages and desserts, and sometimes a light lunch. Many patrons have a favourite kind of coffee or other drink and will drive past other coffee shops to go to one that serves the flavour they like.

Visitors from other countries are often surprised at how roomy these coffee shops can be. Some are as large as regular restaurants. Having a nice bit of space around them encourages people to relax. Some people arrange regular dates and meet every day, or every week, at the same time. For example, retired friends may get together every weekday morning at 10:00 am. Others stop every morning at the drive-in line to get their coffee for work. Even people who have coffee machines at home or at work like to go to coffee shops to get a special kind of coffee or a favourite treat.

It might seem that the business owners would not make much money just selling a few items, but in fact, many coffee shops do extremely well, especially if they are located in a busy traffic area. Then business tends to be steady all through the day. Not only do people come in and sit down, but there is usually a lot of take-out business as well.

People go to coffee shops not only to socialize with family and friends, but also to discuss business or treat their employees to a snack. Others go there to read the newspaper or a favourite magazine. Some people even go there to do work. This article was written in a coffee shop!

Of course, people who come here usually like coffee and donuts. Coffee is the favourite hot drink in North America, but most shops also serve tea, hot chocolate and cappuccino, as well as some other cold beverages. Donuts are usually round, and are small deep-fried breads with various toppings. Most donuts have a hole in the middle. Even these "holes," which are punched out of the donut, can be sold separately, as a kind of mini-donut.

Everywhere you go in North America, you will see coffee shops. So take half an hour to stop in and relax. You'll enjoy the great North American "coffee break!"

28. Choose the best title for this passage.

(a) a nice place-coffee shops
(b) visitors at coffee shops
(c) a special kind of coffee
(d) people who like coffee shops

29. What are the main items at coffee shops?

(a) coffee and donuts
(b) light lunch
(c) drink beverages
(d) dinner

30. Choose one that refers to the underlined word, 'them'?

(a) coffee shops
(b) regular restaurants
(c) countries
(d) cars

31. According to the passage what do donuts have in the middle?

(a) chocolate
(b) sugar
(c) hole
(d) cream

32. In the author's opinion, how are coffee shops in American?

(a) strike
(b) comfortable
(c) gloomy
(d) noisy

기초어휘

shop talk 직업(일) 이야기 / informal 형식을 따지지 않는 / drop in 들르다
patron 단골손님 / roomy 넓은(=large) / deep-fry 기름을 넣고 튀기다

심화어휘

1. regular; 통상의, 정기적인(periodic), 정시의

regular meetings 정규 모임들 / regular salary 고정 월급
regular customers 단골 고객들 / regular train departure 기차의 정시 발차

2. extreme; 극도의, 극한의, 극심한

extreme poverty 극도의 빈곤 / extreme weather 극단적인 날씨
extreme fog 극심한 안개

3. steady; 꾸준한, 안정된

steady increase(growth) 꾸준한 증가(성장)
steady job 안정적인 일자리 / steady seller 꾸준히 잘 팔리는 것

Key Structure

Compared to some other department stores Wal-Mart has relatively fewer employees.

≪문장 맨 앞에 오는 "동사원형+ed"는 언제나 과거분사이고, 줄친 부분은 과거분사가 이끄는 구이므로, 분사구문이다.≫

⊃ 예제 33~37

Wal-Mart is now the world's largest retail organization. Wal-Mart employs around 1.2 million people worldwide. In 2000, Wal-Mart had sales of more than $191 billion, with profits of $6.3 billion. Profits increased 16% from the previous year.

People have come to expect that Wal-Mart's profits will increase substantially every year. Each year more stores are opened, and Wal-Mart expands into new countries. Wal-Mart also enters new areas of business nearly every year. Few people know that Wal-Mart is also a major real estate company.

Sam Walton opened his Walton's Five and Dime in Bentonville, Arkansas, in 1950. Twelve years later he opened the first Wal-Mart in Bentonville. His business philosophy was simple-- good prices, great selection and a friendly greeting. Walton was known for the "Ten Foot Attitude." This means that any employee should greet any customer who is within ten feet of them. He emphasized that it is important to speak to people before they speak to you. Walton also believed that good deals from suppliers should be passed along to customers. The combination of low prices and friendly service is basic to Wal-Mart's success. That one store in Bentonville has become 4,203 stores in the U.S.A., plus another 1,000 outside the United States.

Walton died in 1992, but his business philosophy continues to be preached at Wal-Marts. Each store has greeters who meet the customers at the door, and deal with any special needs they have. Having greeters gives the effect of having more service clerks than Wal-Mart really has. Compared to some other department stores, Wal-Mart has relatively fewer employees.

Wal-Mart also has the Wal-Mart Foundation, which sponsors numerous good causes. Among their programs are high school scholarship, fund-raising for local hospitals and sick children, environmental concerns and community "matching grant' outreach.

So, what's not to like about Wal-Mart? The main complaint is that their business style is extremely aggressive. Wal-Mart's attitudes towards manufacturers and suppliers are: "You do it our way, or we won't do business with you." This puts Wal-Mart at an advantage over smaller retailers who don't have the same retailing power. Wal-Mart has been known to demand that its suppliers provide products at discount for Wal-Mart store openings; levy fines for shipment errors; tell manufacturers what products, styles and colours to make, etc. Wal-Mart expects product delivery in two days, and expects manufacturers to cooperate with its promotional and retailing strategies. In effect, any company that works with Wal-Mart becomes one of their employees.

Any company, which so dominates one area of the market, will have a lot of power. So far, Wal-Mart has been successful in getting what it wants, and providing customers with what they want.

33. What's the main idea of the passage?

(a) Wal-Mart of Sam walton succeeded with special business philosophy.

(b) Walton built Wal-Mart.

(c) There's a behind story.

(d) Wal-Mart is all over the worlds.

34. What percent do the profits about this year increase from the last year?

(a) 1.2 % (b) 8 %

(c) 16 % (d) 6.3 %

35. Where is the first place of Wal-Mart?

(a) Bentonville

(b) all regions of U.S

(c) New York

(d) In front of Walton's Fire and Dime.

36. Which is not mentioned of Sam Walton's business philosophy?

(a) good prices (b) great selection

(c) friendly greeting (d) large store

37. Which of the following is true?

(a) Sam Walton is still alive.

(b) Sam Walton emphasized the size of the store.

(c) Wal-Mart can be found only in America.

(d) Walton was known for the "Ten foot attitude".

기초어휘

retail 소매 / profit 이익/ substantially 충분히, 든든히 / real estate 부동산
sponsor 후원하다 / fundraising 기금조성, 자원조달 / levy 부과하다 / promotional 승진의
In effect 사실상 / dominate 지배하다

심화어휘

1. employ; 고용하다, 사용하다

employ top engineers 최고의 엔지니어들을 고용하다
employ the best materials 최고의 재료를 사용하다
employ a joke 농담을 하다

2. basic; 기초적인, 기초가 되는, 근본적인

basic instinct 원초적 본능 basic pay 기본급
basic elements 기본적인(근본적인) 요소들

Key Structure

Its body temperature drops to near 32° F, it breathes just a few times a minute, and its heartbeat is <u>so slow as to be almost imperceptible.</u>

≪"so slow as to be almost imperceptible"-원급 구문-≫

예제 38~42

Do all bears hibernate? To be perfectly accurate, no bear hibernates. When an animal hibernates, it is near death and may appear to be dead. Its body temperature drops to near 32°F, it breathes just a few times a minute, and its heartbeat is so slow as to be almost imperceptible. If the animal is exposed to warmth, a few hours may pass before it awakens and is alert. Animals that hibernate include bats, hedgehogs, ground squirrels, and marmots.

Although most people say that bears hibernate, hibernation is not the proper term in the case of bears, because during their sleep there is little change in their body temperature, respiration, or metabolic rate. A better term would be "deep winter sleep" (the scientific term is "dormancy"). If left alone they can sleep in the same position for months, yet they awaken quite easily if disturbed.

The reason for hibernation and deep winter sleep is the same. During winter, food is scarce, and it's often difficult for some animals to maintain their normal body temperature. To protect themselves, many animals pass the time away by hibernating or sleeping. They store body fat when food is plentiful, then live off the stored fat when hibernating or sleeping. By sleeping for long periods of time, they keep activity to a minimum and also control their temperature and metabolism so that no growth occurs.

A bear may decide to sleep in a hollow tree, a cave, a pile of brush, or a den that it has dug. Sometimes the bear adds dried leaves and grass to its bed for additional insulation against the harsh cold of winter.

Not all bears sleep all winter. If bears live in an environment with a good year-round food supply, they don't need to go into a deep winter sleep. Tropical bears such as sun bears, sloth bears, and spectacled bears never go into a winter sleep.

The male polar bear never goes into dormancy, but the female does only if she is pregnant.

If a bear is accustomed to dormancy but is kept in a zoo where food is always available, it will not go into dormancy regardless of how cold it may get.

38. The passage is primarily concerned with?

(a) hibernation of bears (b) bears's death
(c) sleeping bears (d) shortage of food

39. Which of the following doesn't hibernate?

(a) bats (b) hedgehogs
(c) marmots (d) sun bears

40. Which is not true of hibernating animals, according to the passage?

(a) It breathes just a few times a minute.

(b) It is near death and may appear to be dead.

(c) Its body temperature drops to near 32°F.

(d) Its heartbeat becomes very fast.

41. What's the proper term instead of "hibernation"?

(a) sleep (b) near death

(c) deep winter sleep (d) none

42. What's the reason for "hibernation"?

(a) food is scarce.

(b) Animals can maintain their normal body temperature.

(c) Animals can awaken easily.

(d) Animals can't move in winter.

기초어휘

hibernate 동면하다 / temperature 온도, 체온 / imperceptible 감지할 수 없는, 미세한
alert 민첩한 / hedgehog 고슴도치 / metabolic 신진대사의 / den 굴
dormancy (동물의)휴면 / scarce 부족한, 드문 / hollow 텅 빈 / insulation 단열, 절연
pregnant 임신한 / is accustomed to ~에 익숙하다

심화어휘

1. bear; …을 낳다, 참다, 간직하다

bear fruits 열매를 낳다
bear extreme weather 극단적인 날씨를 견디다
bear a grudge(ill will) 앙심(악의)을 품다

2. expose; (위험 · 공격 · 위해 따위에) …을 드러내다; (비 · 바람 · 추위 따위에) …을 노출시키다, [마약 따위]를 경험[체험]시키다

expose a secret(scandal) 비밀(추문)을 폭로하다
expose bedding to the sun 이불을 햇볕에 노출시키다

3. harsh; (성격 · 태도 · 기후 · 조건 따위가) 엄격한, 가혹한, 무자비한

harsh discipline 엄격한 훈육 harsh criticism 가혹한 비판
harsh treatment 가혹한 대우 harsh punishment 가혹한 처벌

Key Structure

As parents, you can take solace in the fact that it is only because your children have such faith in your unconditional love that they can use you as a safe target for their resistance and opposition.

≪such~that(접속사)구문이다.≫

➲ 예제 43~47

Sixth graders will argue over homework, school rules, and procedures. They contradict ideas in their classes and their reading. They love to argue -- about anything!

Sixth grade can be a very hard time for both parents, but especially for mothers, because it is usually mothers on whom sixth graders take out their frustration. They'll set up for an argument or push against their mothers in order to establish their independence. Much to your chagrin, your sixth grader might often be fresh, talk back, and no longer seem to value your opinion. A daughter will criticize her mother's hair, clothes, or general appearance. A son might keep such criticisms to himself; however, he might ask his mother not to show up at school or talk to his friends.

This apparent disdain seems to be necessary in order for a child to make the inevitable break from his or her parents. Both genders must begin the process of self-discovery and sound decision making. A daughter needs to gain distance from a mother to establish her identity as a woman in her own right. A son needs to distance from a mother because of his budding sexuality. As parents, you can take solace in the fact that it is only because your children have such faith in your unconditional love that they can use you as a safe target for their resistance and opposition.

As a parent, your biggest challenges are to keep trouble at school or at home in perspective and not to personalize your child's behavior. It usually has nothing to do with you. The number one strategy for helping both you and your child is to maintain your balance -- and your sense of humor. This sounds easy but can actually be very difficult. At times you'll be hurt and angry, but every time you succeed in keeping your cool, give yourself a star.

When your sixth grader tries to engage you in a skirmish, it's best to acknowledge her feelings, state your position firmly, and then bow out. Your child needs you to be fair but to hold your position. Refuse to get pulled into an escalating war of words. She's going to have the last word anyway, so let her have it early Sixth graders must save face.

Your sixth grade daughter, for all her seeming resistance, still desperately needs your unconditional love and support. On good days, she will confide in you, chatting about friends and school and the myriad things that interest her. She'll appreciate times of intimacy, when she can be alone with you without interruption from brothers and sisters. When she's having these back-to-the cocoon days, she'll welcome your affection and might even initiate it herself holding your hand, hugging, or even kissing you. However, on flailing-about days, a simple question such as "How was school?" might be met with the accusation that you're prying. If you try to hug her, she's apt to pull away. It's important that you continue to give her physical affection when you can. Watch for those moments when she's feeling stable, and give her a hug and tell her how much you love her. Bedtime often offers an opportunity for affection.

Your sixth grade son, however, might not show any physical affection. But he might show his love in a different way: by washing the car or mowing the lawn without being asked. When you see these acts of love, make sure you tell him you appreciate them. Also, tell him how proud of him you are when he brings home a good paper or is kind to his sister.

Another positive approach that meets the approval of boys and girls is to plan a special outing with your child. This is especially true if time is set aside for the sixth grader alone, without other siblings along. Take your child to your office, go out to lunch, see a movie together. These are very special times, and they will be talked about at school and possibly remembered for a lifetime.

43. What is the main idea of the passage?

(a) There are various way of treat six graders

(b) Parents concerned about their children.

(c) It's important to know sixth graders' feeling.

(d) It's good to show parents' love to children.

44. Which of the following is NOT the solution, according to this passage?

(a) It's best to acknowledge her feelings.

(b) It's important that you continue to give her physical affection.

(c) You must show physical affection to your sixth grade son.

(d) Another positive approach is to plan a special outing with your child.

45. The way of approaching to boy and girls is ________________.

(a) perfectly same

(b) somewhat different

(c) passionate

(d) perfectly different

46. Why did sixth graders push against their parents?

(a) in order to establish their independence

(b) to keep their secrets

(c) beautiful of amusement

(d) It's necessary to have their own rights

47. Underlined "they" refers to ________________.

(a) children (b) parents

(c) very special times (d) only boys

기초어휘

contradict 반대하다 / frustration 좌절 / independence 독립 / chagrin 억울함
fresh 건방진 / disdain 경멸 / inevitable 피할 수 없는 / budding 나타나기 시작한
sexuality 성적 관심 / solace 위안 / pposition 반대 / in perspective 전체적인 시야로
have nothing to do with ~와는 아무런 관련이 없다 / strategy 전략 / skirmish 작은 논쟁
bow out 물러나다 / seeming 겉으로, 외관상 / myriad 무수 / intimacy 친밀
interruption 방해 / cocoon 고치 / initiate 시작하다
flailing 도리깨질하듯이, 격렬히 움직이는 / accusation 비난, 트집 / prying 엿보는, 캐는
approval 찬성, 동의 / sibling 형제 자매

심화어휘

1. establish; (정부 따위)를 수립하다, [학교 · 회사 따위]를 설립[설치]하다, –을 자리 잡게 하다(확립하다)

establish an independent nation 독립국가를 수립하다
establish a research center 연구소를 설립하다
establish peace 평화를 확립하다

2. value; …을 (금전적으로) 평가하다; …가격으로 견적하다

value honor 명예를 소중히 하다
value friendship 우정을 소중히 여기다
value intimacy 친밀함을 소중히 여기다

3. inevitable; 피할 수 없는, 면할 수 없는; (논리적으로) 당연한, 필연적인

inevitable consequence 피할 수 없는 결과
inevitable conclusion 필연적인 결론
inevitable bankruptcy 면할 수 없는 파산

4. maintain; …을 지속[계속]하다, 유지하다. …을 주장하다

maintain relations 관계를 지속하다
maintain upright posture 곧바른 자세를 유지하다
maintain one's rightness –의 정당성을 주장하다

Key Structure

Printed on the ticket were instructions about how to behave on this occasion.
≪동사(were)의 주어는 "instructions"이고, 보어인 과거분사 "Printed"가 강조되어 문장 맨 앞에 위치하면서, 어순이 도치되었다.≫

예제 48~52

"Etiquette" is a French word. The original meaning was "little tickets." These tickets were given to people who were attending a public ceremony. Printed on the ticket were instructions about how to behave on this occasion. So etiquette came to mean the way to behave on public occasions.

Etiquette today includes how to introduce people; how to eat properly; how to dress for different occasions; how to speak to different people; and what to do on special occasions. Almost every part of social life can have its particular etiquette.

Sometimes, etiquette changes or seems to change. There was much behaviour attached to courtship, such as a man holding the door open for a woman. Nowadays, some people find this outdated. But politeness is always a good idea. It is nice to hold the door open for the next person, whoever they are.

In fact, it sometimes seems like contemporary life encourages bad manners. Etiquette is no longer taught to young people. Moreover, in a youth culture, young people take their examples from other young people. As a result, good manners aren't considered important.

The point of etiquette is to help people to get along with each other. If people behave in an accepted manner, there is less chance of misunderstanding. Moreover, it is important for people to think about treating other people well. If everyone does what they feel like doing, it doesn't seem like they respect other people. Etiquette can help things to go a lot smoother.

Manners vary from culture to culture, but the intention is the same: to treat people with consideration. This is a way to reduce conflict.

Sometimes, we can understand where these customs come from. Originally, shaking hands with your right hand probably meant that you weren't carrying a weapon. Taking off your hat may originally have been taking off your helmet. This meant that you weren't going to fight.

Nowadays, there are new areas of social life. For example, a lot of conversation now takes place on the telephone. Perhaps because there is no traditional telephone etiquette, some people feel free to be rude. Try to treat the person on the phone just the way you would treat them if you were actually talking to them. Most people feel it is rude to interrupt a conversation. But many people seem to think that it is okay to interrupt someone talking on the phone. Children especially need to be taught not to interrupt.

The Internet also needs its own etiquette or "netiquette." Because you cannot see whom you are talking to, and they may be thousands of miles away, it is easy to misunderstand. Also people cannot hear the tone of your voice over the Internet. For this reason, some people use "smiles" – little faces – to show how they are feeling. If they make a joke they can use a smiling face, or print after their remark. This tips off the recipient that their remark is not to be taken seriously.

Using simple words like "please" and "thank you" can make everyday life a lot smoother and happier. Like a lot of other things, we do not realize the importance of etiquette until it starts to disappear.

48. Choose the one that etiquette's original meaning is ______________.

(a) politeness
(b) bus tickets
(c) little tickets
(d) behaviour

49. Etiquette today doesn't include ______________.

(a) how to introduce people

(b) how to eat properly

(c) how to dress for different occasions

(d) how to show your real minds

50. Which of the following is NOT true?

(a) Politeness is always a good idea.

(b) Etiquette is no longer taught to young people.

(c) Young people take their examples from the old.

(d) The point of etiquette is to help people to get along with each other.

51. In the last passage, underlined it refers to ______________.

(a) importance (b) everyday life

(c) smile (d) etiquette

52. The bolded eighth passage, it is concerned with ______________.

(a) the point of etiquette (b) new areas of etiquette

(c) traditional etiquette (d) netiquette

기초어휘

instruction 지시 / occasion 경우 / courtship 예절, 구혼
outdated 구식의(=old-fashioned) / politeness 예의 / contemporary 현대의
consideration 고려 / conflict 충돌 / rude 무례한 / interrupt 방해하다, 중단하다
remark 주목하다, 말하다 / tips off 힌트를 주다

심화어휘

1. public; 공공의, 공중인, 대중의

public service 공공 서비스 public sauna 대중 사우나
public sanitation 공공 위생

2. special; 특수한, 특별한, 각별한

special sauce 특수한 소스 special case 특별한 경우
special friend 각별한 친구

3. hold; …을 붙들다, 잡다, 쥐다, 개최하다, 억누르다

hold tightly 꽉 잡다
hold a meeting(party) 모임(파티)을 개최하다(갖다)
hold the passion 열정을 억누르다

Key Structure

What if they had allowed her to do more of the things she wanted to do?
≪원래는 "What would have happened"였는데 "would have happened"가 생략되었고, 조건절의 동사 "had allowed"는 가정법 과거완료이다.≫

예제 53~56

The story of Anne Shirley, the red-haired orphan, has been popular around the world for almost a century. The opening chapters of "Anne of Green Gables" tell how a brother and sister, living together on a farm, have decided to adopt a boy. Matthew Cuthbert is now 60 years old and needs help working the farm. They have sent away to the orphanage, and the boy will be arriving by train.

When Matthew goes to the train station with his horse and buggy, there is no boy, only a girl-- Ann Shirley. Anne is no ordinary girl. She has a vivid imagination and loves to talk about things that interest her. Matthew, who is shy and quiet, takes an immediate liking to her. When they arrive home, however, his sister Marilla is very upset. She doesn't see what good a girl would be to them. Matthew says, "We might be some good to her."

After a while, Marilla begins to feel sorry for the thin little orphan and decides to keep her. But Marilla finds that teaching Anne how to behave properly is quite a challenge. Anne often does things without thinking first, and Marilla has to be vigilant to keep her out of trouble. As time goes by, Anne becomes accepted in the community and doesn't get into as many difficulties.

One characteristic of the little orphan is a love of big words. While she lived a life of hard work, Anne liked to imagine beautiful things that she didn't have. This was her way of dealing with unhappiness when she worked as a servant for unkind people. Living at Green Gables makes her happy, but she doesn't lose her love of special words or beautiful things.

Anne is also unhappy because she has red hair and freckles. In Anne's day, beautiful women were thought to have light clear complexions and black hair. Her colouring seemed unromantic. However, red hair and freckles are very common on Prince Edward Island, where many of the people are of Scottish descent.

This story tells us a lot about how to be happy. When Matthew and Marilla stop worry about needing a boy, and start taking care of Anne, they find that they enjoy having her around. Their lives become much more interesting now that they have someone who needs them. So happiness involves looking after others, and being needed by them.

There were many stories about orphans when "Anne of Green Gables" was written. Before modern medicine, many parents died before their children were grown up. A lot of mothers died in childbirth. Since fathers didn't usually try to raise young children in those days, someone else had to take the responsibility.

This is what happened to Lucy Maud Montgomery, the author of "Anne." Her mother died when she was a baby, and her father left her with her mother's parents. Montgomery's grandparents provided a good home for her, but they were very strict and stern and didn't have a lot of sympathy with the little girl.

In her story, Montgomery is imagining how she would have liked her own life to have happened. What if her grandparents had been more like Matthew and Marilla? What if they had allowed her to do more of the things she wanted to do? Wouldn't she have been happier then?

The story shows how young children are hurt by bad treatment from the adults looking after them. Even if the adults don't mean to be unkind, sometimes they say or do things that make children very unhappy. "Anne" teaches parents and grandparents to encourage their children and help them to be happy and successful.

Anne Shirley is one little person who changes a whole community and makes it better. We all have special gifts and talents, and if we are allowed to use those abilities, they will benefit everyone around us.

53. What is the original title of this story?

(a) The red-haired Anne (b) Anne's story

(c) Anne of green gables (d) An orphan's story

54. When Matthew goes to the train station, who is there?

(a) Marilla (b) Anne

(c) An orphan boy (d) Nobody

55. Which of the following is NOT mentioned, according to the passage?

(a) Anne likes to imagine.

(b) Anne goes to school.

(c) The story of Anne teaches us many things.

(d) Anne doesn't like her hair

56. What does Anne do when she undergos a hard situation?

(a) She goes to a lake.

(b) She eats food.

(c) She cleans her room.

(d) She thinks about things she doesn't have.

기초어휘

orphan 고아의 / adopt 입양하다 / vigilant 자지 않고 지키는 / freckle 주근깨
stern 엄격한 / benefit ~에게 이익을 주다 / buggy 말 한 필이 끄는 경마차
complexion 피부색

심화어휘

1. immediate; (시간적으로) 곧 일어나는, 즉시[즉각]의, 가까운, (공간적으로) 직접의, 직접 접해 있는, 바로 이웃의

immediate notice 즉각적인 통보 immediate neighbor 가까운 이웃
immediate family 육친

2. common; 공통의, 공공의, 보통의, 흔한, 평범한, 저속한

a common language 공통의 언어 a common belief 일반화되어 있는 신앙
the common people 서민 common manners 버릇 없는 태도

3. raise; 들어 올리다, 높이다, 〈집 등을〉 세우다, 〈먼지 · 소동 · 반란 등을〉 일으키다, 승진[진급, 향상]시키다, 〈문제 · 질문 · 이의 등을〉 제기[제출, 제안]하다, 기르다(grow), 〈돈을〉 모으다

raise the standard of living 생활수준을 높이다
raise a house 집을 세우다 raise a rebellion 반란을 일으키다
raise rents 집세를 올리다 raise one's voice 소리 지르다
raise a question 문제를 제기하다 raise corn 옥수수를 기르다
raise children 아이들을 키우다 raise fund 기금을 모으다

Key Structure

The interest of the story lies <u>in</u> <u>how these very different people come together.</u>
≪전치사 뒤에 올 수 있는 것은 (대)명사, 명사구, 명사절. 여기서는 "how~together"이라는 명사절이 전치사(in)뒤에 와서 그 전치사(in)의 목적어 역할을 한다.≫

예제 57~61

Novels are imaginary stories about people and events. They are written to entertain and amuse. Two thousand years ago, Greek writers told tales of young lovers. Usually the lovers were separated by terrible events and were reunited only after much hardship and suffering. This plot idea is still in use today.

The most popular books for women today in North America are romance novels. Many millions are sold every year. This means that romance publishing is big business and very competitive. Companies survey their readers to determine the kinds of stories they like. One survey asked readers whether or not they would like more references to sex in their novels. Usually, romances are about love, not sex. But in today's market, publishers are ready to give their readers what they want.

The essence of the romance is to create suspense by putting obstacles in the way of the lovers. One simple obstacle is to make the hero and the heroine as different as possible. For example, an Eastern schoolteacher meets a Western cowboy. Of course, at first they don't like each other at all; but in time, they fall in love. Or a female social worker might meet an aggressive businessman.

Quite often the heroine is a spinster who has sworn never to marry. Or perhaps she has a special dislike for the hero and his family. The romance writer must come up with a plausible way to bring the two together. There are a number of popular plots that lead to marriage. Sometimes, the heroine – out of a sense of duty – will move in with the hero to help him raise his children. Or she may be a professional nanny who moves in with a widower.

A favourite plot is the marriage of convenience. Two people who don't like each other get married for financial or political reasons, or for the sake of the children. Later, of course, they fall in love. In most cases, there is some particular obstacle to marriage. Often either the hero or the heroine already has children, and he or she doesn't expect that anyone will want to take on their ready-made family. Sometimes, one or the other has a physical disability, or is of a different race, class, or background. For example, the heroine may come from a very strict and proper family, while the hero may have a dubious reputation, or even be a criminal. The interest of the story lies in how these very different people come together.

Usually, the hero is a very masculine type – a cowboy, engineer, military man, pirate, gambler, etc. The heroine is usually very female, but may have tomboy or spinster traits. She frequently has a strong personality and a temper and is described as feisty or fiery. A good example of the two types is Rhett Butler and Scarlett O'Hara in "Gone With the Wind."

Nearly every romance novel will contain some promotional offer to encourage readers to order more books. Romances can be addictive, and some women read them almost non-stop. Some romances are very well written, but the majority follow a set formula. That way, the reader always knows what to expect.

57. The most popular story told in novels is about ______________.

(a) science (b) romance
(c) terrible events (d) suspence

58. The romance novel usually contains ______________.

(a) sufferings
(b) pretty hero
(c) Unchangeable attitude of man and woman
(d) death

59. According to the passage, which is NOT true?

(a) Novels are imaginary stories.
(b) Many millions of romance novels are sold every year.
(c) Usually, romances are about love and sex.
(d) The essence of the romance is to put obstacles in the way of the lovers.

60. The underlined them refers to ____________________.

(a) readers (b) romance novels
(c) novel for women (d) hero tales

61. What is the favorite plot, according to the passage?

(a) cowboy (b) children
(c) marriage of convenience (d) special dislike

기초어휘

imaginary 상상의 / entertain 즐거움(=amuse) / reunite 하나가 되다 / competitive 경쟁적인
reference 언급 / essence 본질 / suspense 불안, 걱정 / obstacle 장애물, 방해물
spinster (혼기를 놓친) 노처녀 / come up with ~을 따라가다 / plausible 그럴듯한
duty 의무, 책임 / nanny 유모 / disability 무능, 장애 / dubious 의심스러운, 모호한
reputation 평판 / feisty (생각보다)도도한

심화어휘

1. entertain; 즐겁게 하다, 환대하다, 〈감정 · 의견 · 희망 등을〉 간직하다, 지니다

entertain guests(friends) 손님(친구들)을 즐겁게 하다
entertain an ideal(ambition) 이상을 품다
entertain hostility 적대감을 품다

2. suffer; 〈고통 · 상해 · 손해 · 슬픔 등을〉 경험하다, 겪다

suffer great losses 큰 손해를 입다 suffer death 죽다
suffer change 변화를 겪다

3. competitive; 경쟁의, 경쟁적인, 경쟁에 의한, 〈제품 · 가격이〉 경쟁할 수 있는

a competitive examination 경쟁시험 competitive games 경기 종목
a competitive price 경쟁 가격 competitive spirit 경쟁심

4. strict; 엄한, 엄밀한, 정밀한, 완전한(absolute), 순전한

strict rules 엄한 규칙 a stern teacher 엄격한 선생님
strict diet 철저한 다이어트 secrecy 극비

CHAPTER 3

글의 제목 / 주제 / 요지 찾기

Questions about the ideas of the passage

Tips for Fluent Reading

글쓴이가 글을 통해서 말하고자 하는 바를 찾아내는 것이 우리가 글을 읽고 분석하는 가장 큰 목적입니다. 이런 유형의 문제는 주로 topic과 main idea를 찾는 형태로 많이 출제됩니다. 많은 학생들이 이 두 가지를 쉽게 혼동하지만, 둘은 결코 같은 것이 아닙니다. 'Topic'은 'about what', 즉 글쓴이가 무엇에 관해 이야기하고 있는지를 묻는 것으로 단어나 구, 문장의 형태로 나타날 수 있습니다. 'Main Idea'는 바로 글쓴이가 글을 통해 말하고자 하는 요지로 반드시 문장으로 나타나게 되어 있습니다. 'Topic'은 글에 나오는 주요 단어를 모두 포함하는 가장 포괄적인 범위의 단어나 구를 찾아야 하고, 'Main Idea' 역시 지나치게 부분적이거나(too specific) 지나치게 광범위하지(too general) 않은 것으로 선택해야 합니다. 그러기 위해서는 당연히 글의 내용을 전체적으로 이해하는 것이 중요합니다.

Key Structure

They all want <u>many customers to buy</u> their product.

≪many customers가 부정사 "to buy"의 의미상 주어이고, 의미상 주어 앞에 전치사가 없는 이유는, 동사(want)가 타동사라서이다.≫

⊃ 예제 1

Advertising is an important part of the free enterprise system. This is because different businesses are competing for the same market. They all want many customers to buy their product. For this reason, they buy advertising space in newspapers or magazines and advertising time on radio or TV. They each hope that advertisements will cause more demand for their product.

1. What is the main idea of the above passage?

(a) types of ads
(b) people's demands for product
(c) advertising space
(d) importance of ads

기초어휘

enterprise 기업체, 회사 / compete for 경쟁하다, 겨루다

심화어휘

1. compete; 경쟁하다, 겨루다, 경합하다, 맞서다

compete with rivals 맞수들과 경쟁하다
compete with fossil fuels 화석연료와 경합하다
compete with China 중국과 경쟁하다

Key Structure

These were toys for the chimps to play with.

≪부정사 "to play with"의 의미상 주어는 "the chimps"이고, 문장동사가 자동사일 때는 부정사의 의미상 주어 앞에 전치사를 반드시 써 준다.(대부분 "for", 주격보어가 사람의 성질, 태도를 나타내는 형용사일 때만 "of"이다.

예제 2

In a large space at the Delta Primate Center in Louisiana, there were some long wooden poles. These were toys for the chimps to play with. One day, one of the chimps climbed a pole to get something from a high place. In other words, he used this toy as a tool. Soon all of the chimps knew how to use it. With this "ladder", the chimps could achieve their objective: they climbed over the wall and escaped into the trees outside the Prime Center.

2. What is the main theme of the passage?

(a) Chimps can climb a tree.
(b) There were some long wooden tree.
(c) Chimps used poles as a tool.
(d) Chimps can think.
(e) Chimps escaped the Prime Center.

기초어휘

primate 영장류 pole / 막대기, 장대, 기둥/ objective 목표, 목적

심화어휘

1. large; 큰, 대규모의, 〈수 · 양 · 액수 · 인구 등이〉 많은, 도량이 넓은, 허풍떠는

a large family 대가족 　　a large area 광대한 지역
on a large scale 대규모로 　　large insight 탁월한 식견
a large talk 허풍

2. objective; 목적의, 목표의, 객관적인

objective point 목표 지점 　　objective view(opinion)객관적인 견해(의견)
objective standard 객관적인 기준 　　objective analysis(description) 객관적인 분석(묘사)

Key Structure

Pavlov rang a bell <u>every time</u> he gave food to a dog.
≪"every time+주어+동사"는 "whenever+주어+동사"와 같다.≫

예제 3

Conditioning is a way of learning by association-that is, by putting together different ideas. In 1900, Ivan Pavlov, a Russian biologist, studied conditioning in dogs. Dogs innately salivate when they smell food. Pavlov rang a bell every time he gave food to a dog. soon the dog started to associate the sound of the bell with the smell of food. After some time, it salivated when it heard a bell alone, without food.

3. What is the topic of this passage?

(a) Pavlov's studies 　　(b) dogs ability of smelling food
(c) the importance of food 　　(d) a way of learning by association.

기초어휘

conditioning 조건화, 조절 / association 연합, 협회 / salivate 침 흘리다

심화어휘

1. innate; 〈성질 등을〉 타고난, 고유의, 본질적인

an innate instinct(characteristic) 타고난 본능(특성)
innate talent 타고난 재능 　　innate ability 타고난 능력
innate ideas(concepts) 본질적인 개념

Key Structure

They don't have to spend as much time <u>sitting in highway traffic.</u>
≪분사구문의 부대상황으로 "sitting in highway traffic"과 "pend as much time"은 동시발생이다.≫

⊃ 예제 4

Employees like telecommuting because they can have a more flexible working schedule. They can start to work when they want. They can work in the evening and go out in the morning or the afternoon. They don't have to spend as much time sitting in highway traffic. They can take advantage of the fresh air. Moreover, telecommuting gives working mothers and fathers more time with their families.

4. The passage is mainly about ______________________.

(a) the benefits of telecommuting
(b) the work at home
(c) employees who like telecommuting
(d) demands of employees
(e) part time jobs

기초어휘

employee 피고용인, 종업원(↔employer) / telecommuting 재택(자택)근무
flexible 구부리기 쉬운 / take advantage of 이용하다 / spend 시간 돈 (on) ~ing ~에 시간이나 돈을 쓰다, 소비하다

심화어휘

1. flexible; 구부리기[휘기] 쉬운, 〈사람 · 성격 등이〉 유순한, 융통성 있는, 탄력적인
   a flexible cord 마음대로 구부러지는 코드
   a flexible pipe 잘 구부러자는 파이프
   flexible schedule 탄력적인 스케쥴
   flexible working hours 융통성 있는 근무시간
2. fresh; 새로운, 〈식품 등이〉 신선한, 짠맛이 없는, 〈공기 · 기후 등이〉 맑은, 상쾌한, 풋내기의
   fresh paint 갓 칠한 페인트
   fresh eggs 막 낳은 달걀
   fresh bread 갓구운 빵
   a fresh hand 풋내기
   fresh meat 날고기
   fresh footprints 아직 새로운 발자국
   fresh water 민물

Key Structure

They are learning what it means to be a girl and a boy in the culture.
≪목적격 관계대명사 "what"은 "means"의 목적어이고, "it"은 가주어, "to be ~culture"는 진주어이다.≫

예제 5

Both Joy and Tommy are growing up in the culture of the United States. They are learning what it means to be a girl and a boy in the culture. Their sex at birth, female and male, is now becoming a gender—a way of thinking, speaking, and acting that is considered feminine or masculine. Each culture has its own way of defining gender, and very early in life gender becomes a basic part of a person's identity. According to Deborah Tannen, a professor at Georgetown University, gender differences are even reflected in the ways that men and women use language. Tannen and others who study communication believe that these differences begin early.

5. The best title of the passage is ______________________.
   (a) Boys and Girls
   (b) Different playing of boys and girls
   (c) American games
   (d) Best friends

기초어휘

female 여성 / feminine 여자의, 여성다운 / male 남성 / masculine 남성의, 남성다운
gender 성, 성별(특별히 사회적 의미)/ define 정의를 내리다, 규정짓다 identity 정체성
reflect 반영하다, 반사하다

심화어휘

feminine; 여자의, 여성의, 여성다운(womanly);상냥한, 연약한, ≪경멸≫ 〈남자가〉 여자 같은, 나약한
feminine beauty 여성미　　feminine dress 부인복
a man with a feminine walk 여자같이 걷는 남자

Key Structure

Although he was getting on in years, he had a longstanding habit of going out alone to walk in a shoddy part of town late at night.
≪"a long standing habit"은 "going~night"과 동격임.≫

예제 6

To many of his friends, Mr. Jones seemed quite eccentric. Although he was getting on in years, he had a longstanding habit of going out alone to walk in a shoddy part of town late at night. His friends warned him that this was a dangerous practice, and they advised him to do his walking during the day. However, he made no effort to change his routine.

6. Which of the following best expresses the idea of the passage?
(a) He who laughs last, laughs best.
(b) You're never too old to learn.
(c) You can't teach an old dog new tricks.
(d) practice makes perfect.
(e) silence is gold.

기초어휘

eccentric 별난, 비정상적인 / getting on in years 나이 먹다, 늙다
shoddy 초라한 / advise someone to ~ 누군가에게 ~을 하라고 충고하다
routine 일과, 일상의 일

심화어휘

eccentric; 〈사람 · 행동 등이〉 별난, 상궤(常軌)를 벗어난, 괴벽스러운
an eccentric person 괴벽스러운 사람, 기인
eccentric habit 괴이한 습관 eccentric clothes 상궤를 벗어난 옷

Key Structure

It seemed to have been gulped down.
≪"to have been gulped"는 수동형 완료부정사로 그 시제는 문장동사 "seemed"보다 더 먼저 이루어진 동작이다(즉, 과거완료).≫

예제 7

It was a very beautiful day, and I was on a big ship. The sea was calm and quiet, the sky blue and clear, and the sun warm and bright. Suddenly, heavy clouds covered the sky. The sun disappeared, the wind began to blow, and the sea turned to gray. There was such a fierce storm that the ship almost sank. At that moment another ship appeared from out of the dense fog. It was a pirate ship with a black flag and a crew of armed pirates. The pirates jumped onto our ship, and the battle began. I was assailed by three pirates at once. One pirate had a long beard, the second had a big black mustache, and the third had a wooden leg. I had a sword in my hand, and I fought bravely. All around me a violent battle raged. Soon I was wounded and lay bleeding on the deck. Then, all at once, a very beautiful girl appeared on the other ship. She gave some sharp commands, and all the pirates disappeared. Their ship vanished, too. It seemed to have been gulped down. Immediately the storm stopped and the sun came out again. Just then I awoke and found that I was in my own bed. The sun was shining, and there was a ray of light on my face.

7. The title that best expresses the ideas of this passage is ___________.

(a) A beautiful girl (b) An exciting experience
(c) A story of a hero (d) An unusual dream

기초어휘

fierce 사나운, 맹렬한 / sank (sink의 과거) 가라앉다, 침몰하다
dense 조밀한, 짙은 / pirate 해적 / assailed 공격하다 / beard 턱수염
mustache 콧수염 / vanish 사라지다 / gulp 꿀꺽꿀꺽 마시다, 삼키다

심화어휘

1. warm; 따뜻한, 온난한, 열렬한, 열심인, 온정 있는, ≪구어≫(숨바꼭질에서) 숨은 사람에게 가까워진(알아맞히기 · 보물찾기 등에서) 목표물에 가까운

a warm welcome(thanks) 따뜻한 환영(마음에서 우러나오는 감사)
a warm supporter 열광적 지지자 You are warm 너는 정답에 가까이 왔다.

2. cover; 덮다, 감싸다, 숨기다, 엄호하다, 〈어떤 범위에〉 걸치다, 미치다, 〈분야 · 영역 등을〉 포함하다, 〈비용 · 손실 등을〉 보상하다, 〈사건을〉 취재하다, 〈뉴스 등을〉 보도하다

covered with blossoms. 꽃으로 뒤덮여 있다 cover a mistake 과오를 숨기다
covers all cases 모든 경우에 적용된다 cover the accident. 그 사고를 보도하다.

3. black; 검은, 〈손 · 옷 등이〉 (더러워져) 오염된, 비관적인, 불길한, 악마에 관계된, 흉악한, 흑자의

black despair 암담한 절망 black ingratitude 배은 망덕
a black balance sheet 흑자 대차 대조표

4. sharp; 날카로운, 가파른, 〈길 등이〉 갑자기 꺾이는, 〈커브 · 회전 등이〉 급한, 〈윤곽 등이〉 뚜렷한, 〈의견이〉 대립된, 차이가 확실한, 〈맛 등이〉 자극성인, 〈추위 등이〉 살을 에는 듯한, 〈고통 등이〉 찌르는 듯한, 〈행동이〉 활발한, 빈틈없는

a sharp pencil 끝이 뾰족한 연필 a sharp impression 선명한 인상
sharp contrast 현저한 대조 a sharp pain 심한 통증
sharp arguments 격론 sharp criticism 신랄한 비평

Key Structure

It looks like a little pink pig and its eyes <u>remain closed</u> for three to four weeks.
≪동사 "remain"은 언제나 자동사이기에 수동태를 쓸 수 없고, 여기서 "closed"는 과거분사로 주격보어로 쓰였다.≫

예제 8

A new born panda is a tiny, helpless little creature. It looks like a little pink pig, and its eyes remain closed for three to four weeks. Pandas develop fairly slowly, compared to most animals. The babies are completely dependent on their mothers for a long time. In fact, they don't even begin to walk until they are about five months old. The only food they eat for at least a year is their mother's milk. That doesn't stop them from growing, however. Pandas may weigh over 55 pounds by the time they are a year old. Around that time, the young panda begins to eat bamboo, like its mother. By the time it is a year and a half old, a panda bear may weigh over 100 pounds.

8. Choose the main idea of this passage.

(a) A new born panda looks like a little pig
(b) Pandas eats bamboo.
(c) Pandas develop fairly slowly compared to most animals.
(d) Young panda bears gain weight quickly.

기초어휘

compare 비교하다 / be dependent on~ ~에 의지하다, 의존하다

심화어휘

helpless; (제 힘으로) 어찌할 수 없는, 속수무책인

helpless with laughter 아무리 해도 웃음이 멈춰지지 않는
helpless situation(circumstances) 어쩔 수 없는 상황
helpless firefighters 속수무책인 소방대원들

Key Structure

This fact is widely recognized and many governments have passed laws requiring seat belt use.

≪"which require seat belt use"라는 관계대명사절이 분사구로 전환되었다.≫

⊃ 예제 9

Many studies have shown that it is better to wear your seat belt when you are traveling in a car. Seat belts greatly reduce the risk of death or injury in an accident. This fact is widely recognized and many governments have passed laws requiring seat belt use. However, many people still do not wear seat belts. Researchers have found several reasons for this. Some people feel uncomfortable with the seat belt. They are afraid of being trapped in the car in an accident. Others do not think that the seat belt can protect them. They believe that people have no power over their fate. Fate will decide whether they will have an accident and whether they will be injured or die. They think that wearing a seat belt or not will make no difference.

9. What is the main topic of the passage?

(a) Some people don't think that seat belt can protect them.
(b) A car accident happens suddenly.
(c) In spite of the risk, some people do not wear seat belts.
(d) Travelling in a car is good.

기초어휘

recognize 인정하다 / uncomfortable 불편한, 불안한 / trap 가두다, 덫 / fate 운명

심화어휘

wear; 입고[신고, 쓰고, 끼고] 있다, 띠고[휴대하고] 있다, 〈향수를〉 바르다, 〈표정을〉 하고 있다, 닳아지게[해지게] 하다, 지치게[쇠약하게] 하다

wear a tie(socks / glasses / accessaries / shoes / helmet) 넥타이(양말 / 안경 / 악세서리 / 신발 / 헬멧)를 메다

wear perfume 향수를 바르다　　wear thin 닳아서 얇아지다

Key Structure

Traditionally the meats <u>associated with Easter</u> are lamb and ham.

≪원래는 "which are associated with easter"의 관계대명사절에서, "which are"가 생략된 것이다.≫

예제 10

Traditionally, the meats associated with Easter are lamb and ham. Both of these meats have had symbolic meaning since ancient times. In the Old Testament, Abraham used the lamb as a sacrifice after God ordered him not to kill his son Isaac. The lamb has always been a part of the Passover tradition. For Christians, the lamb symbolizes the sacrifice of Christ. For thousands of years, the pig has been a symbol of good luck. On Easter Sunday, smoked or cooked ham is the traditional main course in both Europe and the United States.

10. The passage is mainly about ______________________.

(a) symbolic meaning of lamb and ham　　(b) Abraham's story

(c) Christian's favorite foods　　(d) Easter Sunday

기초어휘

Easter 부활절 / Old Testament 구약성서 / sacrifice 희생물 / passover 유월절
symbolize 상징하다 / smoked 훈제한, 그을린

심화어휘

main; 주된, 주요부[중심]를 이루는

main issue 주요 문제　　main gate 정문

main difference 주요 차이　　main topic 주제

CHAPTER 4

글의 목적/분위기/ 글의 순서

Overall Review Question

Tips for Fluent Reading

앞에서도 계속 강조해 왔듯이, 모든 독해 문제 풀이의 기본은 본문 내용의 이해에 있습니다. 본문 내용에 대한 충분한 이해를 바탕으로 다음의 풀이 전략을 사용해 보세요. 특정 정보를 찾아낼 때에는 문제에 제시된 단어가 포함되어 있는 본문 속 문장을 찾아서 문제를 해결하도록 합니다.
어조나 작가가 글을 쓴 목적 등을 이해하기 위해서는 전반적인 글의 분위기 파악이 중요합니다. 본문 속에서 배경이나 분위기, 기분을 나타내는 단어를 중점적으로 찾아서 문제를 해결하도록 합니다. 주어진 문장을 본문 속에 적당히 끼워 넣는 문제에 있어서는 주어진 문장을 토대로 앞뒤에 들어갈 내용을 유추하는 능력이 필요합니다. 이 때에는 특별히 접속사에 유의하도록 합니다. 위에 제시된 유형 외에도 글의 앞이나 뒤에 올 내용에 대해 묻는 문제가 있을 수 있습니다. 이 때에는 앞에 올 내용을 유추할 때는 본문의 맨 처음 문장을, 뒤에 온 내용을 유추할 때에는 본문의 맨 뒤 문장을 근거로 문제를 풀면 쉽게 해결할 수 있습니다.
잊지 마세요!! 당연한 말 같지만, 모든 독해 문제 풀이의 핵심은 바로 본문에 있습니다.

Key Structure

Whenever it was necessary to discuss matters of public importance all the citizens gathered in the market place.

≪복합관계부사 whenever가 이끄는 양보(비록 −일지라도)의 부사절이고, "it"은 가주어, "to discuss~importance"는 진주어이다.≫

예제 1

In the beginning, all the Greeks were equally rich and equally poor. Every man owned a certain number of cows and sheep. His mud-hut was his castle. He was free to come and go as he wished.

Whenever it was necessary to discuss matters of public importance, all the citizens gathered in the market place. One of the older men of the village was elected chairman, and it was his duty to see that everybody had a chance to express his views. In case of war, one of the strong and able villagers was chosen commander, but the same people who had voluntarily given this man the right to be their leader, claimed an equal right to deprive him of his job, once the danger had gone.

1. Where in the passage those the author mention who chairman was elected?

(a) Lines 1–2　　(b) Lines 3–4
(c) Lines 5–6　　(d) Lines 7–8

기초어휘

castle 성 / duty 의무, 임무 / express 표현하다 / commander 지휘관, 사령관/ deprive 빼앗다

심화어휘

1. gather; 모으다, 〈꽃 · 과실 등을〉 따다, 〈세금 · 회비 · 대금 등을〉 징수하다, 〈속력 등을〉 더하다

gather a crowd 사람들을 모으다　　gather roses 장미를 따다
gather statistics 통계를 내다　　gather information 정보를 수집하다
gather one's strength 기력을 회복하다

2. express; 〈감정 · 생각 등을〉 표현[표명]하다, (기호 · 숫자 등으로) 나타내다, 상징하다, ≪미≫ 〈물건을〉 (지급) 운송편으로 부치다;≪영≫ 〈편지 등을〉 속달로 부치다

express satisfaction 만족을 표하다　　express addition 덧셈을 나타내다
express mail 속달로 부치다

Key Structure

It's this incomparable Irish spirit that makes Bennigan's the perfect place to celebrate anything, <u>no matter how small</u>.
≪"no matter how small it is"에서 "it is"가 생략되었다≫

예제 2~3

When D. Bennigan came to America from his native Ireland, he looked for places like the taverns of his homeland. Places where he could relax with family and friends, enjoy great food, raise a glass, and wish them a hearty Sl?nte!

Sl?nte (pronounced "slawn cheh") is a traditional Irish toast in the ancient Gaelic language meaning 'To your health'. It represents a spirit of good cheer and generosity, trademarks of the kind of Irish hospitality that D. Bennigan had in mind when he founded Bennigan's Grill & Tavern.

It's this incomparable Irish spirit that makes Bennigan's the perfect place to celebrate anything, no matter how small. So, from all of us at Bennigan's Irish American Grill & Tavern to you, Sl?nte! (Bennigan's)

2. Which of the following best describes the author's purpose for writing this passage?
(a) To advertise (b) To entertain
(c) To persuade (d) To motivate

3. Where in the passage those the author mention what the meaning of the Sl?nte is?
(a) Lines 2-3 (b) Lines 4-5
(c) Lines 6-7 (d) Lines 8-9

기초어휘

tavern 선술집 / hearty 마음에서 우러난 / toast 건배의 인사, 축배 / generosity 관대함, 아량
hospitality 환대 / no matter how 아무리 ~하다 할지라도

심화어휘

1. native; 출생지의, 본래의, 〈성격 · 능력 등이〉 타고난, 그 지방 고유의, 향토[지방]적인, 꾸밈없는, 자연스런, 소박한, 〈광물 등이〉 천연 그대로의
one's native country[land] 본국 one's native place 출생지, 고향
native ability 천부적인 재능

[유의어] native, natural은 다 같이 「타고난」의 뜻을 나타내지만, 전자가 후천적이 아님을 강조하는데 대해 후자는 그 사람[물건]의 본질이나 특징으로서 갖고 있는 것을 나타낸다.
native art 향토 예술　　native copper 천연[자연]동(銅)

2. hearty; 마음에서 우러난, 정성어린, 애정 어린
receive a hearty welcome 환대를 받다　　hearty dislike 마음속으로부터의 혐오
hearty support 마음에서 우러나는 지지　　hearty wish 애정 어린 소망

Key Structure

The opening of the galleries marked the return of the magnificent African collections after nearly 30 years at the Museum of Mankind
≪"the+동사원형+ing"에서 "동사원형+ing"는 더 이상 동명사가 아닌 명사이다.≫

예제 4~5

The Sainsbury African Galleries provide a substantial and permanent exhibition space for one of the finest collections of African art and artefacts in the world. The collections comprises over 200,000 objects and encompasses both archeological and contemporary material, which includes both unique masterpieces of artistry and objects of everyday life. Highlights of the collection include a magnificent brass head of a Yoruba ruler from Ife, Nigeria; Asante goldwork from Ghana and the Torday collection of Central African sculpture, textiles and weaponry.

The opening of the galleries marked the return of the magnificent African collections after nearly 30 years at the Museum of Mankind.

(The British museum)

4. Where in the passage those the author mention what the highlight of the collection is?
(a) Lines 1-2　　(b) Lines 3-4
(c) Lines 5-7　　(d) Lines 8-9

5. Which of the following best describes the author's purpose for writing this passage?
(a) To inform the reader　　(b) To entertain the reader
(c) To persuade the reader　　(d) To motivate the reader

기초어휘

substantial 내용 있는, 견고한 / comprise 포함하다(encompass, include)
masterpiece 걸작, 명작 / brass 놋쇠

심화어휘

mark; 표시하다

mark a map 지도에 표시를 하다 　 mark with a cross 가위표를 하다
mark in pencil 연필로 표시하다

Key Structure

There is no law [that states 〈*that* the president of the United States must have a cabinet〉].

≪[that states 〈*that* the president of the United States must have a cabinet〉] 전체는 "law"를 수식하는 형용사절이고 that은 주격관계대명사임. 또한 그 뒤의 〈*that* the president of the United States must have a cabinet〉는 동사 "states"의 목적어이고 "*that*"은 접속사이다.≫

예제 6

There is no law that states that the president of the United States must have a cabinet. The constitution states only that the president "may require the opinion, in writing, of the principal officer in each of the executive department, upon any subject relating to the duties of their respective officer" The President does not have to ask for this advice, and, when it is given, does not have to take it. Nevertheless presidents have looked to this group of officer councilors for information and advice, because no one person can know about everything that is going on in the nation.

Each President chooses the members of the cabinet with the "advice and consent" of the Senate, but these advisers serve at the president's pleasure and can be fired at any time.

They are chosen for their knowledge, their experience, their special talents, or their general wisdom. They maybe old and trusted friends, sometimes even relatives. They can be farmers, diplomats, scientists, or politicians. They meet weekly in the cabinet room next to the President's Oval Office in the west wing of the White House.

6. Where in the passage dose the author mention how often cabinet meets?

(a) Lines 5–7
(b) Lines 8–10
(c) Lines 11–13
(d) Lines 14–15

기초어휘

cabinet 대통령자문위원회 / constitution 헌법 / Senate 상원
President's Oval Office 대통령집무실

심화어휘

1. deliver; 〈물건 · 편지를〉 배달하다, 〈전언 등을〉 전하다, 넘겨주다, 〈연설 · 설교를〉 하다, 〈의견을〉 말하다, 구해내다, 분만[해산]시키다

deliver a package 소포를 배달하다
deliver a verdict of guilty 유죄 평결을 선포하다
deliver a speech(lecture) 연설(강의)하다
deliver a baby 아기를 분만하다

2. improve; 개선[개량]하다, 증진하다, 진보[향상]시키다, 〈토지 · 부동산의〉 가치를 높이다

improve health 건강을 증진하다
improve productivity 생산성을 향상시키다
improve chance 가능성을 높이다
improve farmland 농토를 개량하다

Key Structure

As a result, thousands die each year from diseases [that could have been treated].
≪주격관계대명사 "that"의 선행사는 "diseases"이고, 그 뒤의 동사 "could have been treated"는 가정법 과거완료이다.≫

예제 7~8

"It can't happen to me." That's the unfortunate mind-set that causes many people to skip simple medical screening tests. As a result, thousands die each year from diseases that could have been treated. Consider these figures:

If everyone over 50 followed official colon-cancer screening recommendations, the death rate from colon cancer would be reduced by up to 50%.

※ Widespread blood pressure screening and treatment have cut the death rate from stroke and heart attack by at least 50%.

※ In women over age 50, yearly mammograms reduce the breast-cancer death rate by 30%.

※ Between 1955 and 1992, deaths from cervical cancer declined by 74%, mainly because women started having regular Pap tests.

To help you figure out which tests you need, we've compiled lists of exams for men and women in three age groups. These are recommendations for healthy people at average risk. Talk to your doctor about a schedule that meets your needs. (Reader's Digest)

7. The author's purpose in this passage is to ________.

(a) discuss kinds of the cancer
(b) tell the story of heathy people
(c) canvass for medical tests
(d) explain relations between age and cancer

8. The tone of this passage is ________.

(a) outraged (b) judicial
(c) hypnotic (d) informative

기초어휘

skip 간과하다 / screening 검진 / mammogram 유방 X선 사진 / cervical cancer 자궁경부암
pop test 자궁경부암 조기진단 / compile 수집하다, 편집하다 / colon-cancer 결장암
recommendation 충고

심화어휘

1. cut; 베다, 상처를 내다, 그만두다〈수업을〉 빼먹다, 줄이다, 〈각본 · 영화 등을〉 삭제[컷]하다, 〈비용을〉 삭감하다, 〈값을〉 깎아 내리다

cut a finger with a knife 칼로 손가락을 베다
cut an acquaintanceship 교제를 끊다
cut school[the class] 학교[수업]를 빼먹다
cut price 값을 깍다
cut corners 지름길로 가다

2. attack; 공격, 습격, 비난, (병의) 발작, (일 · 식사 등의 정력적인) 개시, 착수

deliver[make] an attack 공격(을 가)하다
have an attack of fever 열병에 걸리다
fatal attack 치명적인 공격
bomb attack 폭탄 공격

Key Structure

Even though SAMSUNG has had unprecedented growth for the past 50 years, it must continue to survive in an era of even fiercer competition with internationally established rival companies.

≪여기서 "unprecedented"는 동사가 아닌 과거분사로 뒤의 명사 "growth"를 수식한다.≫

⊃ 예제 9~10

The corporate management philosophy of SAMSUNG is present and future visions.

SAMSUNG was established in 1938, and has extended its business to an international level with mottos such as "Economic contribution to the nation," "Priority of the human resources," and "Pursuit of rationalism" for over 50 years. SAMSUNG has acknowledged the need to transform its management philosophy to become more globalization-oriented and specialized in order to keep up with the rapidly changing global economy. Even though SAMSUNG has had unprecedented growth for the past 50 years, it must continue to survive in an era of even fiercer competition with internationally established rival companies. Therefore SAMSUNG changed its group corporate identity and management philosophy to "We will devote our people and technologies to create superior products and services, thereby contributing to a better global society." (SAMSUNG homepage)

9. The tone of this writer can best be described as ___________.

(a) cold (b) sadistic
(c) emotional (d) descriptive

10. Which of the following best describes the author's purpose for writing this passage?

(a) To explain the products and services
(b) To tell the history of the company
(c) To advertise good image of the company
(d) To describe how SAMSUNG was extended

기초어휘

contribution 기여 / priority 우선권 / pursuit 추구 / unprecedented 전례가 없는
fierce 격렬한, 거센 / devote 바치다, 쏟다

심화어휘

unprecedented; 전례가 없는, 전에 없던, 공전의

unprecedented event 전례가 없는 사건 unprecedented promotion 전례없는 승진
unprecedented rate 전례없는 비율(속도)

Key Structure

We see a substantial waste of educated manpower <u>much of which is far from adequately trained.</u>

≪"목적격 관계대명사(전치사 of의 목적어) which"는 계속적 용법으로 쓰였으며, 선행사는 "educated manpower"이다.≫

예제 11~12

The current system of selecting college freshmen leaves room for reform, especially in terms of aptitude and potential and the capacity of society to harness the student's experience. We see a substantial waste of educated manpower, much of which is far from adequately trained. Unfortunately, we have no sage or pundit to prescribe a cure-all for the ills of our education system and examination craze. But at least we should pause to ponder what good education of all about.

11. The author's purpose in this passage is to ____________.

(a) give an opinion of college
(b) demand the educational world's serious reflection
(c) describe the history of college
(d) outline various systems of selecting college freshmen

12. The tone of this passage is ____________.

(a) critical (b) humorous
(c) informative (d) concerned

기초어휘

reform 개혁하다, 재편성하다 / aptitude 적성 / adequately 알맞은 / sage 현인
pundit 전문가 / pause 잠시 멈추다 / ponder 곰곰이 생각하다
leave room for ~여지가 남아있다./ harness 이용하다

심화어휘

1. current; 지금의, 현재의, 현행의, 통용하는, 유통[유포]되고 있는, 현재 유행하는, 초서체의

current issue[number] 최근호　　current news 시사 뉴스
current price 현재 가격　　current writing 초서(체)

2. potential; 가능성이 있는, 잠재하는, 잠재 세력의

a potential genius 천재적 소질을 가진 사람
potential health threat 잠재적인 건강 위협(요인)
potential employer 잠재 고용주

Key Structure

Wherever he is some assault against your person is being committed.
≪"Wherever he is"는 복합관계부사절이고, 복합관계부사(whenever, wherever, however)는 언제나 양보(비록 -일지라도)의 부사절을 이끈다.≫

예제 13~14

Anyone can make friends these days, since the claims to friendship are usually based on "Hello" and a lunch; but the making of enemies, there is an art to that. It is infinitely harder to win enemies than friends, and harder still to hold on to them. Remember: the subject is real enemies, not just those pests of whom one thinks with a dull, bored ache from time to time, or those whose irritating presence makes one pine for Madagascar. A real enemy is in a different league. He is a hated hater, a mirror image of one's meanest desires. He wants to do unto you exactly as you would do unto him. Such people are rare and valuable, and with the proper care and feeding they may last a lifetime. An enemy well nurtured is a joy forever. When he is not maligning you in public, he is maligning you in private ;when he is not maligning you in private, he is contemplating doing so. Wherever he is, some assault against your person is being committed. Wherever he has been, your bones lie heaped. He is enormous. In your dreams his shoulders press against your skull. He himself never sleeps. There is too much mischief to be done, too many calamities begging to be aired. And think: it is you who brought this creature into being. He lives and fumes solely for you. (고려대 대학원)

13. The tone of this writer can best be described as ______________.

(a) bitter (b) cavalier
(c) ominous (d) tongue in cheek

14. Which of the following best describes the author's purpose for writing this passage?

(a) To inform the reader (b) To entertain the reader
(c) To persuade the reader (d) To motivate the reader

기초어휘

irritating 거슬리는, 짜증나는 / mean 비열한 / contemplate 생각하다 / heap 쌓아올리다
mischief 해악 / calumny 비방, 중상모략 / pest 성가신 사람, 골칫거리
pine 애타게 그리워하다, 열망하다 / malign 헐뜯다 / fume (연기나 김 등을)뿜다, 약이 오르다

심화어휘

1. rare; 드문, 진기한, 〈공기 등이〉 희박한≪구어≫ 참 좋은, 매우 뛰어난

rare opportunity 드문 기회 rare animals(plants) 희귀한 동물들(식물들)
rare talent 참 좋은 재능

2. valuable; 금전적 가치가 있는, 값비싼, 귀중한, 매우 유익한

valuable papers 유가 증권 valuable jewelry 값비싼 보석류
a valuable friend(experience) 소중한 친구(경험)
valuable information 유익한 정보

3. proper; 적당[타당]한, 적절한, 알맞은, 예의 바른

at proper time 적당한 때에 a proper person 적절한 사람
a proper young man 예의 바른 젊은 남자

4. enormous; 거대한, 막대한, 엄청난

an enormous difference 엄청난 차이 enormous pressure 엄청난 압력
enormous cellphone bills 엄청난 휴대전화 사용료

Key Structure

Nicotine influences other brain circuits [that fine-tune the dopamine release], Daniel McGehee and his team at the University of Chicago in Illinois have found.
≪"Nicotine influences other brain circuits [that fine-tune the dopamine release]"는 "have found"의 목적어이고, "that"은 주격관계대명사로 동사 "fine-tune" 주어이다.≫

예제 15~16

Smokers who resolve to quit often feel the first painful pangs an hour after their last cigarette. ① Researchers have now identified the brain circuits that trigger this craving, which might offer new routes to beating addiction. ②

One lungful of smoke swamps brain cells with nicotine, causing release of reward chemical dopamine. ③ Within seconds, the same cells become desensitized to nicotine. ④

Nicotine influences other brain circuits that fine-tune the dopamine release, Daniel McGehee and his team at the University of Chicago in Illinois have found. In particular, a hit of nicotine switches off one circuit for about an hour. This circuit normally stops cells releasing dopamine. (Nature)

15. The tone of this passage is _____________.

(a) concerned (b) disinterested
(c) placid (d) exaggerated

16. The following sentence could be added to this paragraph.

> So it is unclear why smokers enjoy a whole cigarette.

Where would it best fit in the passage?

(a) ① (b) ②
(c) ③ (d) ④

기초어휘

resolve 결심하다 / swamp 완전히 적시다 / desensitize 민감성을 줄이다
switch off 절단하다

심화어휘

1. painful; 아픈, 고통을 주는, (정신적으로) 고통스러운

   a painful wound 아픈 상처　　a painful memory 불쾌한(고통스러운) 기억
   a painful life 괴로운 생활

2. trigger; (방아쇠를 당겨서) 쏘다, 발사하다, 폭발시키다, 〈일을〉 일으키다, 시작케 하다, 유발하다

   trigger violence 폭력을 유발하다　　trigger curiosity 호기심을 자아내다
   trigger inflation 물가인상을 촉발하다

Key Structure

The hippocampus is a part of the mesial temporal lobe memory system, and known to be affected early in the course of AD.

≪known to be affected의 주어는 the hippocampus이다.≫

예제 17

Alzheimer's disease(AD) is the most common cause of dementia, yet impossible to diagnose precisely without invasive techniques, particularly at the onset of the disease. ① The hippocampus is a part of the mesial temporal lobe memory system, and known to be affected early in the course of AD. Recent development of imaging techniques, particularly magnetic resonance imaging(MRI), has made the evaluation of diminutive brain structures, such as the hippocampus, conceivable. ② The purpose of this study was to focus on the sensitivity and specificity of different approaches of hippocampal imaging by MRI, and their applications for the diagnosis of incipient AD. ③ Hippocampal pathology was evaluated by means of linear(interuncal distance, IUD), planimetric(hippocampal area) and volumetric measurements, complete with T2 relaxometry using an 1.5 T imager. The accuracy of hippocampal measurements was compared to that of the amygdala and the frontal lobes. Various procedures for normalization of the data to the head and brain size were compared.④

17. The following sentence could be added to this paragraph.

> Therefore, a reliable diagnostic method is needed.

Where would it best fit in the passage?

(a) ①   (b) ②

(c) ③   (d) ④

기초어휘

dementia 치매 / hippocampus (대뇌 측두엽의) 해마회(回), 해마 / mesial 중간의
invasive techniques 수술이나 내시경 검사처럼 환자 신체 내부를 조사하는 기술

심화어휘

1. precise; 〈정의 · 지시 등이〉 정확한, 정밀한, 〈수량 등이〉 정량의, 조금도 틀림없는, 〈사람 · 태도가〉 정확한, 까다로운, 〈발음 등이〉 지극히 명확한
precise meaning 정확한 의미   precise measurement 정확한 측정
precise pronunciation 정확한 발음   precise study 철저한 연구

2. temporal; 시간의, 일시적인, 잠시의, 현세의, 속세의
temporal joy 일시적인 기쁨   temporal prosperity 현세의 번영
temporal power 세속적 권력

CHAPTER 5

글의 추론

Indirectly answered questions

Tips for Fluent Reading

추론(Inference)은 독해에 있어 가장 어려운 부분 중의 하나라고 할 수 있습니다.
본문의 내용이 포함하는 속뜻을 추적해서 찾는 것이죠.
추론을 잘하기 위해서는 먼저 본문의 내용을 잘 이해하는 것이 중요합니다.

Key Structure

Despite their diversity, Harvard students as a group do seem to share a few characteristics.

≪"despite"는 전치사. 전치사 뒤에는 "주어+동사"는 절대 올 수 없고, (대)명사, 명사구, 명사절이 올 수 있음. 여기서는 명사인 "their diversity"가 왔다.≫

⊃ 예제 1~2

Visitors often ask: Who is the typical Harvard student? The answer is that there is no such person. Each student is a unique individual, and the student body is incredibly diverse.

Harvard men and women represent an array of ethnic groups, religious traditions, and political persuasions. They come from every region of the United States and more than 100 other countries. They include undergraduates and graduate, continuing education, and Summer School students. They range from pre-teens to octogenarians; in 1997, Mary Fasano became the oldest person ever to earn a Harvard degree when she graduated from the Extension School at the age of 89.

Harvard College students have a remarkable range of backgrounds and academic and extracurricular interests. Two-thirds come from public schools, and about two-thirds receive some form of financial aid. Despite their diversity, Harvard students as a group do seem to share a few characteristics.

(Harvard University homepage)

1. It can be inferred from the passage that Harvard College students are ____.

(a) greasy grind (b) common
(c) various (d) humorous

2. The underlined word 'They' refers to ________.

(a) Visitors (b) ethnic groups
(c) Summer School students (d) Harvard College students

기초어휘

incredibly 믿을 수 없는, 대단히 / diverse 여러 종류의, 다양한(varied)
an array of 죽 늘어선 / persuasion 설득, 신념

심화어휘

1. typical; 전형적인, 대표적인, 상징적인

typical businessman 전형적인 실업가 typical customers 전형적인 고객
typical sample 전형적인 표본

2. unique; 유일(무이)한, 대신할 것이 없는, 특이한

unique ceremony 독특한 의식 unique way 유일무이한 방식
unique opportunity 유일한 기회

3. diverse; 다른 종류의, 여러 가지의, 다양한

diverse interests 다양한 취미 diverse opinions 다양한 의견
diverse ranges 다양한 범주

Key Structure

Thus loosely understood, 'essay' admits a wide variety of subject, purpose, tone, and style.

≪"when it is loosely understood"라는 절이 분사구문으로 전환된 것이다.≫

⊃ 예제 3~4

As originally used by Montaigne, 'essay' signified a rather brief, loosely organised prose work, personal and informal in style. Today, although writers continue the tradition of Montaigne, 'essay' has broadened its meaning to include much more than the informal, but it has also become a convenient term which would be unwise to restrict too narrowly. Nowadays we take 'essay' to mean a relatively short piece of prose nonfiction, with the purpose of informing, persuading, or entertaining its reader. Thus, loosely understood, 'essay' admits a wide variety of subject, purpose, tone, and style.

3. According to the passage, we can say that the essay ________________.

(a) is a personal and interesting verse (b) is formal in style

(c) is enlightening (d) is boring

4. The underlined expression 'the tradition of Montaigne' means ________.

(a) essay means a brief and loosely organised prose work.

(b) writers must to enlightening its reader.

(c) essay admits a wide variety.

(d) the purpose of essay is to give intelligence to its reader.

기초어휘

signified 나타내다, 의미하다(mean)

심화어휘

1. informal; 형식[격식]을 따지지 않는, 탁 터놓은, 평상복의, 비공식의, 약식의, 〈말 등이〉 평이한, 회화체[구어체]의

an informal meeting(gathering) 격의 없는 회합

an informal visit[talk] 비공식 방문[회의]

informal interview 격의 없는 인터뷰

2. relative; 비교상의, 상대적인, 관계있는

relative merits 우열 a relative concept 상대 개념

relative temperature 상대적 온도 relative humidity 상대 습도

Key Structure

Those five emphatic words waked something in me [that has never slept since.]

≪주격 관계대명사 "that"절은 선행사 "something"을 수식하며, 여기서 "since"는 부사이다.≫

예제 5

Mine has been the limited experience of one who live in a world without color and without sound. But ever since my student days I have had a joyous certainty that my physical handicaps were not an essential part of my being, since they were not in any way a part of my mind. This faith was confirmed when I came to Descartes' maxim, "I think, therefore I am."

Those five emphatic words waked something in me that has never slept since. I knew then that my mind could be a positive instrument of happiness, bridging over the dark, silent void with concepts of a vibrant, light-flooded happiness. I learned that it is possible for us to create light and sound and order within us, no matter what calamity may befall us in the outer world.

(Helen Keller: *The story of My Life*)

5. According to the passage, the author ________________.

(a) is a physically handicapped person.
(b) has psychosis.
(c) feels sad about her handicap.
(d) is a man of weak faith.

기초어휘

certainty 확신 / being 존재 / in any way 어떤 점에 있어서도 / confirm 확립하다
emphatic 힘있는 / void 공간 / vibrant 활기에 넘친 / light-flooded 빛이 가득한
calamity 재난 / befall (재난이) 떨어지다

심화어휘

dark; 어두운, 〈뜻이〉 애매한, 비밀의, 음흉한, 〈얼굴빛 등이〉 흐린

the darkest ignorance 극도의 무지 dark deeds 나쁜 짓, 비행
dark face 시커먼 얼굴 dark side 어두운 측면
dark cloud 먹구름

Key Structure

She was a big woman with very large arms and looked as though she would not hesitate to use them if called upon to do so.

≪"if called upon to do so"는 분사구문이다(원래는 "if she were called upon to do so").≫

예제 6~7

Miss Smith's landlady, Mrs. Baker, admitted Charley without surprise. She was a big woman with very large arms and looked as though she would not hesitate to use them if called upon to do so. "Yes", she said. "Miss Smith is in. You'd better go straight up. Number 12 was on the top floor. I must excuse myself for not going up first to tell Miss Smith, but I have trouble with my feet and can't be expected to wear them out running up and downstairs after my lodger's friend." Charley sympathized with her over her feet and started briskly up the stairs. Mrs. Baker remained standing in the hall for a moment and, as he reached the first floor, called out sharply, "No gentleman visitors after eleven. That's my rule and Miss Smith doesn't need to be reminded of it."

6. According to the passage, Mrs. Baker's character is ______.

(a) timid (b) strict (c) tender (d) amiable

7. The underlined word 'them' refers to ______.

(a) Mrs. Baker's large arms (b) lodger's friends

(c) gentleman visitors (d) Mrs. Baker's feet

기초어휘

landlady (여관, 하숙 등의) 여주인 / excuse 변명하다 / lodger 하숙인, 숙박인

심화어휘

1. big; 큰, 〈사람이〉 훌륭한, 중요한, ≪구어≫ 〈일이〉 중요한, 〈의복이〉 낙낙한, 〈와인이〉 감칠맛 있는, 알코올 도수가 높은

a big man (덩치) 큰 남자
a big voice 큰 목소리
a big event 중대한 사건
a big problem 중대한 문제
a big announcement 중대 발표

2. bright; 빛나는, 밝은, 〈날씨가〉 화창한, 〈색이〉 선명한, 영리한, 〈표정 등이〉 밝은, 〈장래 등이〉유망한

bright red 선홍색
a bright idea 영리한 생각
bright prospects[hopes] 빛나는 전도[희망]

Key Structure

Not much to anyone's surprise but to the disappointment of many, he chose a tract of land on the banks of the Pot ó mac River, a few miles upstream from his beloved plantation Mount Vernon.

≪"not A(much to anyone's surprise) but B(to the disappointment of many)"의 병렬 구문이다.≫

예제 8~9

Washington was the first city in history to be created exclusively for the purpose of governance. Following the Revolution, members of Congress had hotly debated the question of a permanent home for themselves and for those departments—the Department of state, the Treasury, the patent Office, and so on. In 1790, mostly in order to put an end to congressional bickering, George Washington was charged with selecting a site for the newly designated federal district. Not much to anyone's surprise but to the disappointment of many, he chose a tract of land on the banks of the Pot ó mac River, a few miles upstream from his beloved plantation Mount Vernon.

The District of Columbia was taken in part from Virginia and in part from Maryland. At the time its hundred square miles consisted of gently rolling hills, some under cultivation pot ó mac. There is now a section of Washington that is commonly referred to as Foggy Bottom; that section bore the same nickname a hundred and eighty years ago.

Two port cities, Alexandria and Georgetown, flourished within sight of the new capital and gave it access by ship to the most important cities of the infant nation and also to the far-off ports of England and the Continent.

8. We can infer from the passage that the term "foggy bottom" means a section of Washington, D.C that ______________.

(a) used to be mostly swampland

(b) lies underneath Mount Vernon

(c) has not lowest population in the district

(d) was village squares

9. It can be inferred from the passage that Alexandria was important in the eighteenth century because it ______________.

(a) linked the federal district with the ocean.

(b) was the home of the Department of State.

(c) was a strategic point of the east coast.

(d) was a model for building the new federal district.

기초어휘

exclusively 오직 / debated 논쟁하다 / designated 지정된 / far-off 아득히 먼
Mount Vernon 미국 / Virginia 주 북동부 / Potomac 강변, 조지 워싱턴의 옛 집과 묘지
rolling 완만한 / cultivation 경작 / within sight of 보이는 곳에서

심화어휘

1. exclusive; 배타[배제]적인, 독점적인, 폐쇄적인, 〈호텔 · 상점 등이〉 회원[고객]을 엄선하는, 상류의, 고급의

exclusive rights 독점권 　 an exclusive contract 독점 계약
an exclusive story 독점 기사 　 an exclusive club 회원제 고급 클럽

2. permanent; 영속하는, (반)영구적인, 불변의, 상설의, 〈물건이〉 오래 가는, 변색[퇴색]하지 않는

a permanent residence 영주(永住) 　 permanent employment 종신 고용
permanent ink 바래지 않는 잉크

CHAPTER 6

실전 종합 문제

Actual Test

Key Structure

Chocolate is a food made from the seeds of a tropical tree called the cacao.
≪위 문장은 원래 "Chocolate is a food (which is) made from the seeds of a tropical tree (which is) called the cacao."였는데, "which is"가 각각 생략된 문장이다.≫

예제 1~5

Chocolate is a food made from the seeds of a tropical tree called the cacao. The word cacao apparently comes from two Maya Indian words meaning bitter juice. The word chocolate came from two Maya words meaning sour water.

The cacao tree produces the seeds, or cacao beans, from which all chocolate is made. These trees flourish in a warm, moist climate. They live within an area about 20 latitude north and south of the equator. Most of the world's cacao beans come from the west coast of Africa, where Ghana, the Ivory Coast, and Nigeria are the largest producers. Brazil is the largest cacao bean producer in the Western hemisphere.

The cultivated cacao tree grows about 7.6 meters high. It produces leaves, flowers, and fruit in all seasons of the year. The flowers are small. They grow singly and in clusters on the main stem on the branches and on the trunk. The ripe fruit (or pod) may be red, yellow, golden, pale green, or a combination of these colors. The melon-like pod contains 20 to 49 almond-shaped seeds which, when fermented and dried, become the commercial cacao bean.

Because of a mistake in spelling, probably made by English importers many years ago, these beans became known as cocoa beans in English-speaking countries. This causes many people to think ________________.

1. What is the subject of this passage?
   (a) a note on chocolate
   (b) a habitat of coconut palm tree
   (c) a manufacturing process of the commercial cacao bean
   (d) English importers' mistake

2. According to the passage, the cacao trees __________.
   (a) produce the seeds from which all cocoa is made.
   (b) flourish in a cold, dry climate.
   (c) produce fruits in all seasons of the year.
   (d) have beautiful flowers.

3. Which of the following is closest in meaning to 'in clusters'?
   (a) in groups
   (b) in all directions
   (c) thinly
   (d) sparsely

4. The word 'cultivated' is closest in meaning to ______.
   (a) wild
   (b) tilled
   (c) cultured
   (d) refined

5. What is the most appropriate expression for the underlined part?
   (a) the beans come from the coconut palm tree instead of the cacao tree.
   (b) Hawaii is the largest cocoa beans producer.
   (c) chocolate is delicious.
   (d) English importers are smart.

기초어휘

tropical 열대(지방)의 / flourish 번창하다, 무성하게 자라다 / latitude 위도 / equator 적도
cluster 송이, 무리, 집단 / ferment 발효시키다 / commercial 상업상의, 통상의

심화어휘

1. bitter; 쓴, 고통스러운, 비통한, 〈바람 · 추위 등이〉 지독한, 모진, 받아들이기 어려운, 〈말 등이〉 신랄한, 통렬한

a bitter taste 쓴 맛 / a bitter experience 쓰라린 경험
a bitter chill 살을 에는 듯한 추위 / bitter criticism 가혹한 비판

2. sour; 신, 시큼한, 시어진 〈우유 등〉, 신내가 나는, 심술궂은, 〈마음이〉 비뚤어진

sour milk 신 우유 / sour face 심술궂은 얼굴
sour stomach 쓰린 속

3. small; 〈형상 · 규모가〉 작은, 소형의, 〈허리 · 손목 등이〉 가는, 호리호리한, 적은, 얼마되지 않는, 사람 수가 적은, 〈시간이〉 짧은, 근소한, 거의 없는

a small waist 가는 허리 / a small number 소수
small percent(portion) 작은 비율 / a small possibility 희박한 가능성

Key Structure

Research <u>suggests</u> that aerobic exercise <u>helps</u> you learn new things and remember old information better.

≪"suggest"가 "암시하다"의 뜻 일 때는, 그 뒤의 접속사 "that"절에서 직ㅅ ㄹ법 동사가 오고, "제안하다"의 뜻 일 때는 "(should) 동사원형"이 온다.≫

예제 6~10

It won't surprise that aerobic exercise does more than raise the heart rate: It lifts the spirit and builds confidence. But many brain researchers believe that something else happens, too. Just as exercise makes the bones, muscles, heart, and lungs stronger, researchers think that it also strengthens important parts of the brain.

Research suggests that aerobic exercise helps you learn new things and remember old information better. Aerobic exercise sends more blood to the brain and it also feeds the brain with substances that________________. If the exercise has complicated movements like dance steps or basketball moves, the brain produces even more nerve connection – the more connection, the better the brain can process all kinds of information.

Scientists still don't fully understand the relationship between exercise and brain power. For the moment, people just have to trust that exercise is helping them to learn or remember. Scientific research clearly shows, however, that three or more workouts a week are good for you . A study in the Journal of the American Medical Association, for example, shows that walking four to five miles(6.5 to 8km) an hour for 45minutes five times a week helps you live longer. So don't be a couch potato. Get out there and do something!

6. What is the main topic of the passage?
   (a) Important parts of the brain
   (b) Some ways of for good health
   (c) Profits of aerobic exercise
   (d) Couch potato

7. Which of the following best expresses the main idea of the passage?
   (a) Exercise don't lifts the spirit or builds confidence.
   (b) Aerobic exercise is all subtly linked with brain power.
   (c) Aerobic exercise can't help you learn new things and understand old information better.
   (d) If the exercise has complicated movements like basketball moves, the brain get a shock.

8. According to the passage, which of these statements about exercise is false?
   (a) It makes you feel more self-confident.
   (b) It gives you better eyesight.
   (c) It can help you learn things better.
   (d) It helps you live longer

9. In this passage, what does the term 'a couch potato' refer to?
   (a) a picnic　　(b) a underexercised person
   (c)an athlete　　(d) a patient

10. What is the most appropriate expression for the underlined part?

(a) develop new nerve connections.
(b) strengthen memory.
(c) help body stronger.
(d) understand new information.

기초어휘

substances 물질 / complicated 복잡한, 어려운 / for the moment 우선, 당장에는
workout 운동, 체조

심화어휘

1. build; 짓다, 세우다, 〈기계 따위를〉 조립하다, 〈새가〉〈둥지를〉 틀다, 〈불을〉 피우다, 〈부 · 명성 등을〉 쌓아올리다

build a nest 둥지를 틀다
build a ship 배를 만들다
build fund 기금을 모으다
build a fire 불을 지피다

2. strengthen; 강하게 하다, 튼튼하게 하다, 증강하다, 강화하다

strengthen one's body 몸을 튼튼하게 하다
strengthen position 입장을 강화하다
strengthen protection 보호를 강화하다

Key Structure

With one in two marriages <u>ending in divorce,</u> there is an increase in single-parent homes: a father or mother living with one or more children.
≪"ending in divorce"는 "which ends in divorce"가 분사구로 전환된 것이다.≫

예제 11~15

The American family unit is in the process of change. In the first half of the twentieth century, there were mainly two types of families: the extended and the nuclear. An extended family includes mother, father, children, and some other relatives, such as grandparents, aunts, or cousins, living in the same house. A nuclear family is composed of just parents and children living under the same roof.

As the American economy progressed from agricultural to industrial, people were forced to move to different parts of the country to get good jobs. These jobs were mainly in the large cities. Now, in fact, three-quarters of Americans live in urban areas, a mere 2.5 percent of the nation's total land mass. Of the 118 million in the civilian labor force, only 3 million still work on the farm.

Since moving for better jobs often split up the extended family, the nuclear family became more prevalent. At present, 55 percent of the families in the United States are nuclear families. But besides these two types of traditional family groupings–extended and nuclear– the word family is now being expanded to include a variety of other living arrangements.

American families today are made up of many ______ combinations. With one in two marriages ending in divorce, there is an increase in single–parent homes: a father or mother living with one or more children. About one household in ten is headed by a single parent. Divorce has also led to more "blended families." Blended families occur when previously married men and women marry again and combine the children from former marriages into a new family. Some married couples are deciding not to have any children at all, so there is an increase in two–person childless families. Many couples are also deciding not to get married legally, and so there is an increase in couples just living together. There are also more people living alone: single, widowed, divorced. About one in five Americans lives alone.

11. What is main topic of the passage?

(a) Increase of divorce rate
(b) a problem of single parent home
(c) Domestic American
(d) The changing American family

12. The word 'prevalent' is closest in meaning to ____________.

(a) current
(b) old–fashioned
(c) encouraged
(d) extend

13. Which word worst fits blank?

(a) diverse
(b) different
(c) varied
(d) changed

14. According to the passage, the nuclear family ____________.

(a) is composed of grandparents, parents and children.

(b) became more prevalent by industrialization.

(c) still works on the farm.

(d) is 45 percent of the families in the United states.

15. Why occurs 'blended family'?

(a) Industrialization

(b) Breaking of the extended family

(c) Digamy

(d) Bachelorhood

기초어휘

extended 펼친, 확장한 / is composed of ~으로 구성되다 / split up 분열시키다, 나누다(divide)
prevalent 일반적으로 행해지는, 유행하는 / expanded 확대된 / blended 혼합된
combine 결합시키다

심화어휘

1. nuclear; (세포) 핵의, 원자핵[력]의, 핵무기의, 원자력을 동력으로 하는

nuclear division 핵분열 | nuclear charge 핵전하
nuclear war 핵전쟁 | a nuclear reactor 핵원자로

2. prevalent; 일반적으로 행하여지는, 유행하는, 널리 퍼진

prevalent distrust 만연한 불신 | prevalent plague 널리 퍼진 역병
prevalent curruption 널리 퍼진 부패

3. traditional; 전통의, 전통적인, 전설의

traditional grammar 전통 문법 | traditional wisdom 전통적인 지혜
traditional remedies 전통적인 치료법

Key Structure

If you tickle a chimp, it will likely laugh, but the sound doesn't resemble human laughter so much as it does panting, with one sound per inhale and exhale.
≪원급 구문이고, "does"는 "resemble"을 대신하는 대동사이다.≫

⊃ 예제 16~20

To investigate the roots of laughter, scientists have turned to our primate cousins. If you tickle a chimp (carefully; and preferably a baby), it will likely laugh, but the sound doesn't resemble human laughter so much as it does panting, with one sound per inhale and exhale. Neuroscientist Robert Provine of the University of Maryland realized that the reason chimps cannot emit a string of "ho ho ho" is that they cannot make more than a single sound when they exhale or inhale. Humans, ____1____, can chop up a single exhalation into multiple bursts of "ha ha ha"–or words. (Speech results from chopping up an exhalation into separate sounds.) "Laughter," says Provine, "is a probe into such fundamental questions as _______2_________ but other apes can't." No humanlike laughing, no speaking.

16. What is the passage about?
(a) Laughter (b) Breathing
(c) Breeding (d) Sound

17. What is main idea of this passage?
(a) Chimps' laughter is resemble human laughter.
(b) Other apes can speak.
(c) No humanlike laughing, no speaking.
(d) Laughter can help you to get good health.

18. In this passage, what does the term 'our primate cousins' refer to ________.
(a) Human (b) Chimps (c) Laughter (d) Speaking

19. What is the most appropriate conjunction for underlined part 1 ?
(a) Therefore (b) Finally
(c) In contrast (d) In fact

20. Which expression best fits blank 2 ?

(a) Why human can speak

(b) What is laughter

(c) Why human laugh

(d) What is the principle of breathing

기초어휘

primate 영장류 / tickle 간질이다, 기쁘게 하다 / inhale 들이쉬다 / exhale 내쉬다
chop up 자르다, 잘게 썰다

심화어휘

1. investigate; 조사하다, 수사하다, 연구하다

investigate the cause of the car accident 자동차 사고의 원인을 조사하다
investigate the source of the rumor 소문의 출처를 조사하다
investigate the place of crime 범죄 장소를 조사하다

2. fundamental; 기본적인, 근원의, 최초의, 근본적인

fundamental colors 원색
fundamental human rights 기본적 인권
a fundamental principle[rule] 원리, 원칙

Key Structure

With the exception of homework, there is nothing that a student is required to do after school hours.

≪"that"은 목적격 관계대명사(to do의 목적어, 선행사는 nothing)절로 "nothing"을 수식한다.≫

예제 21~25

Mandatory volunteering for high school is not a good idea. First, many students do volunteering, and most do it with full force. By the time a volunteering student becomes a senior, that student could earn as many as 1000+ service hours. If an entering freshman is told that he or she must volunteer for a pre-set number of hours, the student might become resentful, complete the required hours, and never volunteer again. The volunteered hours would end up being less than the hours being volunteered now.

Many students do not have the time to volunteer. School goes from a set starting time to a set ending time. With the exception of homework, there is nothing that a student is required to do after school hours.

_______, mandatory volunteering is an oxymoron. If students are required to volunteer it is no longer volunteering. The performed service becomes one more thing to do in order to graduate from high school. The quality of work can suffer greatly. If a student enjoys volunteering, he or she will volunteer without having to be told.

21. What is the main idea of the passage?

(a) Mandatory volunteering has reverse effects.
(b) Volunteering for high school is good experience.
(c) Senior is very busy due to extracurricular activity.
(d) After-school schedule is more important than volunteering.

22. Which of following does NOT happen when students do volunteer with full force?

(a) never volunteer again
(b) become resentful
(c) don't have time for extracurricular
(d) enjoy volunteering seriously

23. According to the passage, the meaning of 'mandatory' is __________.

(a) obligatory　　(b) spontaneous
(c) extraordinary　　(d) careless

24. What is the most appropriate conjunction for underlined part?

(a) However　　(b) Finally
(c) In contrast　　(d) In fact

25. Choose the same meaning as the following sentence.

(a) Required volunteering is a thing of no worth as sincere volunteering.
(b) Volunteering is mandatory activity originally.
(c) Student must do volunteering.
(d) Volunteering is very hard work to students.

기초어휘

mandatory 강제의(obligatory) 필수의 / with the exception of ~을 제외하고

심화어휘

1. mandatory; 명령의, 통치를 위임받은, 강제의, 의무의, 필수의

mandatory meeting 의무적인 모임　mandatory courses 필수 과정
mandatory rule[administration] 위임 통치

2. full; 가득 찬, 완전한, 〈용적 · 수량 · 정도 등이〉 최대한의, 최고의, 〈계절 등이〉 한창의, 〈회의 · 모임 등이〉 전원 출석의, 배부른

full capacity 최고 용량　full explanation 완전한 설명
full moon 보름달　full speed 최고 속력
full house 대만원

Key Structure

Venus, Earth, and Mars, <u>although comparably endowed with carbon and water,</u> evolved differently from each other owing to size and distance from the Sun.

≪종속접속사+현재분사(혹은 과거분사)가 올 경우, 이는 분사구문이다.≫

예제 26~30

Venus, Earth, and Mars, although comparably endowed with carbon and water, evolved differently from each other owing to size and distance from the Sun.

Venus, closest to the Sun, receives the most solar energy. Early in its history, it may have had an ocean, At that time the Sun shone less brightly than now. But it would have boiled off as the Sun's output increased. Meanwhile, volcanoes were venting carbon dioxide into the atmosphere. Venus lacked the water to return carbon to the crust as carbonate rock, and carbon dioxide levels rose limitlessly. This created a "greenhouse", allowing solar energy to penetrate the atmosphere but blocking the escape of heat. Temperatures on Venus are now too hot to support even primitive life.

Earth is far enough from the Sun to retain water. It recycles its carbon through plate tectonics(changes in the structure of its crust). The prolonged presence of water enabled marine organisms to evolve, and they now serve as a means of removing carbon dioxide from the atmosphere. Plate tectonics with its associated volcanism, continuously returns carbon dioxide to the atmosphere. Thus in equilibrium, Earth's climate is moderate.

Mars, too, probably once had a moderate climate and liquid surface, but it is tectonically less active. The result: carbon dioxide was removed from the atmosphere but not returned to it. Thus the 'greenhouse effect' weakened, water froze, and Mars was left high and dry.

26. What is the main idea of the above passage?
(a) The similarity of Venus, Earth, and Mars
(b) The different development of three planets
(c) Imaginable life forms on planets
(d) The necessity of water to sustain life

27. In their early histories, Venus, Earth, and Mars were similar in which of the following?
(a) Size and distance from the sun
(b) Water and carbon resources
(c) Solar energy
(d) Tectonic action and heat

28. The 'greenhouse' means here ___________.
(a) a place for organisms to grow
(b) a removal of carbon dioxide from the atmosphere
(c) an increase in liquid surface on a plant
(d) an entrapment of heat from the Sun

29. The word 'it' refers to __________.
(a) greenhouse (b) Mars
(c) carbon dioxide (d) the atmosphere

30. It can be inferred from the passage that the climate on Mars is now ______.
(a) high temperature (b) moderate
(c) cold (d) variable

기초어휘

endowed 부여하다, 타고나다 / evolve 진화(발전)시키다/vent 발산하다 / crust 딱딱한 표면 penetrate 꿰뚫다, 스며들다 / plate tectonics 판구조학 / prolonged 장기의 equilibrium 평형 / carbonate 탄산염 / marine organism 수중생물 / volcanism 화산활동

심화어휘

1. lack; …이 없다, 결핍되다, 필요로 하다, …만큼 모자라다

lack water. 물이 없다
lacks common sense 상식이 없다
lack two votes to win 이기는데 두 표가 모자란다.

2. return; 돌려주다[보내다], 보답하다, 대답하다, (정식으로) 제출하다, 보고하다, 〈빛 · 소리 등이〉 반사하다, 반향하다, 〈노동 · 투자 등이〉 〈이익 · 소득을〉 내다, 〈선거구가〉 〈후보를〉 선출하다, 재선하다

return a favor 호의를 호의로 답하다
return a kindness with ingratitude 은혜를 원수로 갚다
return a person to Parliament …을 국회 의원으로 선출하다

3. moderate; 절제[절도] 있는, 온건한, 알맞은, 〈기후 등이〉 온화한, (정치 · 종교에서) 온건[중도]파의

moderate opinions 온건한 의견
moderate prices 적당한 값
moderate exercise 적당한 운동
a moderate winter 온화한 겨울

4. active; 활동적인, 의욕적인, 적극적인, 〈운동 · 경기 등이〉 체력을 요하는

active volcano 활화산
active role 적극적인 역할
active business 활동적인 사업

5. dry; 마른, 물기 없는, 말린 , 가래가 나오지 않는, 목마른, 냉담한, 무미건조한

a dry house 습기 없는 집
a dry cough 마른 기침
a dry season 건기(乾期)
dry thanks 형식적인[성의 없는] 감사

Key Structure

They help build underwater foundations for bridges and piers.

≪"help"동사 뒤에는 "to+동사원형" 또는 "동사원형" 양쪽 모두 올 수 있다. 단, "동사원형+ing"가 올 수도 있는데 그 때는 "help"의 뜻이 "피하다(=avoid)"가 된다.≫

⊃ 예제 31~34

Some people enjoy deep-sea diving as a sport, but for most divers it is a way of reaching jobs that must be done under water. For example, deep-sea divers raise sunken ships. They help build underwater foundations for bridges and piers. Sometimes, divers recover great treasures of gold and silver and other valuable cargoes from the holds of sunken ships. A diver faces danger each time he goes under water.

His life depends on a steady supply of air pumped to him through a hose from the surface. He usually wears a bulky waterproof suit and a metal helmet that make it difficult to move about. Often a diver must grope his way through icy water filled with mud and silt that make it hard to see. Swift currents may hurl him against an obstacle and tangle his air hose. If a diver rises to the surface too rapidly, he may suffer a sickness called the bends.

There are four main kinds of deep-sea divers. Commercial divers salvage sunken ships, cargos, and aircraft, and help build or repair docks, breakwaters, piers bridges and pipelines. Open sea divers harvest sponges, pearl oysters, seaweed, and other products of the sea. Research divers search the bottoms of oceans for oil and conduct scientific investigations of sea life, geology, and oceanography. Military divers blow up harbor defenses, clear mines from harbors, scout shorelines, and also salvage sunken ships and aircraft.

31. The very air a deep-sea diver breathes is supplied by ________.

(a) patient men in a boat above
(b) an automatic engine in his hand
(c) gills
(d) an aqualung

32. Which of the following suggested title gives the best description of the passage?

(a) The modern knight in Armor (b) diving for sunken ship
(c) diving for fun (d) deep-sea diving

33. A diver may suffer a sickness called the bends. The word "bends" most nearly means ______.

(a) yellow fever (b) poliomyelitis
(c) caisson disease (d) rheumatic fever

34. A culture-pearl raiser could be a ______________.

(a) research diver (b) open sea diver
(c) commercial diver (d) military diver

기초어휘

grope 손으로 더듬어 찾다 / tangle 엉키게 하다 /salvage 해난구조, 침몰선 인양
conduct 지도하다, 지휘하다 / pier 부두, 방파제 / sponge 해면동물, 해면체
mine 지뢰 / gills 아가미

심화어휘

recover; 되찾다, 〈시체 등을〉 찾아내다, 〈손실을〉 벌충하다, 개심시키다, 회개시키다, 〈유용한 물자를〉 회수하다, 재생시키다

recover consciousness 의식을 회복하다
recover health 건강을 회복하다
recover popularity 인기를 만회하다

Key Structure

National income available for spending was nearly a third greater than it had been in 1950.

≪"available"은 원래 "which was available"인데 "which was"가 생략된 것임. 즉, "주격관계대명사+be동사+어미가" "ible/able"로 끝나는 형용사에서 "주격관계대명사+be동사"는 생략할 수 있다.≫

예제 35~40

The economy of the United States after 1952 was the economy of a well-fed, almost fully employed people. An economic survey of the year 1955, a typical year of the 1950s, may be illuminating as illustrating the decade. The national output was valued at about 10 percent above that of 1954. The production of manufacturers was about 40 percent more than it had averaged in the years immediately following World War Ⅱ. The country's businesses spent about 30 billion dollars for new plans and machinery. National income available for spending was nearly a third greater than it had been in 1950. Consumers spent about 256 billion dollars; that is, about 700 million dollars a day, or about 25 million dollars every hour, all around the clock. Sixty-five million people held jobs and only a little more than two million wanted jobs but could not find them. Only agriculture complained that it was not sharing in the boom. As farmers' share of their products declined, marketing costs rose. But there were few pessimists among the observers of the national economy. Those few appeared to fear that the prosperity was based on government pump priming on a stupendous scale.

35. The passage is mainly concerned with ___________.

(a) the manufactural trends of the 1950s.

(b) the reduction of agricultural products.

(c) the unemployment rate in 1955.

(d) the general economic situation in the 1950s.

36. According to the passage, income available for spending in the United states was how much greater in 1955 than in 1950 ?

(a) 10%
(b) 33%
(c) 40%
(d) 60%

37. About how many people were unemployed in 1955 ?

(a) One million
(b) Two million
(c) Three million
(d) sixty-five million

38. The passage implies that most Americans in 1955 viewed the national economy with an air of ________.

(a) distrust
(b) cynicism
(c) confusion
(d) optimism

39. Which of the following was LEAST satisfied with the national economy in the 1950s?

(a) Farmers
(b) Manufacturers
(c) Consumers
(d) Economist

40. The word "boom" could best be replaced by ________.

(a) nearby explosion

(b) crashing noise

(c) general public support

(d) rapid economic growth

기초어휘

illuminating 조명하는 / illustrating 설명하다/well-fed 영양이 충분한, 살찐
around the clock 하루종일/pessimist 비관론자 / priming 갑작스러운 주입
stupendous 엄청난, 굉장한 /cynicism 비꼬는 버릇, 냉소주의]

심화어휘

1. economic; 경제학의, 경제(상)의

economic principles 경제학상의 법칙　　an economic policy 경제 정책
economic miracle 경제적 기적

2. share; 분배하다, 나누어 주다, 할당하다

share rent 집세를 분담하다　　share cost 비용 분담하다
share profit 이익을 분배하다　　share burden 부담을 나누다

Key Structure

all <u>that matters</u> is whether the evidence supports their contentions.
≪"that matters"의 "that"은 관계대명사(주격)이고, 선행사는 "all"임. "all"이 셀 수 있는 것을 나타낼 때는 복수취급, 셀 수 없는 것을 말 할 때는 단수 취급한다.≫

⊃ 예제 41~45

But the success of science depends on the self-correcting character of science. There should be a way of testing any valid idea. It should be possible to reproduce any valid experiment. The character or beliefs of scientists are irrelevant; all that matters is whether the evidence supports their contentions. Arguments from authority are useless; too many authorities have been mistaken too often. I would like to see these very effective scientific ways of thought communicated by the schools and the media; and it would certainly be a great surprise and delight to see them introduced into politics. Scientists change their minds completely and publicly when presented with new evidence or new arguments. I cannot recall the last time a politician showed a similar openness and willingness to change.

41. What is the main idea of the passage?
(a) Science and its practical application
(b) The importance of scientific beliefs
(c) An important characteristic of science
(d) Some similarities between politics and science

42. The previous paragraph most like discusses ___________.
(a) the achievements of science
(b) self-correction
(c) faulty information
(d) the schools and the media

43. If a scientist repeats an experiment several times and does not obtain similar results each time, the experiment must be ________.
(a) tested again
(b) very complex
(c) invalid
(d) scientific

44. Choose the one which is most essential to scientist' work.
(a) Success
(b) Authority
(c) Evidence
(d) Willingness

45. The author implies that the scientific mode of thinking should be propagated by ________.
(a) newspapers
(b) businesses
(c) research centers
(d) the medical community

기초어휘

effective 효과적인/irrelevant 엉뚱한, 부적절한, 무관계한
contention 논쟁, 주장 / authority 권위, 근거 /propagate 선전하다, 보급시키다, 전하다

심화어휘

1. valid; 근거가 확실한, 정확한, 정당[타당]한, 유효한
a valid conclusion 타당한 결론 a valid remedy 효과적인 치료
a valid contract 합법적인 계약

2. irrelevant; 부적절한, 무관계한 ≪to≫, 〈증거 등이〉 소송의 쟁점과 관계없는
irrelevant facts 무관한 사실 irrelevant questions 무관한 질문
irrelevant answer 무관한 대답

Key Structure

What they don't understand is the fact [that for centuries this animal has controlled the character of the forests and streams] [*that* it occupies].
≪"[that"~streams]는 접속사 "that"절로 바로 앞 "the fact"와 동격의 명사절이고, [*that* it occupies]는 관계대명사 "*that*"절로 선행사인 "the forests and streams"를 수식한다.≫

⊃ 예제 46~50

Beavers appear to lead such exemplary lives that a trapper once observed that 'beavers follow close to the line of the Ten Commandments.' The Ten Commandments do not mention anything about building dams, lodges, and canals, however, and the beaver's penchant for doing so has got it into a lot of hot water lately. Fishing enthusiasts in the Midwest and New England are complaining about beaver dams that spoil streams for trout and, in the Southeast, lumber companies object whenever the animals flood out valuable stands of commercial timber. But some beaver experts champion a more charitable view. Historically, they say, this creature's impact in the environment has been tremendously significant. 'Some people think of the beaver the same way they think of the gypsy moth.' said a scientist. They think it just comes through and eats and destroys. What they don't understand is the fact that for centuries this animal has controlled the character of the forests and streams that it occupies.'

46. What is the best title for this passage?
(a) North America's Beaver Population
(b) The Influence of Beavers on Lumbering
(c) The Controversy over Beavers and the Environment
(d) The Beaver's Taste for Building Dams

47. Choose the one which best expresses "has got it into a lot of hot water"
(a) violate the Ten Commandments (b) plumb the depth
(c) are in trouble (d) enjoy hot baths

48. It can be inferred from the passage that gypsy moths ________.

(a) follow the Biblical rules. (b) build dams and canals.

(c) eat fish. (d) have a bad reputation.

49. Why do lumber companies complain about beavers?

(a) Because they eat out valuable timbers.

(b) Because they spoil trout streams.

(c) Because they create floods in forests.

(d) Because they conserve wood resources.

50. What does "it" refer to?

(a) the beaver (b) the gypsy moth (c) a fact (d) a character

기초어휘

penchant 경향, 취미 / timber 재목, 목재/charitable 자비로운, 관대한

심화어휘

spoil; 망치다, 상하게 하다, 못쓰게 만들다, 〈음식물을〉 썩히다, 〈흥미 · 식욕 등을〉 깨다, 못되게[버릇없게] 만들다

spoil eggs 계란을 썩히다　　spoil appetite 식욕을 망치다

spoil children 아이들을 버릇없게 만들다

Key Structure

Changes in cognitive function stemming from SDAT of other excessive loss of brain cells are irreversible.

≪여기서 "stemming"은 "which stems"라는 관계사절을 분사구로 전환시킨 것이다.≫

예제 51~59

→[1] Loss of mental function is the number one cause of anxiety in older individuals and their families concerning age related disorders. As individuals get older, occasional forgetfulness may be the only change that healthy individuals experience. However, about 10% of the older population's forgetfulness migrates to moderate confusion. Another 15% of the older population develops two age-related disorders termed Senile Dementia of the Alzheimer type\(SDAT) and Parkinson's Disease. SDAT develops when there is a loss of brain cells resulting from a cerebral hemorrhage or interruption of the blood supply to a particular region of the brain. Delirium of severe dementia can arise from acute electrolyte disturbances involving changes in sodium or potassium levels, thyroid dysfunction, drug toxicity, of illnesses that decreases the oxygen supply to the brain. Changes in cognitive function stemming from SDAT of other excessive loss of brain cells are irreversible.

→[2] About 1 million Americans have Parkinson's disease. Although this disorder is uncommon among people under age 50, the incidence increases with age and peaks about age 75. Parkinson's disease is caused by a loss of neurons from the base of the brain whose function is production of the neurotransmitter dopamine. When dopamine is no longer produced in sufficient quantities, the characteristic symptoms of Parkinson's disease, which are muscular rigidity tremors, difficulty with balance, and a shuffling gait become evident. To treat Parkinson's disease, the drug levodopa is used to supplement the body's natural supply of dopamine. As more neurons are lost, the patient is forced to take ever-increasing levels of the drug to keep symptoms in check.

Current research is directed towards drugs that will slow the rate of neuronal loss, thereby reducing the amount of levodopa required of control.

51. What is the main topic of this passage?

(a) The difference between SDAT and Parkinson's disease
(b) Age related disorders of the nervous System
(c) The treatment of mental disease
(d) The origin of confusion

52. Look at the word <u>anxiety</u> in paragraph 1. Find out another word or expression in paragraph 1 that is closet in meaning to <u>anxiety</u> :

53. Which of following is the first anxiety in older population?

(a) Forgetfulness (b) Loss of mental function
(c) Change of health (d) Loss of brain cells

54. What percentage of the older population has SDAT and Parkinson's disease?

(a) 5% (b) 10%

(c) 15% (d) 25%

55. Which of following was NOT mentioned in the passage as a factor of delirium of dementia?

(a) Electrolyte disturbances (b) Thyroid dysfunction

(c) Drug toxicity (d) Cerebral hemorrhage

56. According to the passage, what is the main factor of SDAT?

(a) Loss of brain cells

(b) Loss of blood supply to the brain

(c) Cerebral hemorrhage

(d) Drug toxicity

57. According to the passage, which age is the peak of Parkinson's disease incidence?

(a) 75 years (b) 50 years

(c) 45 years (d) 80 years

58. Which of the following is NOT mentioned as the symptoms of Parkinson's disease?

(a) Muscular tremors (b) Balance difficulty

(c) shuffling gait (d) Loss of muscle

59. According to the passage, the drug levodopa supplements _________.

(a) Blood (b) Dopamine

(c) Neurotransmitter (d) Levodopa

기초어휘

disorder 무질서, 질병 / occasional 이따금씩의/moderate 적당한
Senile Dementia 노인성치매/cerebral hemorrhage 대뇌출혈/electrolyte 전해질
delirium 일시적인 정신착란/sodium 나트륨 / potassium 칼륨/thyroid 갑상선
toxicity 독성/tremor 경련 / neurotransmitter 신경전달물질/symptom 증상 / rigidity 경직
irreversible 변경할 수 없는/shuffling 질질 끄는/gait 걷는 모양

심화어휘

1. mental; 마음의, 정신의, 심적인, 내적인

mental health 정신 건강 mental shock 정신적 충격
mental fatigue 정신적 피로

2. evident; 분명한(plain), 명백한

evident satisfaction 분명한 만족 evident distress 분명한 피로
evident proof 분명한 증거

Key Structure

It wasn't until the early 1990's that skyscraper buildings began to be constructed with historical as well as architectural design.

≪"It wasn't until the early 1990's that~design."은 "It is(was)~that~강조구문이고, 시간표시 부사구인" until the early 1990's를 강조한다. 또한 상관 접속사 "as well as"는 historical (design)과 architectural design을 병렬한다.≫

예제 60~70

→[1] During the mid 1880's, the Chicago School of Architecture and Engineering successfully researched and tested the **concept** of reinforced concrete and steel. **Their** efforts **lead** to the mass development of theses two products in the design of what was then known as high rise buildings. Shortly thereafter, engineers named Sullivan, Burnham, Root, Holabird and Roche advanced the concept of Skyscraper buildings. This concept was based on skeletal structures made of steel instead of cast iron. Steel framing provided a building with immense verticality.

Next the reinforced concrete, (concrete slabs with one inch steel rods mounted inside of it) were bolted and welded to the steel framing. It wasn't until the early 1990's that skyscraper buildings began to be constructed with historical as well as architechural design. For example, the Woolworth Building, designed by Cass Gillbert in 1911–1913 focused around neo-gothic ornamental form. This design trend continued until the period of 1925. It was during the mid 1920's that architects named McKenzie, Voorhies, and Gemlin intensified construction design towards expression.

→[3] This construction principle became known as International Style Design. Architects Shreve, Lamb and Harmon further developed **this design** in building the Empire State Building in 1931. The Empire State Building achieved the remarkable height of 1250 feet and weighed over 300,000 tons. Finally, an architect named Raymond Hood designed several disk-shaped skyscrapers during the period of 1931 to 1939. An example of this design structure is the immense Rockefeller Center in New York City that caps the utilitarian framework of skyscrapers as an amalgam of beauty.

In summary, one can see that the relationship of steel and reinforced concrete combined the use of technology and architecture in the creation of landmark historical buildings still in use today.

60. Which of the following is the best title for the passage?

(a) The mid 1880's Architecture

(b) The background of skyscraper construction

(c) The development concrete and steel

(d) The design of skyscraper

61. Look at the word concept in paragraph 1. Find another word or expression in paragraph 3 that is closet in meaning to concept :

62. Look at the word Their in paragraph 1. Find another word or phrase in paragraph 1 that Their refers to :

63. Which were used to construct buildings in the early nineteenth century?

(a) Concrete and Steel

(b) Reinforced concrete and steel

(c) Reinforced concrete and cast iron

(d) Concrete and cast iron

64. According to the passage, a skyscraper building could be constructed by changing the material. How?

(a) Iron → Steel

(b) Steel → Iron

(c) Iron → Concrete

(d) Steel → Concrete

65. According to the passage, who focused around neo-gothic style to built skyscraper buiding?

(a) Sullivan (b) Gillbert

(c) Gemlin (d) shreve

66. What is the International style design's main focus?

(a) Expression (b) Intension

(c) Remark (d) constructionism

67. The Author mentions all of the following as architects who designed the Empire State building EXCEPT?

(a) Shreve (b) Lamb

(c) Harmon (d) Raymond

68. Look at the word <u>lead</u> in paragraph 1. Find another word or expression in paragraph 3 that is closest in meaning to <u>lead</u> :

69. Look at the word <u>this design</u> in paragraph 3. Find another word or phrase in paragraph 3 that <u>this design</u> refers to :

70. According to the passage, which building was designed disk-shaped?

(a) New York City hall (b) Rockefeller center

(c) Empire state building (d) Woolworth building

기초어휘

reinforced 강화된 / skyscraper 초고층 건물 /skeletal 골격의 / cast iron 주철, 무쇠
immense 거대한 / verticality 수직상태/rod 막대기 / weld 용접하다
ornamental 장식적인 / intensify 강화시키다 / utilitarian 실용주의의
amalgam 아말감(수은과 다른 금속과의 합금)

심화어휘

1. reinforce; 강화[증강, 보강]하다, …의 힘을 북돋우다, 지원군을 보내다, 증원하다, 〈공급 · 저장 · 경험 등을〉 늘리다, 〈건강을〉 증진하다

reinforce a garrison 수비대를 증강하다 reinforce a supply 공급을 늘리다
reinforce team 팀을 보강하다

2. historical; 역사상의, 사실(史實)에 바탕을 둔, 과거에 속하는, 역사상 실존한

a historical novel[play] 역사 소설[사극]
historical records 역사 기록 문서
historical evidence 사실(史實)

3. remarkable; 주목할 만한, 놀랄 만한, 두드러진, 비범한

a remarkable change 현저한 변화
remarkable achievement 놀랄만한 업적
a remarkable discovery 주목할 만한 발견
remarkable recovery 두드러진 회복

Key Structure

The red panda is smaller than the giant panda, <u>the red panda being about sixty centimeters in length compared to the approximately one hundred and seventy centimeter long giant panda.</u>

≪"the red panda being about sixty centimeters in length"는 분사구문으로 그 뜻은 "and the red panda is about sixty centimeters in length"이다. "compared ~ panda." 또한 분사구문이다.≫

⊃ 예제 71~85

→[1] The giant panda, which comes from, and is only found in the wild in China, is sometimes called a Panda bear, but this bear notion is not absolutely accepted by the scientific, especially the zoological community. Part of this problem stems from the fact that there is another kind of Panda, the red panda. The red panda is smaller than the giant panda, the red panda being about sixty centimeters in length compared to the **<u>approximately</u>** one hundred and seventy centimeter long giant panda. Their weights also vary with the giant panda tipping the **<u>scales</u>** at around ninety to one hundred and forty kilograms but the red panda tops out at near fifty kilograms. Coupled with these differences in size these two mammals digress in appearance as well. The red panda, as you may well assume, is red in color and its fur is long and soft. This animal is often compared to the raccoon due the fact that it too has rings about it's tail. The giant panda on the other hand is black and white in color and it's tail is very short and is completely black in color.

→[2] These two animals do have some things in common though for they both eat bamboo but while the giant panda is exclusive to this plant the red panda is much more likely to have it's dietary requirements partially met by bamboo for it also consumes fruits and berries. ▮a The amount of food that these two animals eat in a day varies for a number of reasons. ▮b One, and perhaps the most obvious, reason is the immense difference in size between those two animals. ▮c Another reason, that has to do with the digestive system, is extremely inefficient and due to this it, the giant panda, has to consume forty kilograms of bamboo a day. ▮d Based primarily upon this actuality we can base the impetus for the differences that appear when we shift our focus to the lifestyles of these two animals. The red panda spends most of it's day sleeping in a tree and it only comes down to eat at either dawn or dusk but sometimes both. The giant panda on the flip side has to spend a vast majority of its day in search of or eating food.

→[3] The premises upon the question that was raised at the beginning of this piece can now be understood but the answer still has some questions surrounding it. For starters some zoologists think that the giant panda should be placed in the bear family for they resemble bears in the sense that they are big, and theirdeoxyribonucleic acid is very similar to that of other bears. The red panda's <u>DNA</u> is a closer match to a raccoon's than it is to a bear's. Also, the red panda, like a raccoon has the ability to grasp things with its front paws. The third option in all of this is to create a new family of animals that would be the panda family and would include the giant panda and the red panda as well.

71. What is the Author's main purpose in the passage?
(a) To describe the Giant panda's shape
(b) To interpret the panda family
(c) To compare the habit of two pandas
(d) To explain the red panda's charactristic

72. Find the sentence in paragraph 1 that the author first compares the giant panda with red panda?

73. Look at the word <u>approximately</u> in paragraph 1. Find another word or expression in paragraph 1 that is closest in meaning to <u>approximately</u> :

74. Look at the word <u>scales</u> in paragraph 1. Find another word or expression in paragraph 1 that is closest in meaning to <u>scales</u> :

75. According to the passage, which of the following is NOT mentioned in the passage as an example the author compared the giant panda with the red panda.

(a) Their size (b) Their color
(c) Their DNA (d) Their inhabitation

76. Look at the word it in paragraph 1. Find another word or phrase in paragraph 1 that <u>it</u> refers to :

77. According to the passage, the red panda has been compared to which of the following rather than giant panda.

(a) Raccoon (b) Giant panda
(c) Bear (d) Polar bear

78. According to the passage, the giant panda spends most of it's day

(a) Sleeping in a tree (b) Eating food
(c) Strolling around a mountain (d) Searching a resting place

79. Look at the word **<u>reason</u>** in paragraph 2. Find another word or expression in paragraph 2 that is closest in meaning to **<u>reason</u>** :

80. The following sentence can be added to paragraph 2 :

"the bigger your are the more you have to eat."

Where would it best fit? Find the square(■) to added the sentence to the paragraph 2

81. Look at the word <u>DNA</u> in paragraph 3. Find another word or expression in paragraph 3 that is closest in meaning to <u>DNA</u> :

기초어휘

habitation 서식(지)(=inhabitation) /zoological 동물학의 /stem from ~에서 유래하다
approximately 대략 /coupled with 연관짓다 / raccoon 너구리/bamboo 대나무
exclusive 오로지/immense 거대한 / digestive 소화의 /inefficient 비효율적인
impetus 자극, 힘/dusk 황혼 / premise 전제/resemble 닮다 / grasp 꽉지다
deoxyribonucleic acid 디옥시리보핵산(DNA, 유전자) /paw 동물의 발

심화어휘

1. short; 〈길이가〉 짧은, 〈거리가〉 짧은, 가까운, 〈시간 · 과정 · 행위 등이〉 짧은, 단기간의, 키가 작은, 간결한, 간단한, 불충분한, 쌀쌀한, 무뚝뚝한

short hair 짧은 머리 / a short walk 단거리의 보행
at a short distance 가까이에 / a short time ago 바로 얼마 전에
a short trip 짧은 여행 / a short speech 간결한 연설short sight 근시

2. exclusive; 배타[배제]적인, 독점적인, 〈기사가〉 특종의

exclusive rights 독점권 / an exclusive contract 독점 계약
an exclusive story 독점 기사, 특종 / mutually exclusive ideas 서로 용납되지 않는 생각

3. obvious; 명백한, 분명한, 알기 쉬운, 〈감정 · 농담 등이〉 환히 들여다 보이는, 뻔한, 노골적인

obvious lie 뻔한 거짓말 / obvious mistake 분명한 실수
obvious precaution 명백한 예방조치

Key Structure

The opposite approach of <u>having</u> students <u>work</u> as individuals produced much lower test results in mastery of material.

≪"having"은 "사역(시키다)"의 뜻을 가진 동명사이고 따라서 그 뒤에 원형부정사(work)가 왔으며, "much"(=far=by far=still=a lot=훨씬)는 비교급을 강조하는 부사이다.≫

⊃ 예제 82~92

→[1] ▮a The sophistication of these research procedures have allowed more precise estimates and tests of assumptions on social academic and personal behavior. ▮b Particular interest of the <u>research</u> efforts goes to three groups of <u>investigators</u> in particular. ▮c They are; Rogers and David Johnson of the University of Minnesota, Robert Slavin of Johns Hopkins University and Shlomo Sharon of Tel Aviv University. ▮d

→[2] The teams of Slavin and Johnson used somewhat different strategies to investigate the assumptions of the teaching models of the social family.

Essentially, their research analyzed whether or not cooperative task and reward structure has a positive learning effect. Additionally, they studied the issue of intergroup relations, cooperative behavior and cohesion to determine if improvements occur in cooperative learning procedures. Furthermore, <u>they</u> examined reward structures and the effects of cooperative tasks when students were presented a "traditional task" they had to master.

→[3] To answer the question if cooperative groups have <u>improved</u> learning with the energy generated from the group, the answer is yes. This is evidenced by classrooms that allow students to work collectively in larger groups, tutor one another and share positive rewards. The opposite approach of having students work as individuals produced much <u>lower</u> test results in mastery of material. Additionally, the cooperative learning model generates better intergroup relations, enhanced self images for those with poor achievement and more positive feelings towards tasks.

→[4] Shlomo sharon's research efforts have focused more on the dynamics of the model. He and his colleagues have analyzed the effects of intergroup relations and high order, low order achievement. Additionally, researchers by the names of Joyce, Showers and Baveja have combined the study of cooperative learning model with other models. Their study ,specifically investigated the concept and inductive procedures in cooperative groups. The study result demonstrated enhanced information processing versus a group of students that received intensive individual study.

82. Which of the following is the best title for the passage?

(a) Teaching model
(b) Cooperative teaching effect
(c) Cooperative learning model
(d) Cooperative learning effect

83. Look at the word <u>research</u> in paragraph 1. Find another word or expression in paragraph 4 that is closest in meaning to <u>research</u> :

84. Look at the word <u>investigators</u> in paragraph 1. Find another word or expression in paragraph 4 that is closest in meaning to <u>investigators</u> :

85. The following sentence can be added to paragraph 1 :

"Cooperative learning models have recently generated renewed research efforts."

Where would it best fit? Find the square(■) to added the sentence to the paragraph 1 :

86. Look at the word they in paragraph 2. Find another word or phrase in paragraph 2 that <u>they</u> refers to :

87. Look at the word <u>improved</u> in paragraph 3. Find another word or expression in paragraph 3 that closest in meaning to <u>improved</u> :

88. Look at the word <u>lower</u> in paragraph 3. Find another word or expression in paragraph 3 that is closest in meaning to <u>lower</u> :

89. Whose research did focus on the dynamics of the learning model?

(a) Shlomo Sharon (b) Tel Aviv University

(c) Johns Hopkins University (d) University of Minnesota

90. According to the passage, who studied about the notion of cooperative groups?

(a) Baveja (b) Slavin

(c) Johnson (d) Sharon

91. According to the passage, due to the result of Joyce's research, which group has enhanced information processing.

(a) Cooperative study group (b) Intensive individual study group

(c) Cooperative teaching group (d) Intensive high order group

92. The paragraph following the passage most probably discusses ___________.

(a) cooperative learning model

(b) cooperative teaching model

(c) risk student's disruptive behavior

(d) risk student teaching model

기초어휘

sophistication 궤변, 정교화 /precise 정확한/assumption 가정 / strategy 전략
analyze 분석하다 / cooperative 협동의 /reward 보상 / intergroup 그룹 사이의
cohesion 응집(력) /tutor 개인적으로 가르치다 /enhance 높이다, 강화하다
dynamics 원동력 / inductive 귀납적인

심화어휘

1. generate; 〈결과 · 상태 · 행동 · 감정 등을〉 일으키다, 초래하다, 가져오다, 〈열 · 전기 등을〉 발생시키다
   generate sensation 파문을 일으키다　　generate electricity 전기를 일으키다
   generate results 결과를 초래하다　　generate profit 이익을 가져오다
2. demonstrate; 논증[입증]하다 ,(모형 · 실험 등으로) 설명하다, 실지로 해보이다
   demonstrate a new car 신차를 보여주다　　demonstrate ability 능력을 보여주다
   demonstrate excellence 탁월함을 입증하다

Key Structure

The point where the muscle is fastened to the unmoving bone is called the origin of the muscle, whereas the point [where the muscle is fastened to the bone] [that is to be moved] is called the insertion.

≪"whereas" 이하에서 주어는 "the point"이고, 동사는 "is called"이다. 또한 [where the muscle is fastened to the bone]은 "the point"를 수식하며, [that is to be moved]는 바로 앞 명사 "the bone"을 수식한다.≫

예제 93~100

→[1] It is in the joints of the human body that movements of the bones take place. The movement itself is caused by the pull of sheets and cords of very tough tissue called muscle. Muscle tissue has the special ability to shorten itself so that the bone on which it pulls has to move. When muscle tissue shortens it also bunches up. Muscle tissue covers the body in sheets and bands that lie between the skin and the skeleton. The bones are the framework of the body, but the muscles fill out the body shape. Most muscles extend from one bone to another. When the muscle between the bones shortens, one bone has to move. The point where the muscle is fastened to the unmoving bone is called the origin of the muscle, whereas the point where the muscle is fastened to the bone that is to be moved is called the insertion. Sometimes the muscle is not <u>attached</u> directly to the bone but to a tough, nonstretchable cord, or tendon that is attached to the bone.

→[2] Muscles do not push; they can only pull. To bend the arm at the elbow, the muscle at the front of the upper arm has to shorten and bunch up. To <u>unbend</u> the arm, other muscles in the back of the arm have to shorten. These two sets of muscles − the front and the back − are said to act in opposition to each other. When one set is working, the other set is usually relaxed. But there are times when both of them work. Sometimes muscles are <u>called upon</u> to do more than simply pull in one direction. They may have to perform a turning motion. To be able to do this, the muscle must be attached to the bone at an angle. By pulling, the muscle can cause the bone to pivot.

→[3] A few muscles have special functions. The diaphragm, for example, forces the lungs to <u>take in</u> air. This part of breathing is not primarily a bone-moving operation.

93. The word it in paragraph 1 refers to ___________.

(a) muscle (b) bone
(c) body (d) joints

94. What is the main subject of the passage?

(a) How human muscle develops
(b) The differences between major muscle groups in the human body
(c) Problems with human muscles
(d) The anatomy and operation of human muscles

95. According to the passage, movement occurs when a muscle ___________.

(a) grows (b) shortens
(c) relaxes (d) pushes

96. The word <u>attached</u> in paragraph 1 is closest in meaning to ___________.

(a) detached (b) fixed in place
(c) associated (d) coalesced

97. The point at which a muscle is attached to the bone that moves is called the __________.

(a) source (b) insertion
(c) tendon (d) diaphragm

98. The word <u>unbend</u> in paragraph 2 is closest in meaning to __________.

(a) upright (b) strain
(c) straighten (d) unbind

99. The phrase <u>called upon</u> in paragraph 2 is closest in meaning to __________.

(a) required (b) visited
(c) permitted (d) subjected

100. The passage implies that reversing the muscle–bone movement used to bend an arm requires __________.

(a) the relaxation of two sets of muscles
(b) the use of different muscles
(c) a different kind of tissue
(d) the enlargement of the muscle

101. Why are some muscles attached to bones at an angle?

(a) To cause the muscles to push
(b) To strengthen the muscle
(c) To shorten tissues
(d) To perform a turning action

102. The phrase <u>take in</u> in paragraph 1 is closest in meaning to __________.

(a) receive (b) permit
(c) descend (d) scan

기초어휘

joint 관절 / sheet 근막 / cord 인대 / tissue 조직/bunch up 주름잡히다 / skeleton 뼈대
attached 붙여진 / tendon 건(like 아킬레스건) /pivot ~을 축으로 하여 선회하다
diaphragm 횡경막

심화어휘

1. tough; 질긴, 단단한, ≪구어≫ 튼튼한, 곤란한, 힘든, 믿어지지 않는

tough meat 질긴 고기　　tough clay 차진 점토
a tough worker 튼튼한 일꾼　　a tough racket≪속어≫ 곤란한 일
a tough story 믿기 힘든 이야기

2. fasten; 단단히 고착[고정]시키다, 〈지퍼 · 단추 · 클립 · 핀 등을〉 죄다, 잠그다, 채우다

fasten seat belt. 좌석[안전] 벨트를 단단히 매다
fasten a glove 장갑의 단추를 채우다
fasten a door with a bolt 문에 빗장을 지르다

3. shorten; 짧게 하다, 〈치수 등을〉 줄이다, 단축하다, 깎다, 삭감하다

shorten a dress 옷을 줄이다　　shorten cooking time 조리시간을 줄이다
shorten distribution process 유통과정을 줄이다

Key Structure

Never during the war did the government suffer from inadequate funds or credit.
≪"부정부사" "Never"와 시간표시 부사구 "during the war"가 강조되면서, 문장 맨 앞으로 오면서, 그 뒤에서 어순이 도치-did the government suffer가 되었다.≫

⊃ 예제 103~113

→[1] The cost of the First World War to the United States, **exclusive of** the loss of life and suffering involved and the subsequent payments to veterans, runs into figures almost beyond human comprehension. Including nearly $9,500,000,000 lent to foreign governments, the direct cost for the three years following the declaration of war was around $35,500,000,000. This was three times the total **expenditures** of the federal government during the first 100 years of its existence, and over $1,000,000 an hour during the 25 months following the declaration of war.

→[2] The first problem to be settled in financing the war was, "What proportion of the cost was to be borne by taxes, and what proportion by loans?" In other words, what part of the cost was to be placed on the backs of **subsequent** generations? As it turned out, about one-third was raised by taxation, and the rest by loans. Beginning with the War Revenue Bill, Congress raised the income, inheritance, and excise taxes, and inaugurated taxes on excess profits and luxuries. Congress, however, stood firm on the principle of low tariffs.

→[3] The money that the government borrowed was obtained by means of four "Liberty Loans" and one "Victory Loan." Unlike their practice during former wars, the government made a direct appeal to the people, and by selling the bonds in denominations as low as $50 received aid from millions who until then had never seen a government bond. Over 22,000,000 people subscribed to the "Fourth Liberty Loan." All of the loans were oversubscribed, and about $21,500,000,000 were allotted. Never during the war did the government suffer from inadequate funds or credit.

103. What is the main topic of the passage?
(a) The patriotism of the United States military
(b) One hundred years of United States finance
(c) Investment opportunities for the middle class
(d) Paying for the First World War

104. The phrase exclusive of in paragraph 1 is closest in meaning to ________.
(a) considering (b) restricted to
(c) not including (d) unacceptable

105. Which of the following is included in the $35,500,000,000 mentioned in the passage?
(a) Payments to retired soldiers
(b) Loans to foreign government
(c) Interest payments on government bonds
(d) Salaries paid to members of Congress

106. The word expenditures in paragraph 1 is closest in meaning to ________.
(a) expenses (b) casualties
(c) losses (d) expensive

107. The word <u>its</u> in paragraph 1 refers to ___________.

(a) war (b) hour

(c) declaration (d) federal government

108. Which of the following represents the $1,000,000 mentioned in paragraph 1?

(a) The hourly cost of the war for approximately two years

(b) One-third the amount spent by the federal government between 1776 and 1876

(c) The amount raised through government bonds for the war effort

(d) The daily interest on short-term loans to foreign government

109. Which of the following was the first matter to be settled in financing the war?

(a) Approximately how much the war was going to cost

(b) How much the United States should lend to foreign government

(c) How to convince taxpayers that the United States should be involved in a European war

(d) What part of the cost of the war should be paid by taxes and what part by borrowing

110. The word <u>subsequent</u> in paragraph 2 is closest in meaning to _________.

(a) subordinate (b) subsidiary

(c) before (d) following

111. The word <u>principle</u> in paragraph 2 is closest in meaning to __________.

(a) integrity (b) importance

(c) fundamental rule (d) arrangement

112. Which of the following kinds of the taxes was NOT raised to help pay for the war?

(a) Luxury (b) Income

(c) Tariff (d) Inheritance

113. The word <u>inadequate</u> in paragraph 3 is closest in meaning to ________.

(a) insufficient (b) indefinite

(c) impiety (d) dissatisfied

기초어휘

exclusive of ~을 제외하고/subsequent 다음의 / expenditure 지출 /borne (비용을) 부담하다
revenue 세입/inheritance 유산 / excise 국내소비세/tariff 관세
subscribe 출자하다, 서명하다/stand firm on ~ 양보하지 않다, 꿋꿋이 서있다
oversubscribed 모집액 이상으로 신청하다/allot 할당하다, 충당하다

심화어휘

1. subsequent; 다음의, 그 후의, 버금가는, (…에) 이어서 일어나는, 수반하는

subsequent generation 다음 세대　　subsequent event 후속 행사
subsequent release of new versions 새 버전의 이어지는 출시

2. direct; 똑바른, 직통의, 직접의, 솔직한, 노골적인, 단도직입적인

a direct flight 직행 항공편　　a direct shot 직격[명중]탄
the direct phone[line] 직통 전화　　a direct question[answer] 솔직한 질문[답변]

Key Structure

Now that there are hardly any left, educators are beginning to think that maybe there is something yet to be learned from one-room schools, something *that* served the pioneers *that* might serve as well today.

≪"now that"은 이유표시의 종속접속사(=because)이고, that은 접속사, 그 뒤에 오는 두 개의 *that*은 모두 주격관계대명사이다.≫

예제 114~123

→[1] One-room schools are part of the **heritage** of the United States, and the mention of them makes people feel a **vague** longing for "the way things were." One-room schools are an endangered species, however. For more than a hundred years, one-room schools have been systematically shut down and their students sent away to centralized schools. As recently as 1930 there were 149,000 one-room schools in the United States. By 1970 there were 1,800. Today, of the nearly 800 remaining one-room schools, more than 350 are in Nebraska. The rest are scattered through a few other states that have on their road maps wide-open spaces between towns.

→[2] Now that there are hardly any left, educators are beginning to think that maybe there is something yet to be learned from one-room schools, something that **served** the pioneers that might serve as well today.

Progressive educators have **come up** with progressive-sounding names like "peer-group teaching" and "multi-age grouping" for educational procedures that occur naturally in the one-room school. In a one-room school the children teach each other because the teacher is busy part of the time teaching someone else. A fourth grader can work at a fifth-grade level in math and a third-grade level in English without the **stigma** associated with being left behind or the pressures of being skipped ahead. A youngster with a learning disability can find his or her own level without being separated from the other students. In larger urban and suburban schools today, this is called "mainstreaming." A few hours in a small school that has only one classroom and it becomes clear why so many parents feel that one of the advantages of living in Nebraska is that their children have to go to school.

114. The word **heritage** in paragraph 1 is closest in meaning to ___________.

(a) fate (b) inheritance

(c) emission (d) hereby

115. What is the author's main purpose in the passage?

(a) To discuss present-day education

(b) To mention some advantages of one-room schools

(c) To persuade states to close down one-room schools

(d) To summarize the history of education in the United States

116. The author implies that many educators and parents today feel that one-room schools ___________.

(a) are too small

(b) put pressure on teachers

(c) are too far apart

(d) provide a good education

117. The word **vague** in paragraph 1 is closest in meaning to ___________.

(a) ambiguous (b) distinct

(c) tenacious (d) abstruse

118. According to the passage why are one-room schools in danger of disappearing?

(a) They skip too many

(b) There are no fourth-grade levels in any of them

(c) There is a trend toward centralization

(d) They all exist in one state

119. The word <u>served</u> in paragraph 2 is closest in meaning to ________.

(a) relieved (b) legalized

(c) aided (d) ejected

120. According to the passage, about how many one-room schools are there in the United States today?

(a) 149,000 (b) 1,800

(c) 800 (d) 350

121. The phrase <u>come up with</u> in paragraph 2 is closest in meaning to _____.

(a) thought of (b) made up with

(c) named (d) predicted

122. In the second paragraph, what is mentioned as a major characteristic of the one-room school system?

(a) It causes many children to be left back.

(b) It must work in conjunction with an urban school

(c) It does not allow teachers to do any individual teaching

(d) It does not limit learning to one grade level at a time

123. The word <u>stigma</u> in paragraph 2 is closest in meaning to ________.

(a) thought (b) bequest

(c) disparity (d) disgrace

기초어휘

heritage 유산 / vague 막연한/longing 갈망 / endangered 멸종될 지경에 이른
progressive 진보적인 / peer 동료 /stigma 오명 / mainstreaming 차별교육철폐론

심화어휘

1. scatter; 흩뿌리다, 〈재산을〉 탕진[낭비]하다, 〈군중 · 적군 등을〉 쫓아버리다, 〈바람이〉 〈구름 · 안개 등을〉 흩날려 버리다;〈희망 · 의혹 · 공포 등을〉 무산(霧散)하다

scatter leaflets 전단을 뿌리다　　scatter seeds 씨앗을 뿌리다
scatter hopes 희망을 무산시키다

2. progressive; 전진하는, 〈사회 · 도시 등이〉 진보하는, 〈제도 · 주의 · 방침 · 정책 등이〉 진보적인, 혁신적인, 〈세금 등이〉 누진적인, 〈병이〉 진행하는, 악화하는

progressive changes 점진적 변화　　progressive spirit 진취적인 정신
progressive taxation 누진 과세　　progressive paralysis 진행성 마비

Key Structure

One of the largest in the world, the pipeline cost approximately $8 billion and is by far the biggest and most expensive construction project ever undertaken by private industry.

≪"by far"는 비교급과 최상급을 강조하는 부사구(훨씬)이고, "undertaken"은 과거분사로 명사 "construction project"를 꾸며준다.≫

예제 124~133

→[1] The Alaska pipeline starts at the frozen edge of the Arctic ocean. It stretches southward across the largest and northernmost state in the United States, ending at a remote ice-free seaport village nearly 800 miles from where it begins. It is massive in size and extremely complicated to operate.

→[2] The steel pipe crosses windswept plains and endless miles of delicate tundra that tops the frozen ground. It weaves through crooked canyons, climbs sheer mountains, plunges over rocky crags, makes its way through thick woods, and passes over or under hundreds of rivers and streams. The pipe is 4 feet in diameter, and up to 2 million barrels (or 84 million gallons) of crude oil can be pumped daily.

→[3] Resting on H-shaped steel racks called "bents," long sections of the pipeline follow a zigzag course high above the frozen earth. Other long sections drop out of sight beneath spongy or rocky ground and return to the surface later on. The pattern of the pipeline's up-and-down route is determined by the often harsh demands of the arctic and subarctic climate, the **tortuous** lay of the land, and the varied compositions of soil, rock, or **permafrost** (permanently frozen ground). A little more than half of the pipeline is elevated above the ground. The remainder is buried anywhere from 3 to 12 feet, depending largely upon the type of terrain and properties of the soil

→[4] One of the largest in the world, the pipeline cost approximately $8 billion and is by far the biggest and most expensive construction project ever undertaken by private industry. In fact, no single business could raise that much money, so 8 major oil companies formed a consortium in order to share the costs. Each company controlled oil rights to **particular** shares of land in the oil fields and paid into the pipeline-construction fund according to the size of its **holdings**. Today, despite enormous problems of climate, supply shortages, equipment breakdowns, labor disagreement, **treacherous** terrain, a certain amount of mismanagement, and even theft, the Alaska pipeline has been completed and is operating.

124. The passage primarily discusses the pipeline's ______________.

(a) operating costs (b) employees
(c) consumers (d) construction

125. The author mentions all of the following as important in determining the pipeline's route EXCEPT the ____________.

(a) climate (b) lay of the land itself
(c) local vegetation (d) kind of soil and rock

126. The word **tortuous** in paragraph 3 is closest in meaning to __________.

(a) cornered (b) rough
(c) heavy (d) crooked

127. The word **permafrost** in paragraph 3 is closest in meaning to ________.

(a) permanently frozen ground (b) free area from frost
(c) land in which people can't dwell (d) rocky ground

128. How many companies shared the costs of constructing the pipeline?

(a) Three (b) Four

(c) Eight (d) Twelve

129. The word particular in paragraph 4 is closest in meaning to ________.

(a) peculiar (b) specific

(c) exceptional (d) equal

130. The word holdings in paragraph 4 is closest in meaning to ________.

(a) pipeline (b) property

(c) company (d) delay

131. Which of the following determined what percentage of the construction costs each member of the consortium would pay?

(a) How much oil field land each company owned

(b) How long each company had owned land in the oil fields

(c) How many people worked for each company

(d) How many oil wells were located on the company's land

132. Where in the passage does the author provide a term for an earth covering that always remains frozen?

(a) Line 3 (b) Line 10

(c) Line 15 (d) Line 25

133. The word treacherous in paragraph 2 is closest in meaning to ________.

(a) strong (b) solid

(c) unstable (d) abbreviate

기초어휘

ice-free 얼음이 얼지 않는 /seaport 항구/massive 거대한/ complicated 복잡한 windswept 바람에 노출된/delicate 미묘한, 섬세한 /crooked 구불구불한 / sheer 똑바로 선 plunge 나아가다 / crag 험한 바위산/diameter 지름 /crude 천연 그대로의/rack 선반, 대 subarctic 북극 가까이의 /tortuous 비비꼬인, 비뚤어진/terrain 지형 / consortium 협회 oil field 유전

심화어휘

1. massive; 크고 무거운[단단한], 큰 덩어리의, 육중한, 〈머리 · 체격 등이〉 큼직한, 우람한, 대규모의, 대량의

massive columns 큰 기둥　　massive fire 엄청난 화재
massive buying spree 대량 구매　　a massive chest 떡 벌어진 가슴

2. endless; 끝이 없는, 영원히 계속하는, 무한의

endless argument 끝없는 논쟁　　endless love 영원한 사랑
endless stream of people 사람들의 끊임없는 행렬

Key Structure

Martha Graham's territory of innumerable dances and a self-sufficient dance technique is a vast but closed territory, <u>since to create an art out of one's experience alone is ultimately a self-limiting act</u>.

≪여기 "since"는 이유 표시 종속접속사로 "왜냐하면"의 뜻이고, "to creat an art out of one's experience alone"이 "is"의 주어이다.≫

예제 134~140

→[1] Martha Graham's territory of <u>innumerable</u> dances and a self-sufficient dance technique is a vast but closed territory, since to create an art out of one's experience alone is ultimately a self-limiting act. If there had been other choreographers with Graham's gifts and her stature, her work might have seemed a more balanced part of the story of American dances. But as she built her repertory, her own language seemed to shut out all other kinds. Even when an audience thinks it discerns traces of influence from other dance styles, the totality of Graham's theatrical idiom, its control of costumes, lights, and every impulse of the dance, make the reference seem a mirage. Dance is not her main subject. It is only her servant.

→[2] Graham had achieved her autonomy by 1931. By that time, three giant figures who had invented the new twentieth-century dance were dead: Sergei Diaghilev, Anna Pavola, and Isadora Duncan. Their era ended with them, and their dance values nearly disappeared. Their <u>colleagues</u> Michel Fokine and Ruth St. Denis lived on in America <u>like whales on the beach</u>. During the twentieth, Martha Graham and her colleagues had rescued art-dance from vaudeville and movies and musical comedy and all the resonances of the idyllic <u>mode</u> in the

United States, but in so doing they closed the channel through which different kinds of dance could speak to one another – and **these** stayed closed for half a century. Modern dance **dedicated** itself to deep significance. It gave up lightness, it gave up a wealth of exotic color, it gave up a certain kind of theatrical wit and that age-old mobile exchange between a dancer and the dancer's rhythmical and musical material. No material in modern dance was neutral. The core of the art became an obsession with meaning and allegory as expressed in bodies. Modern dance excluded its own theatrical traditions of casual play, gratuitous liveliness, the spontaneous pretense, and the rainbow of genres that had formed it. But all these things survived in the public domain, where they had always lived, and they have continued to **surface** in American dance, if only by accident.

134. What is the main purpose of the passage?
(a) To discuss Martha Graham's influences on modern dance
(b) To trace the origins of different dance techniques
(c) To argue the role of modern dance as an artistic form of expression
(d) To compare several famous women choreographers of the twentieth century

135. The word **innumerable** in paragraph 1 is closest in meaning to ________.
(a) numerous (b) heavy
(c) limited (d) respected

136. According to the passage, which of the following most influenced Martha Graham's dances and techniques?
(a) Her own experiences
(b) Exotic and idyllic themes
(c) Familiar classical stories
(d) The works of St. Denis nad Duncan

137. The word **achieved** in paragraph 2 is closest in meaning to ____________.
(a) attained (b) included
(c) ended (d) bought

138. The word <u>colleagues</u> in paragraph 2 is closest in meaning to __________.

(a) co-workers (b) enemies
(c) teachers (d) ancestors

139. In paragraph 2, the author uses the phrase <u>like whales on the beach</u> to indicate that Fokine and St. Denis were ______________.

(a) good swimmers (b) physically large
(c) out of place (d) very sick

140. The word <u>mode</u> in paragraph 2 is closest in meaning to ____________.

(a) manner (b) music
(c) motion (d) movement

141. In lines 16-21, what criticism does the author make of Martha Graham and her colleagues?

(a) They patterned much of their choreographic style after vaudeville.
(b) They insisted that all dancers learn the same foreign language.
(c) They adopted the same dance values of the previous era without interjecting any new ideas.
(d) They prevented modern dance from expanding beyond their personal interp retation.

142. The word <u>these</u> in paragraph 2 refers to ____________.

(a) windows (b) houses
(c) dances (d) channels

143. The word <u>dedicated</u> in paragraph 2 is closest in meaning to __________.

(a) devoted (b) exhausted
(c) consumed (d) influenced

144. The word <u>surface</u> in paragraph 2 is closest in meaning to ___________.

(a) emerge (b) cut
(c) disappear (d) outer covering

기초어휘

territory 영역, 분야 / choreographer 안무가 /stature 재능, 위엄 / theatrical 연극풍의 costume 의상 / impulse 충격, 자극/mirage 신기루 / autonomy 자율, 자치/resonance 반향 idyllic 목가적인, 소박한 /dedicate 바치다, 헌납하다 / exotic 이국적인/obsession 망상, 집념 gratuitous 필요 없는/spontaneous 자발적으로 / pretense 잘난체, 잘함

심화어휘

1. exotic; 이국적인, 〈동식물 등이〉 외국산의, 외래의, 신종의, 실험적인

an exotic hairstyle 별난 헤어스타일 exotic atmosphere 이국적인 분위기
exotic location(place) 이국적인 곳 exotic plants 외래 식물

2. casual; 우연의(accidental), 우발적인, 뜻밖의, 무심결의, 무관심한, 격식을 차리지 않는, 〈의복 등이〉 평상복의, 약식의

a casual meeting 우연한 만남 a casual remark 무심코[되는대로] 한 말
casual wear 평상복

Key Structure

<u>Given the uncertainty in the future growth of nuclear power and in the supply of oil and natural gas,</u> coal-fired power plants could well provide up to 70 percent of the electric power in the United States by the end of the century.
≪여기서 "given"은 "-을 고려한다면(=considering)"의 뜻이다.≫

⊃ 예제 145~150

→[1] The invention of the incandescent light bulb by Thomas A. Edison in 1879 created a demand for a cheap, readily **<u>available</u>** fuel with which to **<u>generate</u>** large amounts of electric power. Coal seemed to fit the bill, and it fueled the earliest power stations (which were set up at the end of the nineteenth century by Edison himself.) As more power plants were constructed throughout the country, the **<u>reliance</u>** on coal increased. Since the First World War, coal-fired power plants have accounted for about half of the electricity produced in the United States each year. In 1986 such plants had a combined generating capacity of 289,000 megawatts and consumed 83 percent of the nearly 900million tons of coal mined in the country that year. Given the uncertainty in the future growth of nuclear power and in the supply of oil and natural gas, coal-fired power plants could well provide up to 70 percent of the electric power in the United States by the end of the century.

→[2] Yet, in spite of the fact that coal has long been a source of electricity and may remain one for many years (coal represents about 80 percent of United States fossil-fuel reserves), it has actually never been the most desirable fossil fuel for power plants. Coal contains less energy per unit of weight than natural gas or oil; it is difficult to transport, and it is associated with a host of environmental issues, among them acid rain. Since the late 1980's problems of emission control and waste disposal have sharply reduced the appeal of coal-fired power plants. The cost of ameliorating these environmental problems, along with the rising cost of building a facility as large or **complex** as a coal-fired power plant, have also made such plants less attractive from a purely economic perspective.

→[3] Changes in the technological base of coal-fired power plants could restore their attractiveness, however. Whereas some of these changes are evolutionary and are intended **mainly** to increase the productivity of existing plant, completely new technologies for burning coal cleanly are also being developed.

145. What is the main idea of the passage?

(a) Coal-fired plants are an important source of electricity in the United States and are likely to remain so.

(b) Generating electricity from coal is comparatively recent in the United States.

(c) Coal is a more economical fuel than either oil or nuclear power.

(d) Coal is a safer and more dependable fossil fuel than oil or gas.

146. The word **available** in paragraph 1 is closest in meaning to ________.

(a) peaceable (b) disposable

(c) affable (d) attainable

147. The word **generate** in paragraph 1 is closest in meaning to ________.

(a) produce (b) rely

(c) increase (d) contain

148. Edison's electric light bulb is mentioned in the passage because it ______.

(a) replaced gas as a light source

(b) increased the need for electrical power

(c) was safer than any other method of lighting

(d) could work only with electricity generated from coal

149. The word reliance in paragraph 1 is closest in meaning to ________.

(a) relocation (b) barrier

(c) reluctance (d) dependence

150. It can be inferred from the passage that coal became the principal source of electricity in the United States because it ____________.

(a) required no complicated machinery

(b) was comparatively plentiful and inexpensive

(c) was easy to transport

(d) burned efficiently

151. In the author's opinion, the importance of coal-generated electricity could increase in the future for which of the following reasons?

(a) The possible substitutes are too dangerous.

(b) The cost of changing to other fuels is too great.

(c) The future availability of other fuels is uncertain.

(d) Other fuels present too many environmental problems.

152. Acid rain is mentioned in the passage for which of the following reasons?

(a) It reduces the efficiency of coal-fired plants.

(b) It increases the difficulty of transporting coal.

(c) It is an environmental problem associated with coal use.

(d) It contains less energy per unit of weight than coal does.

153. The word complex in paragraph 2 is closest in meaning to _________.

(a) expensive (b) enormous

(c) complicated (d) tremendous

154. According to the passage, which of the following is one of the goals of the new technology in coal-fired plants?

(a) To adapt the plants to other kinds of fuel

(b) To reduce the cost of building more plants

(c) To lengthen the lives of plants already in use

(d) To increase the productivity of existing plants

155. The word <u>mainly</u> in paragraph 2 is closest in meaning to ___________.

(a) largely (b) in the name of

(c) at the beginning (d) heavily

기초어휘

incandescent 백열의 / bulb 전구 /readily 쉽사리 / set up 세우다/reliance 신뢰 accounted for 책임지다/uncertainty 불확실성 / desirable 호감이 가는/emission 방출 disposal 처리 / ameliorating 개선하다

심화어휘

1. desirable; 바람직한, 탐나는, 호감이 가는 〈사람 · 물건〉, 〈여성이〉 탐나도록 매력적인

a desirable woman 성적 매력이 있는 여자 desirable results 바람직한 결과
desirable surroundings 바람직한 환경

2. attractive; 사람의 마음을 끄는, 매력적인, 눈에 뜨이는, 흥미를 돋우는, 인력이 있는

an attractive woman 매력적인 여성 attractive market 매력적인 시장
attractive salary and benefits 흥미를 돋우는 월급과 복지 혜택

해설 및 정답

CHAPTER 1

문맥속의 어휘

Vocabulary

⊃ 예제 1

저는 오늘 오후에 한 꿈을 꾸었는데, 사람 사이의 형제의 연이 오늘날 현실이 되는 것이었습니다. 이 믿음을 가지고, 나는 밖으로 나가 절망의 산을 통과하는 희망의 터널을 뚫을 것입니다. 이 신념을 가지고, 나는 당신과 함께 나가서 어두운 과거를 밝은 미래로 바꾸어 놓을 것입니다. 이 믿음을 가지고, 우리는 모든 하나님의 자녀, 즉 흑인과 백인, 유대인과 이방인, 개신교도나 천주교도가, 흑인과 더불어 손을 맞잡고 함께 영가를 부를 수 있는 새 날을 맞이할 수 있을 것입니다. 마침내 자유하리라! 마침내 자유하리라! 높으신 하나님께 감사를!

1. 본문의 "despair"와 가장 의미가 유사한 단어는?

| 풀이 | 위의 글은 흑백인 평등과 관련된 글입니다. 작가는 절망을 희망으로, 어두운 과거를 밝은 미래로 바꾸기를 원하고 있습니다. 따라서 'despair'는 'hope'와 반대의 의미를 지녀야 합니다.

| 정답 | (c) hopelessness

| 오답 | (a) insult 모욕 (b) slaughter 학살, 살육 (d) rapture 환희, 미칠 듯이 기뻐함

⊃ 예제 2~3

오랜 세계의 역사 속에서 오직 몇몇 세대만이 극도로 위험한 때에 자유를 수호하는 역할을 부여받았습니다. 나는 이 책임(자유를 위해 싸울 책임)을 회피하지 않고, 기꺼이 받아들입니다. 나는 우리 중 누구도 다른 사람이나 다른 세대와 이 입장을 바꾸지 않을 것이라고 믿습니다. 우리가 (자유를 수호하려는) 이 노력 위에 쏟는 힘과 믿음, 그리고 헌신은 우리나라와 우리나라를 위해 일하는 사람들을 밝게 비출 것이고, 그 타오르는 불꽃은 이 세계를 진정으로 밝힐 것입니다.

그러므로 사랑하는 미국시민이여: 국가가 여러분을 위해 무엇을 해 줄 것인지를 묻지 말고, 여러분이 국가를 위해 무엇을 할 수 있는지를 물으십시오.

사랑하는 세계의 시민 여러분: 미국이 여러분을 위해 무엇을 해 줄 수 있는지를 묻지 말고, 우리 모두가 함께 인간의 자유를 위해 무엇을 할 수 있을지를 물으십시오.

끝으로, 여러분이 미국의 시민이건 세계의 시민이건, 우리가 여러분에게 요구하는 것과 같은 수준의 힘과 희생을 우리에게 요구하십시오.

2. "shrink from"과 가장 같은 의미를 가진 것은?

| 풀이 | 위의 표현이 들어있는 문장을 살펴보면, do not shrink와 welcome이 같은 의미로 쓰이고 있다. 따라서 shrink는 환영하지 않는, 기꺼이 받아들이지 않고 회피하는 것을 의미한다.

| 정답 | (d) evade; 피하다, 모면하다

3. "endeavor"와 가장 비슷한 의미를 나타내는 단어는?

| 풀이 | 주어진 단어가 들어있는 문장 앞 부분의 내용을 살펴보면, 계속 자유를 수호하기 위해 노력하겠다는 내용이 나온다. 따라서 우리가 힘과 신념과 헌신을 다해 해야 할 것은 바로 자유 수호를 위한 '노력'이 된다.

| 정답 | (a) effort

| 오답 | (b) negligence 태만, 부주의 (c) inattention 무심 (d) procrastination 지연

예제 4~5

미국에 있는 경영학교가 그 어느 때보다도 위기를 맞고 있다. 최근 하버드대학교의 경영대학만이 실질적인 입학률 증가추세를 보이고 있고 프린스턴과 예일대학은 그 반대 추세를 보이고 있다. 1990년부터 MBA학위를 받는 사람의 수가 전체 5%에 해당하는 85,000명이 줄어들었고 이렇게 저조한 입학 추세는 계속될 것 같다. MBA학위를 찾는 학생의 수가 줄어드는 이유를 다음의 두 가지에서 찾아볼 수 있다. 첫째 이유는 4년제 경영대학의 학생들이 더 이상은 MBA학위가 월가에서의 고위급 직업을 보장해 주지 않는데다가 미국의 주요도시지역의 금융계에로의 진출도 보장하지 않는다는 사실을 알아가고 있는 데 있다. 많은 신규 취업 단계의 경영 관련 직종이 MBA학위를 취득한 학생뿐만 아니라 영어와 인류학 분야의 석사학위를 취득한 학생을 필요로 하고 있기 때문이다. 학생들은 "MBA 학위가 과연 내가 좋은 직장을 얻기 위해 준비해야 하는 가장 좋은 것일까?"라는 질문을 던지고 있다. 두 번째 이유는 미국의 급료지불총액이 줄어들고 있고, 사원 신규채용의 수가 점점 줄어들고 있기 때문이다. 기업의 요구는 변해가고 있고, MBA 학교들은 이러한 새로운 요구를 충족시키기 위해 힘겨운 싸움을 싸울 것이다.

4. 'trend of'와 가장 가까운 의미를 나타내는 것은?

| 풀이 | 글의 전반에 걸쳐 경영대학에 입학하는 학생이 줄어들고 있는 현상을 우려하고 있다. 이러한 입학 감소를 하나의 경향 내지는 사회적인 추세로 보고 있다.

| 정답 | (c) movement toward

| 오답 | (a) reluctance of ~을 꺼려함 (b) drawback to 약점, 결점 (d) extraction 추출

5. 'plush'는 다음 중 무엇을 의미하는가?

| 풀이 | MBA 학위를 따려는 학생들의 최고의 꿈은 미국 최대의 증권가인 월가에서 좋은 직업을 가지고 편안한 삶을 사는 것이다. 그러나 최근에는 이런 것들이 보장되지 못하고 있음을 걱정하고 있다.

| 정답 | (c) fancy

6. 다음의 단어 중 'struggling'과 가장 가까운 의미를 지니고 있는 단어는?

| 풀이 | 더 많은 것을 요구하는 경영계의 흐름을 경영대학에서 쫓아가야 하는 현실을 묘사하고 있으며, 그러기 위해서는 거의 투쟁에 가깝게 힘을 쏟을 것이라고 말한다.

| 정답 | (d) striving 애써서 노력하다.

예제 7~8

오사마 빈 라덴은 CIA가 가장 붙잡기를 원하는 인물이면서 동시에 많은 아랍 세계 젊은이들의 우상이기도 하다. 라덴과 그의 일당은 이미 1998년 아프리카에서 미국 대사관 폭파사건과 지난해 예멘에서 발생했던 US Cole 공격사건을 포함한 각종 국제 테러 관련 혐의로 추적 당하고 있는 중이다.

엄청난 부자이면서, 베일에 쌓여있는 빈 라덴은 아프가니스탄의 탈레반 정부로부터 안전한 은신처를 제공받았다. 그는 숨어 지내는 동안에 미국을 상대로 성전(거룩한 전쟁)을 일으킬 것과, 미국인과 유대인을 죽일 것을 요청했다. 그는 그의 주변에 삼천 명에 달하는 군사들을 모을 수 있는 것으로 알려졌다. 그는 체치니아와 다른 구소련 국가에 군사들을 훈련시키는 이슬람 훈련기지 설립을 도운 혐의도 또한 받고 있다.

7. "immensely"와 가장 가까운 의미를 띄는 단어는?

| 풀이 | 빈 라덴은 알려진 바와 같이 엄청난 부자이다.

| 정답 | (b) greatly

8. 'rally'가 의미하는 바는?

| 풀이 | 라덴은 자기를 위해 싸울 군사를 3천명 정도는 모을 수 있다고 알려져 있다.

| 정답 | (a) reassemble

| 오답 | (b) recoil 후퇴하다 (c) rebel 반역하다 (d) rebound 돌이키다

예제 9~10

우리로 하여금 억지로 "please; 해 주세요"라고 말하게 하는 법은 없는 것이 사실이지만, 법보다 더 오래되고, 잘 지켜지는 사회적인 관습이 있으며, 그 관습이 우리가 예의바르게 행동하기를 요구한다. 그리고 예절이 요구하는 첫 번째는 우리가 봉사를 인정해야 한다는 것이다. "실례합니다"와 "감사합니다"는 작은 변화이고, 우리는 이 말들로 사회를 형성하는 길을 만든다. 이 말들은 기본적인 예의이며 이것으로 인하여 우리는 삶이라는 기계에 기름을 칠하여 원활히 움직이도록 하는 것이다. 그것들은 우리 관계를 우월한 사람의 열등한 사람에 대한 지시가 아닌 우호적인 협력과 편안한 상호관계 위에 둔다. 명령하기를 원하는 것은 저속한 마음이며, 원하기만 하면 거저 봉사할 수 있는 곳에서 분노가 아니라 좋은 느낌과 기꺼이 하고자 하는 마음으로 봉사하라.

9. 'civility'가 의미하는 것은?

| 풀이 | 주어진 단어가 포함되어 있는 문장 앞에서 보편적으로 지켜지는 사회적 관습이 우리가 예의바르게 행동하기를 요구한다고 했고, 뒤이은 문장에서 봉사를 인정해야 한다고 했기 때문에, 계속해서 다른 사람에 대한 예의에 관해 말하고 있다는 것을 쉽게 알 수 있다.

| 정답 | (c) politeness

| 오답 | (a) honesty 정직 (b) integrity 성실 (d) fidelity 충실, 성실

10. 'resentment'가 뜻하는 바를 가장 잘 나타낸 것은?

| 풀이 | 글의 마지막 부분에서 봉사를 할 때, '이것' 대신에 기꺼이 하는 마음과 좋은 느낌을 가지라고

했기 때문에, '이것'은 이런 마음과는 반대되는 부정적인 의미를 가진 단어임을 생각해 낼 수 있다.

| 정답 | (d) grudge 원한(怨恨), 인색함(willingness; 기꺼이 하는 마음과는 상대적으로 인색하여 하기 싫은 마음이 잘 대조된다.)

| 오답 | (a) grief 슬픔 (b) madness 광기 (c) delight 기쁨

예제 11~13

무엇이 비를 내리게 하는가? 비는 어떤 것이 지구에 떨어지는 것과 마찬가지의 이유로 구름에서 내린다.

지구의 중력이 비를 당긴다. 그러나 모든 구름이 물방울이나 얼음 결정을 만들지는 않는다. 왜 모든 구름에서 비나 눈이 끊임없이 떨어지지 않을까? 구름의 물방울이나 얼음 결정은 엄청나게 작다. 그들에 미치는 중력의 영향은 하찮은 것이다. 공기의 흐름은 물방울을 움직이고 들어올려서 아래쪽으로 향하여 이동하고자 하는 힘은 0이고, 그럼에도 불구하고 물방울은 일정하게 움직인다. 물방울과 얼음 결정들은 마치 공기 속의 먼지가 한줄기의 햇빛 속에서 보이는 것처럼 움직인다. 무관심한 연구자들에게는 먼지는 일정한 방향이 없이 무질서하게 움직여 일정하지 않게 움직이는 것같이 생각된다. 그러나 실제로는 먼지 입자들은 물방울입자들보다 훨씬 크고 그들은 결국은 떨어지게 된다. 구름 속의 물방울의 평균 크기는 단지 지름이 0.0004인치밖에 되지 않는다. 이것은 너무나 작아서 지름 0.008인치가 되려면 16개의 물방울이 모이거나 큰 것이 구름으로부터 떨어질 수 있다. 빗방울은 평균적으로 아주 작은 구름 속 방울의 백만 개를 포함하고 있다. 구름 속 방울이 구름에서 떨어질 만큼 충분히 성장하면 비나 다른 강수형태의 원인이 된다. 이 중요한 성장과정은 유착이라고 불려진다.

11. 다음 중 "minute"와 가장 가까운 의미를 갖고 있는 단어는?

| 풀이 | 중력은 질량에 비례하여 작용한다. 따라서 아주 작은 물방울에 미치는 중력은 자연히 작을 수밖에 없다.

| 정답 | (b) tiny

12. "motion"이 나타내는 의미와 가장 가까운 것은 무엇인가?

| 정답 | (c) movement

13. "random"이 나타내는 의미는?

| 풀이 | 아무런 관심 없이 먼지를 보는 사람에게 먼지는 아무런 방향이나 질서 없이 마구 떠돌아다니는 것처럼 보인다.

| 정답 | (a) unpredictable → 방향도 질서도 없기 때문에 당연히 예측 불가능하다.

| 오답 | (b) perplexing 복잡한 (c) independent 독립적인 (d) abnormal 비정상의

예제 14~16

19세기의 농업은 다음의 두 가지를 포함한다: 노동력을 절감하는 기계류의 개발과 과학적인 농업 기술의 개발이다. 노동 절약형 기계는 당연히 노동력이 부족한 곳에서 먼저 나타났다. "유럽에서는, 노동력이 풍부해서 토지로부터 가장 좋은 산출을 얻는 것이 목표이고; 이곳에서는 토지가 풍부하므로 노동력으로부터 가장 많은 것을 얻어내야 한다."라고 토마스 제퍼슨이 말했다. 따라서 19세기에 농기계류가 가장 진보한 곳은 바로 미국이다.

세기 초에, 조잡한 쟁기를 제외하고, 농부들은 모든 농사 기구를 등에다 지고 옮길 수 있었다; 1860년까지 사용되던 대부분의 기계류는 초기의 형태로 디자인되었다. 초기의 발명품 중 가장 중요한 것은 철제 쟁기였다. 1790년대와 같이 이른 시기에 뉴저지의 찰스 뉴볼드는 주철로 된 쟁기를 만들고 있었고, 자신의 발명품을 알리는 데에 전 재산을 썼다.

그러나 농부들은 철이 토지로 하여금 독성을 띄게 하고 잡초를 자라게 한다는 이유로 발명품에 관심이 없었다. 그럼에도 불구하고, 1869년 사우스 벤드의 제임스 올리브가 냉각된 금속으로 쟁기를 만들 때까지, 많은 사람들이 쟁기에 관심을 가졌었다.

14. "naturally"가 나타내는 뜻과 가장 비슷한 것은?

| 풀이 | 노동력이 부족한 국가에서 노동력을 절약하기 위한 기계를 발명하는 것은 지극히 당연하므로 놀랄 일이 아니다.

| 정답 | (a) unsurprisingly

| 오답 | (b) gradually 점차적으로 (c) apparently 분명히 (d) safely 안전하게

15. "make the most of"라는 표현이 의미하는 것과 가장 가까운 것은?

| 풀이 | 문자 그대로 '가장 많은 것을 만들어낸다'는 의미는 무엇으로부터 가장 많은 산출을 얻는다는 것과 같은 의미이다.

| 정답 | (a) get the best yield from

| 오답 | (b) raise the price of －의 가격을 올리다
(c) exaggerate the worth of －의 가치를 과장하다
(d) earn a living on － 생계를 세우다

16. 본문 속의 밑줄 친 "here"는 무엇을 지칭하는가?

| 풀이 | 영국은 노동력이 풍부하고, 이곳(here)은 토지가 광활하다고 앞 문장에 소개되고 있고, 뒤 이어 미국은 노동력을 절약하기 위한 기계류가 가장 먼저 개발된 곳이라고 하고 있다. 따라서 토지가 많은 대신 노동력이 부족한 미국이 바로 here가 된다.

| 정답 | (b) the United States

➲ 예제 17~18

앞으로 다가올 여러 세기동안 그랜트가 영웅의 모습으로 기억되리라는 것은 확실하다. 하지만, 그의 미래의 모습은 과연 어떠할까? 그를 추앙하는 사람들이 나보다 더 깊이 알고 있던 매력적인 인물은 한사람과의 만남에서 얼굴을 마주하고 그의 인상을 만들었다. 두 번째나 10번째 만남에서 이 개인적 인상의 생생함은 잃어버린 바 되고, 시간이 지남에 따라 모두 사라질지도 모른다. 그는 위대한 군인으로 기억될까? 당연히 그도 한 인간이었다. 그러나 나는 내가 옳다고 믿으며, 그가 이룬 군대에서의 훌륭한 업적이 그를 다른 국가적 영웅과 구별되게 하는 최고의 자질은 아니었다고 주장한다.

17. "intimately"와 가장 가까운 의미를 지니는 단어는?

| 풀이 | 위 글은 사람이 업적에 의해 계속적으로 기억되는 것이 아니라, 대개는 마주한 인상에 의해 기억되며, 따라서 시간이 지날수록 인상은 점점 사라지게 되고 동시에 기억에서도 점점 사라지게 된다는 내용을 담고 있다.
어떤 영웅이나 인물의 추종자들은 그렇지 않은 사람보다 그 대상에 대해 더 깊고 친밀하게 알고 있는 것이 당연하다.

| 정답 | (a) friendly

| 오답 | (b) famously 유명하게 (c) fatally 치명적으로 (d) stately 위풍당당한

18. "Without question"이라는 표현이 담고 있는 뜻은?

| 풀이 | '아무런 질문 없이'라는 표현은 너무나도 당연하거나 확실하기 때문에 질문이 필요 없다는 뜻과 일맥상통하다.

| 정답 | (b) certainly

| 오답 | (a) utterly 완전히 (c) deceitfully 허위로 (d) exaggeratingly 과장되게

➲ 예제 19~20

우리가 그것을 자연적이고 양도할 수 없는 권리로 인정하든 않든 간에 언론, 출판의 자유의 민주주의 원리는 어떤 가정에 기초를 두고 있다. 그것들 중 하나는 사람은 진실을 알고 싶어하는 욕망이 있으며 그것에 의해 인도될 생각이 있다는 것이다. 또 다른 것은 진실에 도달하는 단 하나의 방법이 결국은 개방된 시장에서의 자유로운 의견경쟁에 있다는 것이다. 또 다른 가설은 사람은 피할 수 없는 의견의 차이를 직면하게 될 것이므로 다른 사람도 같은 권리를 지니고 있다고 인정해야 한다는 것이다. 그리고 마지막 가설은 이러한 상호간의 관용과 다른 의견과의 비교가 가장 이성적으로 여겨지므로 이러한 태도가 확대될 것이고 일반적으로 받아들여질 거라는 것이다.

19. 'rest upon'이 나타내는 의미와 가장 가까운 것은?

| 풀이 | 언론과 출판의 자유가 어떠한 가설 위에서 성립되었음을 설명하는 글이다.

| 정답 | (a) base on

| 오답 | (b) depend on 의존하다, 의지하다 (c) hold on 유지하다 (d) keep on 유지하다

20. "in the long run"이라는 표현이 나타내는 의미와 가장 가까운 것은?

| 풀이 | 문자 그대로 해석하면, '오래 달리고 난 후'라는 뜻이 된다. 이 말은 '긴 안목으로 보면, 결국은'이라는 뜻을 의미한다.

| 정답 | (c) in the end

| 오답 | (a) in large quantities 많이 (b) frequently 자주 (d) for a long time 오랫동안

예제 21~22

이식의 주요 목적은 재생이 불가능한 혼수상태를 죽음의 새로운 기준으로 정의 내린다는 것이다. 정의가 필요한 데에는 두 가지 이유가 있다: 환자를 소생시키고 치료를 돕는 방법의 향상은 심하게 부상당한 환자를 살리기 위해 더욱 노력하게 했다. 때때로 이러한 노력은 부분적으로만 성공해서 심장은 여전히 뛰지만 두뇌는 심하게 손상당한 개인을 만들었다. 영구적인 지력의 상실로 고통받는 환자와 그들의 가정 또는 혼수상태에 빠진 환자들이 이미 차지하고 있는 병상에서의 부담은 너무 크다. 시대에 뒤떨어진 죽음에 대한 정의 기준은 이식을 위한 장기를 얻는 문제에 있어 논쟁을 불러일으킬 수 있다.

21. 아래의 단어 중 "resuscitative"와 뜻이 가장 유사한 것은?

| 풀이 | 혼수상태에 빠진 환자를 대상으로 한 치료방법 내지는 소생시키는 방법의 진보를 말하고 있다.

| 정답 | (c) reviving

| 오답 | (a) rewarding 보답하는 (b) retaliatory 보복적인 (d) retroactive 반동하는

22. "Obsolete"의 의미는?

| 풀이 | 혼수상태가 사망이 아니라 살아있는 상태라고 주장하는 것은 최근의 일이다. 장기 이식을 하려고 할 때 뇌사는 사망 상태라는 기존의 사망 정의 기준을 고수하는 사람은 반대를 할 것이므로 논쟁의 여지가 있다.

| 정답 | (a) Outmoded 유행에 뒤진

| 오답 | (b) Operatic 가극의 (c) Resultant 결과로 생기는 (d) Sordid 더러운

CHAPTER 2

직접 정보 찾기

Directly answered questions

예제 1

장래 배우자감의 직업에 대한 선호도에 대해서, 여학생들은 공무원을 최고로 꼽은 반면, 남학생들의 대부분은 교사를 선호했다. 조사기관의 대변인은 이번 조사가 최근의 경제 침체로 인해 안정된 직업에 대한 선호가 증가되었음을 보여준다고 말했다.

1. 최근 학생들은 그들의 배우자가 어떠한 직업을 갖기를 원하는가?

| 풀이 | growing preference among students for stable jobs~

| 정답 | (c) firm jobs

예제 2

작년에 미국에서의 인터넷 사용이 급격히 증가했고, 정부의 새로운 자료는 2001년 미국의 인터넷 사용자 수가 최초로 전체 인구의 50%가 넘었음을 보여주었다. 화요일 발표된 통상부의 보고에 따르면, 1억 4300만 명의 미국인, 즉, 전체 인구의 54%가 작년 9월 1일 현재 인터넷을 사용 중이었다. 이 수치는 재작년에 비해 26%가 증가한 것이다.

2. 위 글에 따르면, 2001년에 미국 인구의 몇 퍼센트가 인터넷을 사용했는가?

| 풀이 | found that 143 million Americans, or 54 percent of the country, were using the internet ~

| 정답 | (a) 54%

예제 3

일상적인 삶의 길에서 탈출하고 싶으신가요? 인도의 국내 운송업체인 사하라항공에서 승객들에게 라이브로 세레나데를 연주해드립니다. 항공사에서는 한 달 동안의 기내 뮤직 페스티벌을 시작했고, 연주자들은 승객들의 신청곡을 받을 뿐만 아니라 기타와 바이올린으로 생생한 멜로디를 들려줄 것입니다.

3. 사하라항공은 어떤 서비스를 준비합니까?

| 풀이 | ~began serenading its passengers to live music.

| 정답 | (c) Live music

예제 4

니코틴은 정상적인 환경에서보다 체내의 칼로리를 더 많이 소비할 수 있는 것처럼 보인다. 니코틴이 체내에서 빠져나갔을 때는, 몸무게는 담배를 피지 않았을 때의 상태로 되돌아올 것이고, 특히 당신이 (담배를 피울 때와) 똑같은 식습관과 운동 습관을 유지한다면 더더욱 그럴 것이다. 그러나 축적되는 칼로리의 양을 줄이기 위해서 조금만 먹고, 타서 없어지는 칼로리의 양을 늘리기 위해 운동을 더 많이 한다면 이러한 현상을 막을 수 있다.

4. 위 글에서 언급되지 않은 한 가지를 찾아라.

| 풀이 | Nicotine does seem able to make the body burn more calories than~
더 많은 칼로리를 소비하면 그 만큼 체중은 줄어든다.

| 정답 | (d) Smoking can't reduce the weight.

| 오답 | (a) Nicotine make the body burn more calories. (Line 1)
(b) To stop smoking can make the weight return. (Line 2-3)
(c) Getting exercises can reduce the weight. (Line 4-7)

예제 5

프랭클린은 사십대에 인쇄업에서 은퇴를 했다. 그가 일을 그만뒀을 때, 그는 다른 흥미 거리, 이를테면 과학, 발명, 정치 등에 시간을 쏟았다. 프랭클린은 전기에 특히 관심이 많았다. 그는 한가지 이론을 주장했는데, 번개가 실제로는 전기라는 것이었다. 이것을 증명하기 위해서 그는 유명한 연 실험을 했다. 연의 맨 꼭대기에 금속조각을 붙이고, 폭풍우가 칠 때 그 연을 날렸다. 번개가 연에 붙어있는 금속 조각을 때렸을 때, 프랭클린은 열쇠를 만졌다. 그가 (번개로 인한) 충격을 받았을 때, 그는 자기의 이론이 옳았다는 것을 깨달았다.

5. 위 글에 근거해서 옳지 않은 문장은?

| 풀이 | he has performed famous kite experiment ~
연 실험을 했을 뿐이지 연 날리는 것을 좋아하는지는 알 수 없다.

| 정답 | (c) Franklin enjoyed to fly a kite.

| 오답 | (a) Franklin is interested in invention. (Line 2-3)
(b) Franklin believed lightning was really electricity. (Line 4-5)
(d) Franklin had gotten a shock by lightning. (Line 8)

예제 6

바이킹들은 재빨리 공격해왔고, 공격을 할 때는 어떠한 경고도 하지 않았다. 그들은 공격하는 마을 사람들에게 무척이나 잔인했고, 때로는 건물들을 모두 태워버려서 마을을 파괴했다. 유럽의 몇몇 나라는 그 지역의 왕이 종종 바이킹과 맞서 싸웠다. 하지만 때때로 왕들은 바이킹이 자기들을 공격하지 않도록 설득하기 위해 돈을 바치기도 했다.

비록 바이킹들이 흉악한 전사들로 알려져 있긴 하지만, 그들은 멋진 배를 만들기도 했다. 대형보트라고 불리는 나무로 만든 바이킹의 배는 아주 나쁜 일기 속에서도 항해가 가능했다. 대부분의 바이킹 배는 약 20미터 정도였지만, 어떤 것들은 거의 90미터 정도나 되었다. 바이킹 항해사들은 배를 움직이기 위해 돛과 노를 모두 사용하였다.

6. 위 글의 내용과 맞지 않는 것은?

| 풀이 | 바이킹들이 그들의 집을 지었다는 언급은 없다.

| 정답 | (c) The vikings sometimes built their houses.

| 오답 | (a) The vikings are fierce. (Line 7)
(b) The vikings built excellent ships. (Line 7–8)
(d) The viking ships are made of woods. (Line 8)

예제 7

수천 명의 중국인들이 철도 건설 작업을 하기 위해서 북아메리카로 끌려왔다. 그들은 열심히 일했지만, 그들의 고용주들은 심하게 중국인들을 대했다. 중국인들의 근무일수는 매우 길었고, 작업 환경도 매우 위험했다. 많은 중국인들이 철도를 건설하는 동안 사고로 죽었다. 중국 여성들도 북 아메리카로 왔지만, 여성의 수보다는 남자의 숫자가 훨씬 더 많았다.

1900년 경, 철도공사가 완료된 후에, 매우 적은 수의 중국인만이 북아메리카로 올 것을 허가받았다. 캐나다와 미국에 사는 대부분의 사람들이 중국인에 익숙하지 않았고, 그래서 낯선 사람들이 자기네 나라에 오는 것을 원하지 않았다. 북아메리카로 오는 중국인들은 많은 세금을 내야만 했다. 이것이 중국인으로 하여금 그들의 아내와 가족들을 북아메리카로 데리고 오는 것을 어렵게 만들었다. 후에 캐나다와 미국 정부는 중국인의 이민을 불법화했다.

7. 밑줄 친 This가 의미하는 바는?

| 풀이 | 중국인으로 하여금 가족을 못 데려오게 하는 원인은 바로 북아메리카로 오는 중국인에게 요구되는 비싼 세금 때문이다. 따라서 'This'는 바로 세금을 내야하는 그 사실 자체를 가리킨다.

| 정답 | (a) Any Chinese person who came to North America had to pay an expensive tax.

예제 8

요즘에 가장 알려져 있고, 널리 논쟁을 불러일으키는 말 중의 하나가 "세계화"이다. 세계화가 실제로 무엇이냐에 관해서 의견의 일치는 없지만, 세계가 점점 밀접하게 연결되고 있다는 사실은 의심의 여지가 없다. 대중 매체와 운송수단 기술, 거기다 더하여 다국적 공동 문화의 증대는 새로운 지구촌 문화를 형성하기 위해 결합되었다.

8. 여섯째 줄에 나와 있는 "a new global culture"가 나타내는 것은?

| 풀이 | 이 글은 세계화에 대하여 소개하고 있다. 새로운 지구촌 문화란 바로 세계화를 의미하는 것이다.

| 정답 | (b) globalization

예제 9

불행하게도 어떤 여성들은 매우 날씬해지는 것에 관심을 가지는 반면에 다른 여성들은 자신의 신체와 관련해서 다른 각도의 관심을 가진다. 예를 들면, 어떤 여성들은 자신의 가슴이 충분히 크지 않다고 생각하고는, 가슴을 확대하기 위해 수술을 받는다. 이 수술은, 가슴을 크게 하기 위해서 가슴 안쪽에다가 어떤 인공 물질을 삽입하는 것이다. 많은 여성들이 이 수술을 받지만, 그 결과 그들 중 많은 사람들이 수술 후 심각한 건강상의 문제로 고통받고 있다.

9. 많은 여성들이 성형 수술을 받는 이유는 무엇인가?

| 풀이 | ~have different concerns related to the appearance of their body.
많은 여성들이 단순히 날씬해지는 것 외에 외모가 더 괜찮아 보이기 위해 걱정을 한다고 말하고 있다.

| 정답 | (c) to look better

예제 10

셰익스피어의 연극에서, 그는 인생의 많은 분야에 대한 폭넓은 지식을 드러내었다. 셰익스피어 연극의 주인공들은 아주 다양한 주제를, 때로는 전문가의 지식을 필요로 하는 주제를 논의한다. 하지만, 그의 연극에서 더욱 감명 깊은 것은 셰익스피어의 영어 사용이다. 그의 어휘는 굉장히 풍부하고, 마치 언어에 많은 새로운 단어들을 소개하는 것 같다. 또한, 셰익스피어 연극의 주인공들이 말했던 여러 문구가 이제는 일상 대화에서도 사용된다. 오늘날에는 작가들도 그들의 작품에 종종 셰익스피어의 연극에서 인용구를 따온다.

그러나 셰익스피어의 연극에서 가장 감명 깊은 점은 바로 연극 속에 나왔던 등장인물들이다. 그의 연극에 등장했던 많은 등장인물들은 각자가 서로 많이 달랐지만, 너무나도 현실적으로 느껴진다. 그들이 느끼는 감정이나, 그들이 하는 말, 또 그들이 하는 행동들은 모두 쉽게 이해가 된다. 셰익스피어의 연극을 보는 많은 사람들은 연극 속에 등장하는 인물들이 상기시켜주는 사람을 안다는 것을 발견하게 될 것이다.

10. 밑줄 친 대명사 them이 말하는 것은?

| 풀이 | 셰익스피어 연극에서 가장 인상 깊은 것으로 연극에 등장하는 인물을 꼽고 있다. 따라서 인물이 등장하는 것은 연극이다.

| 정답 | (b) Shakespeare's plays

예제 11

비록 만우절이 국경일은 아니지만, 많은 사람들, 특히 젊은이들은 이 날을 기념한다. 만우절의 기원은 여러 가지로 설명된다. 가장 인기 있는 기원은 16세기 프랑스로 거슬러 올라가 시작되었다는 이야기일 것이다. 그 당시, 새해의 첫 날, 즉 설날은 3월 25일이었다. 이 날은 또한 춘분과도 일치했다. 그 날은 새해의 시작이었을 뿐 아니라, 새 생명의 시작과 땅의 소생의 시작이기도 했다. 지금도 그런 것처럼 예전에도 새해를 축하하는 것은 파티와 많은 향락을 의미했다. 사실, 프랑스 사람들은 새해를 축하하는 일을 4월 1일까지 중단하지 않았다고 알려진다.

11. 프랑스 사람들은 얼마나 오랫동안 새해를 축하했나?

| 풀이 | 3월 25일에 시작된 새해 축하 행사는 4월 1일까지 계속되었다고 소개하고 있다.

| 정답 | (b) for a week

예제 12

신용카드를 갖는 것은 까다로운 일이다. 무이자 카드를 이용할 수도 있지만, 약관에 나와 있는 많은 규칙들을 따라야만 한다. 만약 당신이 할부금을 하루라도 늦게 낸다면, 당신의 무이자는 최고 22%까지 올라갈 것이고, 최고 30달러의 벌금(연체료)을 물어야 한다. 가장 좋은 방법은 온라인으로 지불하는 것이다. (카드)회사는 당신의 은행 계좌에서 자동으로 돈을 빼가고, 그것은 대개 무료이다. 전화로 수표 결제를 하는 것은 거의 돈이 든다. 월초에 총 차감 잔액을 지불하는 것은 이상적인 일이다.

12. 위 글에 따르면 신용카드를 갖는 것은 어떠한가?

| 풀이 | Having a credit card is a tricky thing.
글쓴이는 결제 문제와 관련해서 신용카드 소지가 불편하고 까다로운 일이라고 말하고 있다.

| 정답 | (c) complicated 복잡한, 어려운

| 오답 | (b) beneficial 유익한, 이로운 (d) convenient 편리한

예제 13

전 세계에 걸쳐서 표준화된 인삼 추출물만을 모은 가장 효과적인 500mg짜리 GinsEnergy를 소개합니다. GinsEnergy는 지속적이고 힘있는 안정된 에너지를 제공하는데, 이것은 신체의 지구력과 기능을 돕고, 면역 체계를 강화시킵니다. 거기다가, 그것은 캡슐 형태라 비슷한 제품들이 지녔던 역겨운 냄새도 나지 않습니다.

GinsEnergy는 강력한 효력이 있는 미국산, 중국산, 그리고 한국산 인삼 추출물 500mg에 지속적으로 에너지를 발산하게 해 주는 일곱 가지의 다른 고 에너지 약초를 첨가했습니다. 여기다가 벌꿀도 첨가했는데, 과학자들과 건강 전문가들은 벌꿀이 비타민과 미네랄을 공급받는 데 놀라운 효능이 있음을 알았습니다.

13. 위 글에서 추론할 수 있는 GinsEnergy은?

| 풀이 | 위에서 소개하는 인삼 제품은 인체의 지구력을 강화하고, 면역 체계를 향상시켜 주며, 비타민과 미네랄도 공급받을 수 있는 영양제라고 할 수 있다.

| 정답 | (d) a dietary supplement

예제 14

케니우드는 아름다운 몽가 강과 우뚝 솟은 가나 산악지대 사이에 위치한다. 그것은 서양에서 가장 아름다운 전통적인 유원지이다. 그 유원지는 롤러코스터와 두 종류의 물 타기, 그리고 스무 종류의 육상 탈 것을 포함하여 25개의 주요 탈 것들이 있다. 또한 서른 다섯 종류의 게임과 두 군데의 비디오 게임센터, 그리고 네 군데의 기념품 가게가 유원지 전체에 걸쳐서 있다. 그리고 까페식 레스토랑인 Park Terrace가 있다. 예약은 온라인에서만 가능하다. 주차는 무료이다.

14. 티켓은 어떻게 미리 구입할 수 있는가?

| 풀이 | Advanced reservations are available online.

| 정답 | (d) via(=through) internet

예제 15

경제가 남부로 옮겨갔을 때, 의욕(사기)도 경제와 함께 옮겨갔다. 소유주들은 그들이 해오던 방식대로 근로자들에게 보수를 줄 수 없다면 어떻게 근로자들에게 동기를 부여할 수 있을지를 궁금해 하기 시작했다. 그러나 모든 소유주들은 피고용인들이 가장 원하는 보상-존중을 제공하기 위한 자원을 가지고 있다.

원하기만 하면 부수입이 생길 때 실시한 한 조사에서 근로자들은 그들이 정말로 원하는 것은 그들의 고용주나 경영인들이 자신들이 한 일에 대해 개인적으로 축하하거나 감사하고, 그들의 업무를 칭찬하는 개인적인 메모를 쓰고, 그들의 노력을 공개적으로 인정해주고, 성공을 축하하기 위해 직원 모두를 모으는 것이었다.

15. 위 글에 따르면, 근로자들이 그들의 고용주나 경영인들에게 가장 원하는 것은 무엇인가?

| 풀이 | personally congratulate or thank them for doing a good job, write a personal note praising their performance, publicly recognize their efforts, gather the staff together to celebrate success.

| 정답 | (b) getting proper compliments for what they've done
compliment 찬사, 인사

예제 16~18

아메리카 카우보이의 황금기는 짧게 지속되었다. 그것은 1860년대 텍사스에서 캔서스로 많은 소들을 데려오면서 시작되었다. 1890년까지 외딴 지역에도 철길이 연결되면서, 더 이상 대규모의 소를 이용한 이동은 필요하지 않게 되었다.

물론, 카우보이는 1860년 이전에도 역사가 있다. 사실, 그보다 오래 전에도 멕시칸 카우보이들이 있었다. 1521년에 스페인 정복자인 헤르난 코르테스가 멕시코에 소를 끌고 왔던 것이다. 코르테스는 자기 소에다가 세 개의 십자형 모양의 상표를 붙였다. 스페인의 뾰족한 뿔을 가진 소는 사막과 초원을 자유롭게 거닐었다. 결국 그들은 텍사스로 가는 길을 발견했다. 텍사스에 정착한 미국인들은 자기네 동물을 스페인 종과 교배시켰다. 텍사스 롱혼(뿔이 긴 소)종이 바로 그 결과였다. 롱혼 종은 나쁜 성격과 공격성으로 유명했다. 롱혼 종은 3.5피트나 되는 뿔을 가진 위험한 동물이었다.

1865년에 남북전쟁이 끝난 이후에, 전에는 흑인노예였던 제대한 군인들과 모험을 찾는 젊은이들이 서부로 향했다. 당시에, 텍사스에는 약 오백만 마리의 소가 있었다. 동부에서는 소고기에 대한 수요가 많았다. 이 때까지, 동부에서 시작되는 철길은 캔서스만큼 먼 서부까지 확장되었다. 남부 텍사스에서 철도까지는 여전히 600마일 이상 떨어져 있었다. 이 두 지역 사이에는 건너야 할 강도 있었고, 인디언 부족, 황무지를 비롯해 다른 많은 어려움이 있었다. 제스 키스홀름이라는 모피 판매업자가 1865년 마차를 끌고 북쪽으로 왔다. 카우보이들과 소들은 키스홀름의 행로를 따라 북쪽 캔사스의 아빌렌까지 따라갔다. 이 행로가 1884년 가시철사로 가로막힐 때까지 소를 몰아가는 가장 유명한 길이 되었다.

16. 이 글에 어울리는 제목은?

| 풀이 | 이 글은 처음에 스페인에서 들어온 소가 텍사스 토종 소와 교배되면서 롱혼 종이 생겨나고, 이후 텍사스에서 캔서스로 소들이 옮겨오면서 카우보이의 황금기가 시작되었음을 소개하는 글이다.

| 정답 | (a) American cowboy's history

| 오답 | (b), (c), (d)는 카우보이의 역사를 소개하기 위한 세부적인 요소에 불과하다.(too specific)

17. 누가 멕시코에 소를 들여왔는가?

| 풀이 | The Spanish conqueror of Mexico, Hernan Cortes, brought cattle ~.

| 정답 | (d) Hernan cortes

18. 위 글에 들어있지 않은 것은?

| 풀이 | ~ cowboys have a history before 1860.

| 정답 | (a) Cowboys have a history after 1884.

| 오답 | (b) Line 10 (c) Line 14-15 d) Line 17-18

⊃ 예제 19~23

사람과 동물의 행동에 관심이 있으신가요? 그렇다면, 당신은 아마 심리학을 좋아할 것입니다. 심리학은 행동을 연구하는 학문이지만, 매우 광범위한 연구 범위를 가집니다. 몇 가지의 다양한 심리학의 분야가 있고, 각각의 분야는 행동의 서로 다른 측면을 연구합니다.

사회 심리학은 사람 사이의 상호작용을 연구합니다. 예를 들어, 사회 심리학자는 사람들로 하여금 공격적으로 행동하게 하는 상황에 관한 연구를 시도합니다. 사회 심리학자들이 연구하는 또 다른 문제는 왜 사람들이 특정 사람에게 서로 끌리는가 하는 것입니다. 사회 심리학에서 재미있는 주제 중에 하나는 일치에 관한 것입니다. 무엇이 사람으로 하여금 같은 방식으로 행동하게 하고, 다른 사람이 행하고 말하는 대로 따라하게 만드는가? 하는 것입니다.

인지 심리학자들은 생각과 기억, 그리고 언어에 관해 연구합니다. 인지 심리학자들이 연구하는 하나는 어떻게 사람들이 숫자를 기억하느냐 하는 것입니다. 예를 들어, 어떤 번호를 기억하는 가장 좋은 방법은 무엇인가? 숫자를 반복해서 익히는 게 좋을까, 아니면 숫자에다가 어떤 의미를 부여하는 것이 좋을까? 하는 것입니다. 인지 심리학자들은 언어도 연구합니다. 예를 들어, 어떻게 해서 어린 아이들이 제2외국어를 쉽고 빨리 배울 수 있는가? 하는 것입니다. 인지 심리학자들은 또한 사람들이 새로운 장소를 찾아내는 것처럼 문제를 해결하는 것을 배우는 방법에도 관심이 있습니다.

임상 심리학자들은 정신질환을 연구합니다. 예를 들어, 임상 심리학자들은 우울증의 원인을 찾아내어 우울증에 걸린 사람들을 도울 방법을 찾아내기 위해 노력합니다. 다른 임상 심리학자들은 마약 중독으로 고통받는 사람들의 행동을 연구하여 이 문제가 예방되고 치료될 수 있도록 합니다. 임상 심리학자들이 관심을 가지는 또 다른 문제는 폭력적인 행동입니다. 폭력을 예방하고 폭력적인 사람의 행동을 변화시키는 방법을 찾아내는 것은 매우 중요합니다.

어떤 심리학자들은 심리학적 특성을 측정하는 것에 관심이 있습니다. 예를 들어, 심리학자들은 사람의 지능과 성격적인 특성, 또는 흥미를 알아내기 위한 검사를 발전시키고자 합니다. 이러한 검사들은 사람들이 교육과 직업, 그리고 임상치료를 선택함에 있어서 도움을 줄 수 있을 것입니다.

동물의 행동을 연구하는 심리학자는 동물 행동학자로 불립니다. 동물 행동학자들은 종종 새와 물고기 그리고 다른 동물들의 행동을 관찰하기 위해서 야생 지대로 나가기도 합니다. 이 분야의 심리학자는 어떻게 해서 특정 동물들이 양육과 교미, 싸움 등의 다양한 행동과 관련한 "본능"을 지니는지를 알아내기 위해 노력합니다. 어떤 동물 행동학자들은 많은 동물들에게서 보여지는 특이한 행동에 대해 많은 것들을 연구합니다.

이것들은 심리학의 다양한 분야 중 일부일 뿐입니다. 정말로 심리학은 가장 흥미 있는 지식 분야 중의 하나입니다.

19. 이 글의 main idea는 무엇인가?

| 풀이 | 글쓴이는 사회심리학, 인지심리학, 임상심리학, 동물행동학 등의 예를 들면서 궁극적으로 심리학 관련 분야가 다양함을 소개하고 있다.

| 정답 | (a) There are several different kinds of psychology.

20. branches와 바꿔 쓸 수 있는 단어는?

| 풀이 | 다양한 심리학 분야를 소개하기 위해 도입하는 부분으로 직역하면 가지이지만, 이것을 학문에 적용해 볼 때는 중심에서 뻗어져 나온 하위 분야 또는 영역을 뜻한다.

| 정답 | (b) part

| 오답 | (a) stick 나뭇가지 (c) study 연구 (d) behaviour 행동

21. 위 글에 나타나 있지 않은 것은?

| 풀이 | Cognitive psychologists study thinking, memory, and language.

| 정답 | (c) Cognitive psychologists don't study languages.

| 오답 | (a) Psychology is the study of people and animals. (Line 1–2)
(b) Social psychologists study interactions among people. (Line 5)
(d) Clinical psychologists study mental illnesses. (Line 18)

22. 이 글의 어조는 어떠한가?

| 풀이 | 이 글은 심리학의 여러 하위 분야에 대해 설명하는 글이다.

| 정답 | (b) informative

| 오답 | (a) ironic 반어의, 빈정대는 (c) comparative 상대적인 (d) negative 부정적인

23. 'Ethologists'는 무엇인가?

| 풀이 | Psychologists who study the behaviour of animals are called ethologists.

| 정답 | (b) psychologists who study the behaviour of animals

예제 24~27

알코올은 서양에서 이용된 가장 오래된 약품이다. 수천 년 동안, 사람들은 알코올 음료를 만들어왔다. 이 음료들은 발효라고 불리는 과정이 일어나게 함으로써 만들어졌다. 알코올의 발효는 어떤 액체에서 효모나 박테리아가 설탕을 분해하고, 그 설탕의 일부를 알코올 성분으로 바꿀 때 일어난다. 과일주스와 같은 많은 액체가 발효한다.

수천 년 전에, 알코올 음료는 중동지방에서 흔했다. 그러나 이슬람 종교에서 알코올을 금했기 때문에, 그 지역에서는 알코올을 거의 마시지 않았다. 유럽의 여러 나라와 세계 다른 지역에서는 다양한 종류의 알코올 음료가 만들어지고 소비된다.

유럽의 따뜻한 지역에서는 사람들이 포도주스를 발효시켜 와인을 만든다. 유럽의 시원한 지역에서는 물과 다양한 곡류를 섞어 만든 액체를 발효시켜서 맥주를 만든다. 발효과정은 "화주"라고 알려진 더 독한 술을 만들기 위해서도 이용된다. 이 술에는 보드카와 위스키 그리고 럼주가 포함된다. 좋은 와인과 맥주, 화주를 만들기 위한 기술은 수 백년에 걸쳐서 발전되어 왔고, 과학적인 신중함이 요구된다. 어떤 사람들은 잘 만들어진 와인과 맥주, 화주를 잘 구별하는 훌륭한 감각을 발전시켜왔고, 이러한 다양한 종류의 음료에 관한 전문가가 되었다.

많은 사람들이 알코올 음료의 맛을 느끼지만 많은 사람들은 또한 알코올이 가져다주는 느낌을 즐긴다. 알코올은 중앙신경계를 진정시켜서 사람으로 하여금 덜 억제되고 긴장되게 느끼게 하기 때문에 "진정제"라고 불리는 약품으로 분류된다. 많은 사람들이 이러한 느낌을 즐기지만, 너무 많이 술을 마시면 그 사람은 조정력과 균형, 판단력을 잃게 된다. 말이 불분명해지고, 또 말을 지나치게 많이 할지도 모른다. 어떤 사람들은 공격적으로 변하거나 의기소침해진다. 사람이 이러한 알코올의 영향아래 놓이게 되면, 그 사람은 취했다고 말해진다.

술을 마심으로써 생길 수 있는 문제 중의 하나는 "음주운전"이다. 어떤 사람들은 술을 마신 후에 운전을 하려고 하지만, 이것은 정말로 위험하다. 매년, 수천 명의 사람들이 차에 대한 통제력을 상실한 음주 운전자들에게 죽임을 당한다. 최근에는 공공 계몽 캠페인, 엄격한 법률과 처벌로 이 문제를 줄이려는 노력이 있어왔다. 만약 술을 마셨다면, 운전하지 말라!!

술과 관련된 또 다른 문제는 알코올 중독으로 알려진 중독이다. 어떤 사람들은 술을 너무 자주 마셔서 생리적으로 술에 중독이 되 버렸다. 이 문제는 그 사람의 건강과, 인간관계, 그리고 직업에도 엄청난 결과를 초래할 수 있다.

알코올 음료는 서구의 문화이면서 동시에 다른 많은 나라의 문화이다. 한편으로 술은 많은 사람들에게 즐거움과 만족을 가져다준다. 그러나 다른 한편으로 술은 사고와 중독을 가져다주는 악용될 수 있는 마약이기도 하다.

24. 제목으로 적당한 것은?

| 풀이 | 문단별로 살펴보면, 알코올을 발표시켜 술을 만드는 원리, 알코올이 가져다주는 다양한 감정과 알코올을 인한 영향, 음주가 가져다주는 문제들에 대해서 이야기하고 있다. 결국, 이 글은 알코올 음료와 관련한 여러 이야기를 소개하고 있는 것이다.

| 정답 | (a) Alcoholic beverages
문단별 내용을 모두 포함하는 것은 알코올 음료이다.

| 오답 | (b), (c), (d)는 각 문단의 소제에 불과하다.(too specific)

25. 위 글에서 언급되지 않은 것은?

| 정답 | (d) Price of alcoholic beverages

| 오답 | (a) Ways of making alcoholic beverages (paragraph 1)
(b) Problems of alcoholic beverages (paragraph 5 & 6)
(c) History of alcohol (paragraph 2)

26. paragraph 4에 나타나는 글쓴이의 태도는?

| 풀이 | 글쓴이는 넷째 문단에서 술이 가져다주는 다양한 느낌에 대해 언급하면서, 적당한 음주는 사람을 덜 긴장시키지만, 지나치게 취하게 되면 통제력과 균형을 상실하고, 공격적으로 변할 수 있다고 하면서 부정적인 견해를 내비치고 있다.

| 정답 | (c) negative

| 오답 | (a) positive 긍정적인
(b) careful 신중한
(d) angry → 부정적이긴 하지만, 그렇다고 분노하고 있지는 않다.

27. 위 글에 따르면, 사람이 술을 많이 마시면 어떻게 되는가?

| 풀이 | ~ when a person drinks a lot of alcohol, he or she loses co-ordination, balance, and judgment.

| 정답 | (d) loses balance

예제 28~32

"커피 마시러 갑시다!" 미국에서는 친구들끼리 커피숍에서 만나는 걸 좋아한다. 여기서 사람들은 앉아서 그 날의 업무나 뉴스, 스포츠, 개인적인 이야기, 자기 일 이야기, 또는 단순한 잡담을 한다. 커피숍은 대화를 할 수 있는 편안한 분위기를 만든다. 당신은 또 옷을 잘 차려입을 필요도 없다. 학생들은 티셔츠와 청바지를 입고 커피숍에 와서 정장에 넥타이를 맨 회사원들 옆에 앉는다. 많은 커피숍들이 일요일과 공휴일까지 포함하여 24시간 영업을 하기 때문에 밤에 일하는 사람이나 잠을 잘 못 자는 사람들도 아무 때나 들를 수 있다.

커피와 도넛츠는 상대적으로 싸기 때문에 사람들은 자기들이 돈을 많이 쓰고 있다고 생각하지 않고 잠시 앉아 있는 것을 편안하게 여긴다. 비록 커피와 도넛츠가 커피숍에서 파는 주 메뉴이긴 하지만, 많은 곳에서 다른 음료와 디저트, 때로는 가벼운 점심거리도 판다. 많은 단골손님들은 가장 좋아하는 커피나 다른 음료가 정해져 있기 때문에 자기가 좋아하는 것을 찾아 다른 가게를 지나쳐 올 것이다.

다른 나라에서 온 방문객들은 이 커피숍들이 얼마나 넓은지를 보고 종종 놀라기도 한다. 어떤 것들은 일반 식당만큼이나 넓다. 커피숍 주위에 좋은 자리를 마련해 놓고 사람들로 하여금 쉴 수 있게 해준다. 어떤 사람들은 매일이나 매주, 또는 같은 시간에 정기적으로 약속을 정해놓는다. 예를 들어, 퇴직한 친구들이 매일 10시에 모일 것이다. 다른 사람들은 매일 아침 회사로 가져갈 커피를 사기 위해 자동차용 판매대에 들를 것이다. 심지어는 가정이나 직장에 커피 메이커가 있는 사람들도 특별한 커피나 가장 좋아하는 음료를 사기 위해 커피숍에 가는 것을 좋아한다.

단지 몇 개의 제품만 팔아서는 커피숍 소유주들이 많은 돈을 벌지는 못할 것이라고 여길 수도 있겠지만, 사실 많은 커피숍들이 장사가 잘되고, 특히 번잡한 도로 가에 위치한다면 대단히 잘 된다. 그래서 그 사업이 늘 안정되는 경향이 있다. 사람들이 커피숍에 들어와서 앉지 않아도, 외부용 사업이 있게 마련이다.

사람들은 가족이나 친구와 친해지려고 뿐만이 아니라 직원에게 간식을 사주고, 업무를 의논하기 위해서도 커피숍에 간다. 또 다른 사람들은 신문이나 좋아하는 잡지를 읽기 위해서 커피숍에 간다. 어떤 사람들은 심지어 일을 하러 가기도 한다. 이 글도 커피숍에서 쓰여진 것이다!

물론, 이곳에 온 사람들은 대개 커피와 도넛츠를 먹는다. 물론 커피가 미국에서 가장 인기 있는 뜨거운 음료이지만, 대부분의 가게에서는 여러 가지 시원한 음료와 함께 차와 코코아, 그리고 카푸치노도 판다. 도넛츠는 둥글고 작으며 기름을 넣고 튀겨 위에 다양한 토핑을 얹은 빵이다. 대부분의 도넛츠는 중간에 구멍이 있다. 심지어 도넛츠에서 잘라낸 이 구멍도 작은 도넛츠의 형태로 따로따로 팔린다.

미국에서 당신이 어디를 가든지, 당신은 커피숍을 볼 수 있을 것이다. 반시간만 시간을 내서 들어가 쉬어라. 당신은 미국의 유명한 "coffee break!"를 즐길 수 있을 것이다.

28. 이 글의 제목으로 적당한 것을 골라라.

| 풀이 | 글쓴이는 이야기를 나눌 수 있는 편안한 분위기, 격식을 차릴 필요 없는 매장, 휴식 공간의 확보 등 커피숍의 장점에 대해 긍정적으로 열거하고 있다.

| 정답 | (a) a nice place–coffee shops

29. 커피숍에서 파는 주메뉴는 무엇인가?

| 풀이 | Although coffee and donuts are the main items sold at coffee shops, ~

| 정답 | (a) coffee and donuts

30. 밑줄 친 'them'이 나타내는 것은?

| 풀이 | 커피숍 주위에 사람들이 쉴 수 있는 공간이 확보되어 있어야 하므로, 'them'이 가리키는 것은 결국 커피숍이다.

| 정답 | (a) coffee shops

31. 위 글에 따르면 도넛츠의 중간에는 무엇이 있는가?

| 풀이 | Most donuts have a hole in the middle.

| 정답 | (c) hole

32. 글쓴이의 견해에 따르면, 미국의 커피숍들은 어떠한가?

| 풀이 | Coffee shops have an informal atmosphere that encourages conversation.
~ people feel comfortable sitting for a while, ~
So take half an hour to stop in and relax.
글쓴이는 커피숍을 싼 가격에 편안히 쉬다 갈 수 있는 공간으로 여기고 있다.

| 정답 | (b) comfortable

| 오답 | (c) gloomy 우울한 (d) noisy 소란스러운

예제 33~37

월마트는 이제 세계에서 가장 큰 소매기업이다. 월마트는 전세계에 걸쳐서 120만 명의 사람을 고용하고 있다. 2000년에 월마트는 1,910억 달러의 매출을 올렸고, 이윤이 63억 달러였다. 이윤은 전년도에 비해 16%가 증가했다.

사람들은 월마트가 매년 든든하게 성장할 것이라고 예상하게 되었다. 해마다 새로운 상점이 문을 열고, 월마트는 새로운 국가로 확장하고 있다. 월마트는 또한 거의 매년 새로운 사업 영역으로 진출한다. 월마트가 거대한 부동한 회사라는 것을 아는 사람은 거의 없다.

Sam Walton은 1950년 Arkansas Bentonville에 Walton's Five and Dime을 열었다. 12년 후에 그는 Bentonville에 최초의 월마트를 열었다. 그의 경영 철학은 간단했다. 좋은 가격, 많은 선택권 그리고 친절한 인사가 그것이었다. 월튼은 "열 걸음 태도"로도 유명했다. 이것은 모든 직원이 그들로부터 열 걸음 안에 손님이 들어오면 반드시 인사를 해야 한다는 것을 의미한다. 그는 다른 사람이 당신에게 말을 걸기 전에 당신이 먼저 다른 사람에게 말을 하는 것이 중요하다고 강조했다. 월튼은 또한 공급자와의 좋은 거래가 고객에게도 전해져야한다고 믿었다. 낮은 가격과 친절한 서비스가 잘 어우러져서 월마트의 성공의 기본이 되었다. Bentonville에 있던 가게 하나가 미국에만 4,203개, 그리고 미국 외의 국가에 천 개의 점포가 되었다.

월튼은 1992년에 죽었지만, 그의 경영철학은 계속해서 월마트에 전해졌다. 각각의 매장은 입구에서 손님을 맞고 손님이 필요로 하는 어떠한 요구도 충족시킬 직원(greeters)을 고용한다. greeters를 고용하는 것은 월마트가 실제로 고용한 직원의 수 보다 더 많은 직원을 고용한 것과 같은 효과를 가져다주었다. 다른 백화점들과 비교해볼 때, 월마트는 상대적으로 적은 종업원을 확보하고 있다.

월마트는 또한 월마트 재단이 있어서 수많은 좋은 운동을 후원한다. 그들의 프로그램 중에는 고등학교 장학금, 지역 병원과 아픈 어린이들을 위한 기금 조성, 환경 문제, 지역사회의 기부금 조성 활동이 있다.

그렇다면, 월마트에 대한 안 좋은 점은 무엇인가? 주요한 불만은 그들의 경영 방식이 대단히 공격적이라는 것이다. 월마트의 제조업체와 공급자에 대한 태도가 "우리 방식대로 일을 하시오. 그렇지 않으면, 당신들과 거래하지 않겠소." 식이라는 것이다. 이것은 월마트가 그와 같은 힘이 없는 다른 작은 소매업체보다 더 유리하게끔 했다. 월마트는 매장 개업을 위해 공급업자들이 할인된 가격으로 상품을 제공할 것을 요구하는 것으로, 수송상의 문제에 대해 벌금을 부과하는 것으로, 또 제조업체에 만들어야 할 상품의 종류와 스타일, 색상까지 일일이 지시하는 것 등으로 알려져 있다. 월마트는 제품이 이틀 내에 배달될 것과, 제조업자들이 그들의 승진과 소매 전략에 협력해 줄 것을 기대한다. 사실상 월마트와 함께 일하는 회사는 그들의 종업원이 되는 것이다.

시장의 어느 한 부분을 완전히 장악하고 있는 회사는 많은 힘을 가질 것이다. 지금까지, 월마트는 그들이 원하는 것을 얻으면서, 그리고 고객들에게 원하는 것을 제공하면서 성공해왔다.

33. 이 글의 main idea는 무엇인가?

| 풀이 | 글쓴이는 월마트가 지금의 위치에 이르기까지 그 바탕에는 설립자의 독특한 경영 철학과 다양한 소매 사업 전략이 있었다는 것을 소개하고 있다.

| 정답 | (a) Wal-Mart of Sam walton succeeded with special business philosophy.

| 오답 | (b), (c), (d)는 월마트의 시작부터 지금까지의 역사와 성공을 설명하는 세부적인 내용에 해당된다.(too specific)

34. 월마트의 이윤은 작년에 비해서 몇 퍼센트가 증가했는가?

| 풀이 | Profits increased 16% from the previous year.

| 정답 | (c) 16%

35. 최초의 월마트는 어디에 생겼는가?

| 풀이 | ~ he opened the first Wal-Mart in Bentonville.

| 정답 | (a) Bentonville

36. Sam Walton의 경영철학에서 언급되지 않은 것은?

| 풀이 | His business philosophy was simple~
good prices, great selection and a friendly greeting.

| 정답 | (d) large store

37. 아래에서 맞는 것은?

| 정답 | (d) Walton was known for the "Ten foot attitude". (Line 10-11)

| 오답 | (a) Sam Walton is still alive. (Line 17)
(b) Sam Walton emphasized the size of the store. (Line 10)
(c) Wal-Mart places only in America. (Line 15-16)

예제 38~42

모든 곰이 동면을 할까요? 정확하게 말하자면, 어떤 곰도 동면하지 않습니다. 동물이 동면을 할 때는, 거의 죽은 상태이거나 죽은 것처럼 보일 것입니다. 체온이 거의 화씨 32도까지 떨어지고, 일분에 겨우 몇 번만 호흡하며, 심장박동 또한 너무 느려서 거의 표가 안 날 정도입니다. 만약 그 동물이 따뜻함에 노출된다면, 잠에서 깨어 민첩해지기까지는 몇 시간이 걸릴 것입니다. 동면하는 동물에는 박쥐, 고슴도치, 얼룩다람쥐, 그리고 마모트가 있습니다.

비록 대부분의 사람들이 곰이 동면한다고 말하지만, 곰의 경우에는 동면이라는 용어가 적당하지 않습니다. 왜냐면 곰이 자는 동안에는 체온이나, 호흡, 신진대사율에 거의 변화가 없기 때문입니다. "깊은 겨울 잠"(과학 용어로는 "휴면")이 더 나은 용어입니다. 만약 곰들이 같은 자리에서 혼자 몇 달을 잘 수 있다고 해도, 방해를 받으면 쉽게 깨어납니다.

동면과 깊은 겨울잠의 원인은 같습니다. 겨울동안, 먹이가 귀해져서 어떤 동물들은 정상적인 체온을 유지하기가 때때로 어렵습니다. 스스로를 보호하기 위해서, 많은 동물들이 동면이나 휴면으로 시간을 보냅니다. 동물들은 먹이가 풍부할 때 체내 지방을 저장해두었다가 동면이나 휴면 중에 저장해 둔 지방을 사용합니다. 긴 시간동안 잠을 잠으로써 그들은 최소한의 운동만을 유지하고 또한 체온과 신진대사를 조절해서 성장은 일어나지 않습니다.

곰은 속이 텅 빈 나무, 동굴, 덤불 더미나 자기가 판 굴속에서 자려고 결정할지 모릅니다. 때때로 곰은 혹독한 겨울 추위를 피해서 마른 나뭇잎이나 풀을 단열재처럼 잠자리에 보태기도 합니다.

모든 곰이 겨울 내내 자는 것은 아닙니다. 만약에 일년 내내 먹이가 풍부한 환경에서 사는 곰이라면 그 곰들은 깊은 겨울잠에 빠질 필요가 없습니다. 말레이곰이나 인도산곰, 안경곰과 같이 열대지방에 사는 곰은 절대 겨울잠을 자지 않습니다.

수컷 북극곰은 절대로 휴면에 들어가지 않지만, 암컷 북극곰은 새끼를 가졌을 때에만 휴면에 들어갑니다.

만약 휴면에 익숙한 곰이라고 하더라도 항상 먹이가 있는 동물원에서 살게 된다면, 그 곰은 날씨가 얼마나 춥다고 하더라도 휴면에 들어가지 않을 것입니다.

동면과 깊은 겨울잠의 원인은 같습니다. 겨울동안, 먹이가 귀해져서 어떤 동물들은 정상적인 체온을 유지하기가 때때로 어렵습니다. 스스로를 보호하기 위해서, 많은 동물들이 동면이나 휴면으로 시간을 보냅니다. 동물들은 먹이가 풍부할 때 체내 지방을 저장해두었다가 동면이나 휴면 중에 저장해 둔 지방을 사용합니다. 긴 시간동안 잠을 잠으로써 그들은 최소한의 운동만을 유지하고 또한 체온과 신진대사를 조절해서 성장은 일어나지 않습니다.

곰은 속이 텅 빈 나무, 동굴, 덤불 더미나 자기가 판 굴속에서 자려고 결정할 지 모릅니다. 때때로 곰은 혹독한 겨울 추위를 피해서 마른 나뭇잎이나 풀을 단열재처럼 잠자리에 보태기도 합니다.

모든 곰이 겨울 내내 자는 것은 아닙니다. 만약에 일년 내내 먹이가 풍부한 환경에서 사는 곰이라면 그 곰들은 깊은 겨울잠에 빠질 필요가 없습니다. 말레이곰이나 인도산곰, 안경곰과 같이 열대지방에 사는 곰은 절대 겨울잠을 자지 않습니다.

수컷 북극곰은 절대로 휴면에 들어가지 않지만, 암컷 북극곰은 새끼를 가졌을 때에만 휴면에 들어갑니다.

만약 휴면에 익숙한 곰이라고 하더라도 항상 먹이가 있는 동물원에서 살게 된다면, 그 곰은 날씨가 얼마나 춥다고 하더라도 휴면에 들어가지 않을 것입니다.

38. 이 글은 근본적으로 무엇에 관한 것인가?

| 풀이 | 지은이는 사람들이 흔히 말하면 동면과 곰들이 하는 휴면(겨울에 자는 긴 잠)의 차이를 설명하면서 곰의 겨울잠의 특성, 겨울잠을 자는 원인 등을 설명하고 있다.

| 정답 | (a) hibernation of bears

39. 다음 중 동면하지 않는 것은?

| 풀이 | Animals that hibernate include bats, hedgehogs, ground squirrels, and marmots. Tropical bears such as sun bears, ~ never go into a winter sleep.

| 정답 | (d) sun bears

40. 위 글에 따르면 올바르지 않은 것은?

| 풀이 | When an animal hibernates, it is near death and may appear to be dead. Its body temperature drops to near 32° F, it breathes just a few times a minute, and its heartbeat is so slow ~.

| 정답 | (d) Its heartbeat becomes very fast.

41. "hibernation" 대신 적당한 용어는?

| 풀이 | A better term would be "deep winter sleep"(the scientific term is "dormancy").

| 정답 | (c) deep winter sleep

42. "hibernation"(동면)의 이유는?

| 풀이 | During winter, food is scarce, ~ .

| 정답 | (a) food is scarce.

⊃ 예제 43~47

6학년생들은 숙제나 학교 규칙, 절차를 가지고 논의할 것이다. 그들은 교실에서나 읽기 시간에 어떤 생각들을 반대한다. 그들은 모든 것에 관해 논쟁하기를 좋아한다!

6학년은 부모님에게도 매우 힘든 시기가 될 테지만, 특히 엄마들에게 더 그렇다. 왜냐하면 엄마들이 주로 6학년생들이 화풀이하는 대상이기 때문이다. 아이들은 자기들의 독립을 확립하기 위해서 엄마에게 대들거나 논쟁을 벌일 것이다. 억울하게도 당신의 6학년짜리 자녀는 종종 건방지고, 말대꾸를 하고, 더 이상 당신의 의견은 중요하게 여기지 않는 것 같을 것이다. 딸들은 엄마의 머리와 옷, 또는 전반적인 모습을 비판할 것이다. 아들은 그런 비판들을 간직하겠지만, 엄마에게 학교에 찾아오거나 자기 친구들에게 말을 걸지 말라고 부탁할지도 모른다.

이런 명백한 업신여김은 아이들이 그들의 부모로부터 필연적으로 떨어지기 위해서 필요한 것처럼 여겨진다. 남자아이나 여자아이 모두 자기 발견과 건전한 의사결정의 과정을 시작해야만 하는 것이다. 딸은 자신의 고유한 권리 안에서 여자로서의 정체성을 확립하기 위해 엄마로부터 거리를 유지할 필요가 있다. 아들은 싹트기 시작하는 성적인 욕구 때문에 엄마로부터 거리를 두어야 할 필요가 있다. 부모로서, 당신은 당신의 자녀들이 그들의 저항과 대립을 위한 안전한 목표로 당신을 이용할 수 있는 것은 당신의 무한한 사랑에 대해 믿음을 가지고 있기 때문이라는 사실에서 위안을 얻을 수 있다.

부모로서 당신이 직면하는 가장 큰 도전은 학교나 집에서 전체적인 관점에서 문제를 다루고, 아이의 행동을 개인으로 한정시키지 않는 것이다. 그러한 문제들은 대부분 당신과는 상관이 없다.

당신과 당신의 자녀를 함께 돕는 가장 좋은 전략은 균형과 유머감각을 유지하는 것이다. 말은 쉬운 것 같지만 매우 어려운 일이다. 때때로 당신은 상처를 입기도 하고 화가 나기도 하겠지만 항상 냉정함을 유지하고 스스로를 칭찬하는데 성공했다.

6학년 짜리 자녀가 당신과 함께 논쟁을 벌이려고 한다면 자녀의 기분을 알고, 당신의 위치를 확고히 하며, 물러나는 것이 가장 좋다. 자녀는 당신이 공정할 것을 요구하지만 또 당신의 위치를 지킬 것을 필요로 한다. 점점 심해지는 말싸움으로 말려들기를 거부하라. 어쨌든 당신의 자녀는 최후의 한마디를 할 것이고, 그냥 그 말을 빨리 하도록 해서 6학년 짜리 자녀가 체면을 유지하도록 해주어라.

당신의 6학년 된 딸은 겉으로 보기에는 저항하는 것 같아도 여전히 당신의 무조건적인 사랑을 필요로 한다. 좋은 날마다 딸은 친구나 학교 이야기 그리고 관심 있는 많은 것들을 이야기하면서 당신을 신뢰할 것이다. 그녀는 오빠나 여동생으로부터 방해받지 않고 당신과 단 둘이 있을 때, 그 친밀한 시간을 감사히 여길 것이다. 그녀가 이렇게 이전의 누에시기로 돌아오면, 딸은 당신의 애정을 받아들이고 당신의 손을 잡고, 끌어안고, 심지어는 뽀뽀를 하면서 그러한 애정을 나타내기 시작할 것이다. 하지만, 또 격동하는 날에는 "학교는 어땠니?" 같은 단순한 질문도 마치 무언가를 캐묻기 위한 트집으로 여겨질 수도 있다. 당신이 딸을 안으려고 하면, 딸은 빠져나가기 쉽다. 할 수만 있다면 계속해서 신체적인 애정 표현을 하는 것이 중요하다. 딸이 안정을 느끼는 때는 잘 살펴서 그녀를 안아주고 당신이 얼마나 딸을 사랑하는지를 말해주어라. 잠자리에 드는 시간이 종종 애정표현을 할 기회를 제공한다.

그러나 당신의 6학년 짜리 아들은 어떠한 신체적 애정표현도 보이지 않을 것이다. 하지만 아들은 세차를 한다든지, 시키지 않아도 잔디를 깎는다든지 등의 다른 방식으로 자기의 사랑을 표현할 것이다. 당신이 이러한 사랑의 표현을 본다면 감사의 뜻을 반드시 아들에게 전해야 한다. 또한, 아들이 성적을 잘 받아왔거나 여동생에게 친절하게 대할 때 얼마나 자랑스러운지를 말해주어라.

아들과 딸이 받아들일 만한 또 다른 좋은 접근 방법은 자녀들과 함께 특별한 외출을 계획하는 것이다. 이것은 특별히 다른 형제나 자매 없이 6학년 짜리 자녀만을 위해 시간이 마련될 때 효과가 있다. 아이를 사무실로 데려가고, 외식을 하고, 함께 영화를 봐라. 매우 특별한 시간이 될 것이고, 아이들은 그 시간을 학교에서 이야기하고, 평생 기억할지도 모른다.

43. 이 글의 main idea는 무엇인가?

| 풀이 | 외부 세계에 대해 가장 저항적이고 반항적인 6학년 시기에 아이들과 가장 많이 부딪혀야하는 부모, 특히 어머니가 아이의 성별에 따라, 또는 아이의 심리적인 상태에 따라 어떻게 대처해야 할지를 설명해 주는 글이다.

| 정답 | (a) There are various way of treat six graders.

| 오답 | (c), (d)는 부모가 아이를 다루는 구체적인 방법 중의 하나이다. (too specific)

44. 위 글에 근거해서 옳지 않은 것은?

| 풀이 | Your sixth grade son, however, might not show any physical affection.
아들의 경우에는 신체적 접촉보다 칭찬이 더 큰 효과가 있다고 설명하고 있다.

| 정답 | (c) You must show physical affection to your sixth grade son.

| 오답 | (a) It's best to acknowledge her feelings. (paragraph 5)
(b) It's important that you continue to give her physical affection. (paragraph 6)
(d) Another positive approach is to plan a special outing with your child.(paragraph 8)

45. 아들과 딸에게 접근하는 방식은 어떠한가?

| 풀이 | It's important that you continue to give her physical affection ~.
Your sixth grade son, however, might not show any physical affection.
6~7문단을 살펴보면 딸과 아들을 대하는 방법이 각각 잘 설명되어 있다.

| 정답 | (b) somewhat different

46. 왜 6학년 짜리 자녀들이 부모들에게 대항하는가?

| 풀이 | They'll set up for an argument or push against their mothers in order to establish their independence.

| 정답 | (a) in order to establish their independence

47. 밑줄 친 "they"가 가리키는 바는?

| 풀이 | 주의 깊게 보지 않으면 'they'를 부모와 6학년 짜리 자녀로 보기 쉽다. 그러나 'they'가 포함되는 문장을 잘 살펴보면, 아이들이 학교에서 이야기하고, 평생동안 기억할 대상이 바로 'they' 임으로 그것이 앞에서 말한 즐거운 외출, 즉 'special outing' 또는 'very special time'을 가리킴을 알 수 있다.
※ <u>they</u> will be talked about at school and possibly remembered for a lifetime.(by children)
→ Children will talk about <u>them</u> at school and possibly remember <u>them</u> for a life time.

| 정답 | (c) very special times

예제 48~52

"에티켓"은 프랑스어이다. 원래의 의미는 "작은 티켓"이다. 이 티켓은 공식 행사에 참석하는 사람들에게 주어졌다. 티켓에는 행사에서 사람들이 어떻게 행동해야 하는지에 대한 안내가 인쇄되어 있었다. 따라서 에티켓은 공식적인 경우에 행동하는 방식을 의미하게 되었다.

오늘날 에티켓은 사람을 소개하는 방법, 식사하는 방법, 경우에 따라 옷을 입는 방법, 다른 사람에게 이야기하는 방법, 그리고 특별한 날 해야 하는 것 등을 포함한다. 사회생활의 거의 대부분에서 (상황에 맞는) 특정한 에티켓이 필요하다.

때때로, 에티켓은 변하고, 또 변하는 것 같다. 에티켓은 남자가 여자를 위해 문을 열어주는 것 같은 예의와 관련된 행동이 많다. 오늘날, 어떤 사람들은 이것을 구식이라고 생각한다. 그러나 예절은 언제나 올바른 것이다. 누구든지 뒷사람을 위해 문을 열어주는 것은 멋진 행동이다.

사실, 현대의 생활은 나쁜 매너를 권장하는 것 같기도 하다. 더 이상 젊은이들에게 에티켓을 가르치지 않는다. 게다가, 젊은이들의 문화에서는 젊은이들이 다른 이들의 행동을 모범으로 삶는다. 그 결과, 좋은 매너가 중요한 것으로 여겨지지 않는다.

에티켓의 핵심은 사람들이 서로 잘 어울리도록 돕는 데 있다. 만약 사람들이 용인되는 매너를 따라 행동한다면, 서로 오해할 소지가 거의 없을 것이다. 그리고 사람들이 다른 사람을 잘 대하는 것에 관해 생각하는 것은 중요하다. 만약 모든 사람이 자기가 하고 싶은 대로 행동한다면, 다른 사람을 존중하는 것처럼 여겨지지 않을 것이다. 에티켓은 상황이 더 부드럽게 흘러갈 수 있도록 돕는다.

매너는 문화에 따라 다양하지만, 의도는 같다. 사람들을 신중하게 대하는 것이다. 이것은 충돌을 줄이는 방법이기도 하다.

때때로, 우리는 이러한 관습이 어디에서 연유되었는지를 이해할 수 있다. 원래 오른손으로 악수하는 것은 당신이 무기를 가지고 있지 않다는 걸 의미했다. 모자를 벗는 것은 원래 당신의 헬멧을 벗는 것을 의미하고, 이것은 싸우지 않을 것이라는 것을 의미했다.

오늘날에는 사회생활의 새로운 영역이 있다. 예를 들면, 많은 대화가 이제는 전화상에서 이루어진다. 아마 전통적인 전화 에티켓이 없기 때문에, 어떤 사람들은 맘 놓고 무례하게 굴지도 모른다. 전화상에서도 당신이 실제로 만나서 얘기하는 것과 똑같이 상대방을 대하라. 대부분의 사람은 대화를 방해하는 것을 무례하게 여긴다. 하지만 많은 사람들은 전화상에서 누군가가 말하는 것을 방해하는 것을 괜찮게 여긴다. 아이들은 특히 끼어들지 않도록 교육을 받을 필요가 있다.

인터넷 역시 고유의 에티켓 또는 "네티켓"이 필요하다. 말하는 상대방을 볼 수 없고, 상대방과 수 천 마일을 떨어져 있을 수도 있기 때문에, 오해가 생기기 쉽다. 또한 상대방은 인터넷을 통해서는 당신의 말하는 톤을 들을 수가 없다. 이러한 이유로 인해, 사람들은 그들이 어떻게 느끼는 지를 알려주기 위해 작은 얼굴인 "스마일"을 사용한다. 만약 농담을 한다면 웃는 얼굴을 사용할 수 있고, 아니면 말한 후에 스마일을 인쇄할 수도 있다. 이것은 상대방에게 그들의 말을 심각하게 받아들이지 말라는 힌트를 제공한다.

"please"나 "thank you" 같이 간단한 말을 하는 것도 매일의 삶을 훨씬 더 부드럽고 행복하게 만들 수 있다. 다른 많은 것들처럼, 우리는 에티켓이 사라져버리기 시작할 때까지 에티켓의 중요성을 인식하지 못한다.

48. 에티켓의 원래의 의미를 골라라.

| 풀이 | The original meaning was "little tickets."

| 정답 | (c) little tickets

49. 에티켓이 포함하지 않는 것은?

| 풀이 | Etiquette today includes how to introduce people; how to eat properly; how to dress for different occasions; how to speak to different people; ~.

| 정답 | (d) how to show your real minds

50. 옳지 않은 것은?

| 풀이 | ~ in a youth culture, young people take their examples from other young people.

| 정답 | (c) Young people take their examples from the old.

| 오답 | (a) Politeness is always a good idea. (Line 10)

(b) Etiquette is no longer taught to young people. (Line 13)

(d) The point of etiquette is to help people to get along with each other.(Line 16)

51. 마지막 문단에 밑줄 친 it이 가리키는 것은?

| 풀이 | 공기나 물과 같은 것들이 사라져야 그 소중함을 알듯이, 'it'이 사라지기 시작하면서 우리가 에티켓의 중요함을 깨닫게 될 것이라고 했기 때문에, 결국 'it'은 에티켓을 가리킨다.

| 정답 | (d) etiquette

52. 진하게 표시되어 있는 여덟 번째 문단은 무엇에 관한 것인가?

| 풀이 | 앞에서 글쓴이는 에티켓의 기원과 기존에 있는 에티켓의 종류, 에티켓이 있어야 하는 이유, 그러나 예절이 잘 가르쳐지고 있지 않은 요즘의 세태 등을 설명하고 있다.
그러다가 여덟 번째 문단을 시작하면서, new areas of social life를 소개하고, 그에 따라 새로이 요청되는 에티켓의 필요성을 주장하고 있다.

| 정답 | (b) new areas of etiquette

예제 53~56

빨간 머리의 고아였던 Anne Shirley의 이야기는 거의 백 년 가까운 시간이 지나도록 유명하다. 책 앞 부분의 "Green Gables의 앤"이라는 장에서는 농장의 한 남매가 어떻게 소년 한 명을 입양하기로 결정하는지 얘기해준다. Matthew Cuthbert는 60살 먹은 노인으로 농장 일을 도울 사람이 필요했다. 그들은 고아원에 의뢰했고, 그 곳에서 보내주는 소년이 기차를 타고 도착하기로 되어 있었다.

Matthew가 그의 말과 마차를 타고 역에 마중 나갔을 때, 그 곳에서 기다리고 있는 것은 소년이 아니라, Ann Shirley라는 소녀뿐이었다. Anne은 특이한 소녀였다. 그녀는 풍부한 상상력을 가지고 있었고, 그녀가 관심 있어 하는 것들에 관해서 이야기하기를 좋아했다. 수줍음이 많고, 말이 없는 Matthew는 곧 그녀를 좋아하게 된다. 하지만 그들이 집에 도착했을 때, 그의 여동생 Marilla는 매우 당황했다. 그녀는 소녀가 그들에게 아무 도움이 안 될 거라고 생각했다. Matthew는 "우리가 그 소녀에게 도움이 되면 되지."하고 말한다.

조금 뒤, Marilla는 그 작고 가녀린 고아 소녀가 불쌍하다고 느끼고는 그녀를 돌봐주기로 결심한다. 하지만 Marilla는 Anne에게 어떻게 행동하는 것이 옳은 것인지 가르치는 일이 매우 어려운 일임을 알게 된다. Anne은 종종 미리 생각해 보지 않고 행동을 하기 때문에, Marilla는 그녀가 일을 저지르지 않도록 하기 위해 쉴 틈 없이 지켜보아야 한다. 시간이 지나면서 Anne은 그들의 공동체 안에 적응하게 되며, 예전처럼 문제도 많이 일으키지 않게 된다.

이 작은 고아소녀의 특징은 말하기를 무척 좋아한다는 것이다. Anne은 어려운 일을 하고 있을 때에도 그녀가 갖고 있지 않은 아름다운 것들에 대해서 상상하기를 좋아했다. 이것은 그녀가 예전에 불친절한 사람들의 시중을 들면서 일했을 때 불행하다는 느낌을 달래기 위해서 사용했던 방법이었다. 이제 그녀는 Green Gables에 살면서 행복했지만, 그 특별한 말들과 아름다운 것들은 잊지 않고 간직하고 있다.

Anne은 또한 빨간 머리와 주근깨 때문에 불행해한다. Anne의 시대에 아름다운 여성상이란 밝고 깨끗한 얼굴색과 검은색의 머리의 여성이었다. 그녀의 색깔은 낭만적이지 않게 보였다. 하지만 Prince Edward 섬에서는 많은 사람들이 스코트랜드인의 후예였기 때문에, 빨간 머리와 주근깨를 가지고 있었다.

이 이야기는 행복이라는 것에 대해서 많은 이야기를 해 준다. Matthew와 Marilla는 더 이상 소년을 구하려고 애쓰지 않고, Anne을 돌보기로 하면서 그녀가 있다는 것을 좋아하는 그들 자신을 발견하게 된다. 그들의 삶은 누군가 그들을 필요로 하는 사람이 생기자 훨씬 더 활기차게 된다. 이처럼 행복은 다른 사람을 돌보는 것과 그들에게 필요한 사람이 되는 데에서도 찾을 수 있다.

"Green Gables의 Anne"이 쓰여졌을 당시에는 고아에 관한 이야기들이 많았다. 현대의학이 발달되기 전에, 많은 부모들이 그들의 아이가 다 자라기 전에 죽어버렸다. 많은 엄마들이 아이를 낳다가 죽곤 했다. 이 당시 대부분의 아버지들은 어린 아이들을 키우려고 하지 않았기 때문에 다른 누군가가 책임을 맡아야 했다.

이와 같은 일이 "Anne"의 저자인 Lucy Maud Montgomery에게도 일어났다. 그녀의 엄마는 그녀가 아기일 때 죽었고, 그녀의 아버지는 자기의 장인·장모를 떠나버렸다. Montgomery의 할머니와 할아버지는 그녀에게 좋은 집을 제공했지만, 그들은 매우 단호하고 엄격해서 이 작은 소녀에게 정을 주지 않았다.

그녀의 이야기에서 Montgomery는 그녀가 이미 살아온 삶을 어떻게 하면 더 좋아할 수 있었을지 상상해보고 있다. 만약 그녀의 조부모님들이 좀 더 Matthew와 Marilla 같았다면? 조 부모님들이 좀 더 그녀가 하고 싶은 일을 하도록 허락했더라면? 그녀는 보다 행복했을까?

이 이야기는 아이들이 그들을 돌봐주는 어른들의 나쁜 대우로부터 어떻게 상처를 입게 되는지 보여준다. 어른들이 불친절하게 대하려고 의도하지 않더라도, 그들은 때때로 아이들이 불행하다고 느끼게 하는 말이나 행동을 한다. "Anne"은 부모와 조부모들이 그들의 아이들을 격려하고 행복하고 잘 지낸다고 느낄 수 있도록 돕는 방법을 가르쳐준다.

Anne Shirley는 작지만 그녀의 공동체 전체를 바꾸어놓고, 더 멋지게 만들어 놓는 소녀이다. 우리는 모두 특별한 재주와 재능을 가지고 있다. 그리고 우리가 그 능력들을 사용할 수 있도록 여건만 주어진다면 우리 주위의 모든 사람들이 그 능력들로 인해 유익을 얻을 것이다.

53. 이 이야기의 원래 제목은 무엇인가?

| 풀이 | The opening chapters of "Anne of Green Gables" tell ~.

| 정답 | (c) Anne of green gables

54. Matthew가 역에 갔을 때, 누가 거기 있었나?

| 풀이 | When Matthew goes to the train station ~ , there is no boy, only a girl ~.

| 정답 | (b) Anne

55. 위 글에서 언급된 것 중에 옳지 않은 것은?

| 오답 | (b) Anne goes to school.

| 정답 | (a) Anne likes to imagine. (Line 18)
(c) The story of Anne teaches us many things. (Line 26)
(d) Anne doesn't like her hair. (Line 22)

56. Anne은 힘든 상황을 겪을 때 어떻게 행동했나?

| 풀이 | While she lived a life of hard work, Anne liked to imagine beautiful things that she didn't have.

| 정답 | (d) She thinks about things she doesn't have.

예제 57~61

소설은 사람과 사건에 관한 상상의 이야기이다. 그것들은 오락과 즐거움을 위해 쓰여진다. 이천 년 전에, 그리스의 작가들은 젊은 연인에 대한 이야기를 들려주었다. 보통 연인들은 끔찍한 사건으로 인해 헤어지게 되고 많은 어려움과 고통을 겪은 후에야 만 비로소 다시 만나게 되었다. 이 플롯 아이디어는 지금도 여전히 사용된다.

미국에서 여성들에게 가장 인기 있는 책은 연애소설이다. 매년 수백만 권이 팔린다. 이것은 연애소설 출판업이 크고 매우 경쟁력 있는 사업이라는 것을 의미한다. 회사들은 독자들이 좋아하는 이야기를 알아내기 위해서 조사를 한다. 어떤 조사는 독자들에게 소설 속에 좀 더 많은 성적 표현이 있으면 좋겠는지를 물었다. 보통, 로맨스는 섹스가 아니라 사랑에 관한 이야기이다. 하지만 오늘날의 시장에서 출판업자들은 독자들이 원하는 것을 제공할 준비가 되어있다.

로맨스의 본질은 연인들의 사랑에 장애물을 둠으로써 불안감을 조성하는 것이다. 장애물을 만드는 가장 쉬운 방법은 주인공을 가능한 한 다르게 만드는 것이다. 예를 들어, 동부의 교사가 서부의 카우보이를 만나는 식이다. 물론, 처음에는 그들은 서로를 전혀 좋아하지 않는다. 하지만, 시간이 흐르면서 그들은 사랑에 빠진다. 아니면 여성 사회사업가가 공격적인 실업가를 만나게 한다.

아주 빈번히 여주인공은 결코 결혼을 결심해본 적이 없는 숙녀이다. 아니면 그녀는 남자 주인공이나 그의 가족을 특히 싫어한다. 로맨스 작가는 둘을 엮을 그럴듯한 방법을 만들어내야만 한다. 결론으로 이어지는 수많은 유명한 이야기가 있다. 때때로, 의무감에 사로잡힌 여주인공은 남자 주인공의 아이들을 키우기 위해 그와 함께 떠날 것이다. 아니면 그녀는 사별한 남자와 함께 사는 전문적인 유모일지도 모른다.

가장 인기 있는 이야기는 편의에 의한 결혼이다. 서로 사랑하지 않는 두 사람이 경제적이거나 또는 정치적인 이유로, 아니면 아이들 때문에 결혼을 하는 것이다. 물론, 결국에는 그들은 사랑에 빠진다. 대부분의 경우, 결혼에는 어떤 특정한 장애물이 있다. 남주인공이나 여주인공 중 한 명이 이미 아이가 있고, 그들은 누군가가 자신의 가정을 맡아주기를 바란다고 기대하지 않는다. 때때로, 둘 중 한 명이 신체적 장애가 있거나, 다른 인종 또는 계층이거나, 환경을 가진다. 예를 들어, 여자 주인공은 매우 엄격하고 훌륭한 집안 출신인 반면, 남자 주인공은 평판이 안 좋거나, 심지어는 범죄자일 수도 있다. 이야기의 재미는 이렇게 서로 다른 사람들이 어떻게 해서 함께 하게 되느냐에 달려있다.

보통, 남자 주인공은 카우보이나 엔지니어, 군인, 해적, 도박꾼 등과 같이 굉장히 남성적인 타입이다. 여자 주인공은 대체로 아주 여성적이지만, 선머슴이나 노처녀의 성격을 가지기도 한다. 그녀는 강인한 성격과 기질을 가지고 허세를 부리거나 불같은 성격을 가진 것으로 묘사된다. 이 두 유형을 잘 보여주는 좋은 예가 "바람과 함께 사라지다"의 레트 버틀러와 스칼렛 오하라이다.

거의 모든 연애 소설이 독자로 하여금 더 많은 책을 읽게 하기 위해서 무언가를 제공한다. 로맨스는 중독될 수 있고, 그래서 어떤 여성들은 쉬지 않고 로맨스를 읽는다. 어떤 로맨스는 아주 잘 쓰여지기도 했지만, 대다수는 정해진 공식을 따른다. 그래서 독자들이 언제나 전개될 내용을 아는 것이다.

57. 가장 인기 있는 소설의 장르는?

| 풀이 | The most popular books ~ are romance novels.

| 정답 | (b) romance

58. 연애소설은 주로 무엇을 담고 있나?

| 풀이 | 첫 번째 문단에 잘 나와 있다. 로맨스 소설의 기원은 2천년전 그리스의 소설로 볼 수 있는데, 그 주요 줄거리는 사랑하는 여인이 고통과 어려움을 이기고 다시 결합한다는 내용이다.

| 정답 | (a) sufferings

59. 위 글에 따라서 맞지 않는 것은?

| 풀이 | Usually, romances are about love, not sex.

| 정답 | (c) Usually, romances are about love and sex.

| 오답 | (a) Novels are imaginary stories. (Line 1)
(b) Many millions of romance novels are sold every year. (Line 6)
(d) The essence of the romance is to put obstacles in the way of the lovers. (Line 11)

60. 밑줄 친 them이 가리키는 것은?

| 풀이 | 'them'은 읽는 것의 목적어가 되기 때문에, 당연히 로맨스 소설이다.

| 정답 | (b) romance novels

61. 위 글에 따르면 가장 인기 있는 이야기는 무엇인가?

| 풀이 | A favourite plot is the marriage of convenience.

| 정답 | (c) marriage of convenience

CHAPTER 3

글의 제목/ 주제/요지 찾기

Questions about the ideas of the passage

예제 1

광고는 자율 회사 (경쟁) 체제에서 중요한 부분을 차지합니다. 왜냐하면 서로 다른 회사들이 같은 시장을 놓고 경쟁하기 때문입니다. 그들은 모두가 많은 소비자들이 자기회사의 제품을 사주기를 원합니다. 이런 이유 때문에, 각 회사는 신문이나 잡지의 광고란을 사들이고, 라디오나 텔레비전의 광고 시간대를 사들입니다. 그들은 모두가 광고를 통해 소비자의 그들 제품에 대한 더 많은 욕구를 불러일으키기를 희망합니다.

1. 위 글에서 글쓴이가 말하고자 하는 바(main idea)는 무엇인가?

| 풀이 | 지은이는 자율 경쟁 체제에서 회사의 이익을 증대시키기 위해서는 경쟁사보다 더 많은 고객을 확보해야 하고, 그러기 위해서 광고의 역할은 중요하다고 강조하고 있다.

| 정답 | (d) importance of ads

예제 2

루이지애나에 있는 델타영장류센터의 한 넓은 공간에는 길다란 나무 장대가 몇 개 있었습니다. 이 나무 장대들은 침팬지들이 가지고 노는 장난감이었습니다. 어느 날, 침팬지 중 한 마리가 높은 곳에 달려있는 어떤 물건을 얻기 위해 장대를 타고 올라갔습니다. 다시 말해서, 그 침팬지는 나무 막대 장난감을 도구로 사용한 것이었습니다. 곧 모든 침팬지들이 어떻게 그 장난감을 사용하는지 알았습니다. 이 '사다리'를 가지고, 침팬지들은 자신들의 목적을 달성할 수가 있었습니다. 그들은 벽을 타고 올라가서 영장류 센터 바깥에 있는 나무들로 도망가 버렸습니다.

2. 이 글의 main theme(중요 요지)은 무엇인가?

| 풀이 | 일단 이 글은 나무 막대를 이용하는 침팬지에 대해 이야기하고 있다. 침팬지가 나무 막대를 단순히 가지고 노는 장난감이 아니라 목적 달성을 위한 수단으로 사용함을 알리고 있는 것이다.

| 정답 | (c) Chimps used poles as a tool.

| 오답 | a, b, e는 too specific하고, 위의 사실 한 가지만으로는 침팬지가 생각을 할 수 있다고((d)) 단정짓기 어렵다.

예제 3

조건화는 연합, 즉 서로 다른 개념을 한데 묶어 학습하는 한 방법입니다. 1900년에 러시아의 생물학자인 이반 파블로프는 개를 가지고 조건화를 연구했습니다. 개는 음식 냄새를 맡으면 선천적으로 침을 흘립니다. 파블로프는 개에게 음식을 줄 때마다 종을 쳤습니다. 곧 개는 종소리와 음식냄새를 서로 연관짓기(연합하기) 시작했습니다. 얼마가 지나서, 개는 음식 없이 종소리만 들려주어도, 침을 흘렸습니다.

3. 이 글의 topic은 무엇인가?

| 풀이 | 이 글에서는 조건화, 즉 연합에 의한 학습 방법에 관해 이야기하고 있다.

| 정답 | (d) a way of learning by association.

| 오답 | 혹시 topic이 '무엇에 관한-'에 대한 대답이라고 하여 이 글의 topic을 (a)의 파블로프의 연구나, (b)의 개의 침을 흘리는 본능이라고 답을 택한 사람도 있을 것이다. 그러나 중요한 것은, topic이나 main idea는 너무 세부적이거나 너무 일반적이지 않은 글의 내용 전체를 포괄하는 것이어야 한다는 사실이다.

예제 4

피고용인들은 재택근무를 선호하는데, 그 이유는 좀 더 유연한(자유로운) 작업 스케줄을 짤 수가 있기 때문이다. 그들은 원할 때 일을 시작할 수가 있다. 그들은 밤에 일하고 낮이나 오후에는 외출을 할 수도 있다. 그들은 복잡한 도로 위에서 많은 시간을 낭비할 필요가 없다. 그들은 맑은 공기를 마실 수도 있다. 게다가, 재택근무를 하면, 아빠나 엄마는 그들의 가족과 더 많은 시간을 함께 보낼 수가 있다.

4. 이 글은 주로 무엇에 관한 것인가?

| 풀이 | topic을 묻는 문제이다.
글을 잘 살펴보면 'They can~'이라는 구문이 반복되면서 자택근무를 할 경우 피고용인들이 누릴 수 있는 혜택에 대해 설명하고 있는 글이다.

| 정답 | (a) the benefits of telecommuting

예제 5

조이와 토미는 둘 다 미국 문화권에서 자라고 있다. 둘은 그 문화권 안에서 소년이 되고, 소녀가 되는 것이 무엇인지를 배우고 있다. 남성과 여성이라는 태어날 때부터의 성(sex, 생물학적 성)은 이제 사회적인 성(gender), 즉 남성 또는 여성답게 생각하고, 말하고, 행동하는 방식을 나타내는 성으로 바뀌어가고 있다. 각 문화권은 그러한 성을 정의하는 그들 고유의 방식이 있고, 이러한 성은 인간의 생애 초기에 그들의 정체성을 형성하는 기본이 된다. 조지타운 대학의 대보라 타넨 교수에 의하면, 이러한 성의 차이는 심지어 남성과 여성의 언어를 사용하는 방법에 있어서도 반영된다고 한다. 의사소통을 연구하는 타넨과 다른 연구자들은 이러한 차이가 생애 초기에 나타나기 시작한다고 믿는다.

5. 이 글에 가장 잘 어울리는 제목은?

| 풀이 | 제목은 글쓴이의 생각을 반영해야 하므로 topic과 main idea를 모두 포함하는 것이어야 한다. 이것 역시 지나치게 부분만 반영하지도, 또 글의 범위를 벗어나서 지나치게 일반화하지도 않은 적당한 것이어야 한다.

| 정답 | (b) Different playing of boys and girls

| 오답 | (a) Boys and Girls는 제목의 범위가 글의 내용에 비해 지나치게 넓다(too general).

예제 6

존스 씨는 그의 많은 친구들에게 꽤나 별나 보인다. 비록 나이가 들었지만, 존스 씨는 밤늦게 초라한 마을의 일부를 혼자서 걸어다니는 오랜 습관이 있다. 그의 친구들이 그에게 밤늦게 다니는 것은 위험한 일이라고 경고도 하고, 낮에 산책을 하라고 충고도 한다. 하지만, 존스 씨는 자신의 일상을 바꾸기 위해서 아무런 노력도 하지 않는다.

6. 지은이의 생각을 가장 잘 표현한 것은?

| 풀이 | 주제가 담겨있는 속담을 찾는 문제이다. 위 글에서는 친구들이 아무리 경고를 하고 충고를 해도 존스 씨의 습관이 쉽게 고쳐지지 않음을 이야기하고 있다.

| 정답 | (c) You can't teach an old dog new tricks.

➡ 나이가 든 개에게 새로운 재주를 가르칠 수 없다는 말로, 오랫동안 몸에 밴 기질은 변하기가 어렵다는 주제를 잘 포함한다.

| 오답 | (a) 마지막에 웃는 자가 진정한 승리자이다.

(d) 연습이 최고를 만든다.

(b) 배움에 늦음이란 없다.

(e) 침묵이 금이다.

예제 7

참 아름다운 날이었고, 나는 큰배를 타고 있었다. 바다는 고요하고 평온했으며, 하늘은 푸르고 맑았고, 태양은 따뜻하고 밝았다. 갑자기, 음산한 구름이 하늘을 뒤덮었다. 태양은 자취를 감췄고, 바람이 불기 시작했으며, 바다가 회색빛으로 변하였다. 사나운 폭풍이 일어 배는 거의 침몰할 지경이었다. 그 때 짙은 안개를 헤치고 다른 배가 나타났다. 그것은 검은 깃발을 달고, 무장한 해적들이 승무원인 해적선이었다. 해적들이 우리 배로 뛰어 들어왔고 전쟁은 시작됐다. 나는 세 명의 해적에게 한꺼번에 공격을 당했다. 한 명은 턱수염이 있었고, 두 번째 해적은 콧수염이 있었으며, 세 번째 해적은 나무로 된 다리를 하고 있었다. 나는 손에 쥔 칼로 용감하게 싸웠다. 도처에서 격렬한 싸움이 벌어졌다. 나는 곧 부상당했고, 갑판 위에 피를 흘리면서 쓰러졌다. 그 때, 갑자기 한 아름다운 소녀가 다른 배 위에 나타났다. 그녀가 날카롭게 명령하자, 모든 해적들이 사라졌다. 그들의 배도 역시 사라졌다. 마치 아래로 삼켜져버린 듯 했다. 곧, 폭풍우가 멈췄고, 태양이 다시 고개를 내밀었다. 그 순간 나는 일어났고, 내가 침대에 있다는 걸 깨달았다. 태양이 빛나고 있었고, 내 얼굴에 한 줄기 빛이 비치고 있었다.

7. 글쓴이의 의도를 가장 잘 표현한 제목으로 적당한 것은?

| 풀이 | 화창한 어느 날, 배를 타고 가다가 해적을 만나서 싸움을 하고, 부상을 당하지만, 결국 알고 보면 모두 꿈이었음이 글의 마지막 부분에서 드러난다.

| 정답 | (d) An unusual dream

| 오답 | (a)와 (b)는 꿈의 일부 내용만을 담고 있는 'too specific' 한 것이다.

예제 8

새로 태어난 팬더는 작고, 무기력한 어린 생명체입니다. 그것은 마치 작은 분홍 돼지처럼 보이고, 눈은 삼사주동안 감겨진 채로 있습니다. 팬더는 다른 대부분의 동물에 비해서 꽤 천천히 성장합니다. 아기 팬더는 오랫동안 엄마 팬더를 전적으로 의지합니다. 사실, 아기 팬더는 생후 다섯 달이 될 때까지 걷지도 못합니다. 적어도 일년 동안은 엄마의 젖이 팬더가 먹을 수 있는 유일한 음식입니다. 하지만, 이런 것들이 팬더가 자라는 것을 막지는 않습니다. 팬더는 한 살이 되면 거의 55파운드의 무게가 나갑니다. 그 때쯤 되면, 팬더는 엄마처럼 대나무를 먹기 시작합니다. 생후 1년 6개월 정도가 되면, 팬더곰은 100파운드가 넘게 됩니다.

8. 이 글의 main idea를 찾아라

| 풀이 | main idea는 글쓴이가 글을 통해 독자들에게 꼭 하고자 하는 말을 의미한다.
이 글에서는 팬더가 다른 동물에 비해 성장이 느리다는 것을 중심으로 내세우고, 그 근거로 팬더의 의존성, 걷기, 식습관 등을 들고 있다.

| 정답 | (c) Pandas <u>develop</u> fairly slowly compared to most animals.
➡ 혹시 뒷 부분에 언급된 팬더의 무게 때문에, (c)가 답이 아니라고 생각하는 사람이 있을지도 모르겠다. 하지만 여기서 말하는 <u>develope</u>은 신체적인 발육 외에 정서적, 생활적인 면을 모두 포함하는 성장으로 보는 것이 맞다.

| 오답 | (a), (b), (d)는 too specific 하다.

예제 9

많은 연구에서 자동차로 여행을 할 때는 안전벨트를 착용하는 것이 더 낫다는 것을 밝혀냈다. 안전벨트는 사고로 인한 사망이나 부상의 위험을 놀라울 정도로 감소시켜 준다. 이 사실은 널리 인정되고 있고 많은 정부에서도 안전벨트 착용에 관한 법률을 통과시켰다. 그러나 많은 사람들이 여전히 안전벨트를 착용하지 않는다. 연구가들이 이것에 대한 여러 이유를 찾아냈다. 어떤 사람들은 안전벨트를 불편하게 여긴다. 그들은 사고가 났을 때 차에 갇히게 될까봐 겁을 낸다. 다른 사람들은 안전벨트가 그들을 보호하지 못할 것이라고 생각한다. 그들은 인간은 운명을 거스를 힘이 없다고 믿는다. 운명이 사고가 날지, 그래서 다치거나 죽을지를 결정할 것이다. 그래서 그들은 안전벨트를 매든 안 매든 달라지는 건 없다고 생각한다.

9. 위 글의 main topic은 무엇인가?

| 풀이 | 지은이는 안전벨트가 사고에서의 사망이나 부상의 위험을 줄여준다고 앞에서 소개하면서, 그럼에도 불구하고 어떤 이유로 안전벨트를 착용하지 않는 사람들을 소개하고 있다.

| 정답 | (c) In spite of the risk, some people do not wear seat belts.

| 오답 | (a) Some people don't think that seat belt can protect them.
➡ 안전벨트를 착용하지 않는 사람들 중 두 번째 그룹에 해당된다(too specific).

예제 10

전통적으로, 부활절과 관련된 고기는 양고기와 햄(돼지 허벅다리 고기)이다. 이 두 고기에는 고대로부터 전해오는 상징적인 의미가 있다. 구약성서를 보면, 아브라함은 하나님이 그의 아들 이삭을 죽이지 말라고 명령한 직후에 희생 제물로 양을 사용했다. 양은 언제나 유월절 전통의 일부로 존재해왔다. 기독교인들에게 양은 예수님의 희생을 상징한다. 수천 년 동안, 돼지는 행운을 상징했다. 매년 부활절 아침이 되면, 훈제하거나 요리한 햄이 유럽과 미국에서는 전통적인 주요리이다.

10. 위 글은 무엇에 관한 것인가?

| 풀이 | 'topic'을 묻는 문제이다.
부활절 음식인 양고기와 햄의 상징적인 의미에 대해 소개하고 있다.

| 정답 | (a) symbolic meaning of lamb and ham

CHAPTER 4

글의 목적 / 분위기 / 특정정보 / 글의 순서

Overall Review Question

예제 1

초기에, 모든 그리스 시민들은 똑같이 부유하거나, 똑같이 가난하였습니다. 모든 사람이 일정한 수의 소와 양을 소유했습니다. 진흙으로 만든 사람들의 오두막은 그들의 안식처였습니다. 사람들은 원하는 대로 자유롭게 왕래할 수 있었습니다.

공공의 중요한 문제를 의논할 필요가 있을 때에는 시민들은 언제나 장터로 모여들었습니다. 마을의 노인들 중 한 명이 의장으로 선출되고, 모든 사람들이 공평하게 자기 견해를 밝힐 기회를 가지는지를 감시하는 것이 의장의 의무였습니다. 전쟁시에는, 힘세고 능력 있는 마을 사람들 중 한 명이 지휘관으로 선택되지만, 일단 위험이 지나가면, 자발적으로 그 한 사람에게 자신들의 지도자가 될 권리를 부여했던 마을 사람들이 그의 권리를 빼앗고, 동등한 권리를 주장하게 됩니다.

1. 작가가 의장으로 선출된 사람에 대해 언급한 부분은 어디인가?

| 풀이 | One of the older men of the village was elected chairman, ~

| 정답 | (c) Lines 5–6

예제 2~3

베니건이 자신의 고향 아일랜드를 떠나 미국에 왔을 때, 그는 자기 고향의 선술집 같은 곳을 찾았다. 바로 가족이나 친구와 함께 쉴 수 있고, 맛있는 음식을 먹으면서, 축배를 들고, 진심으로 'Sl?nte'를 기원할 수 있는 장소 말이다.

'slawn–cheh'로 발음되는 'Sl?nte'는 '건강을 위하여'라는 의미가 담긴 고대 갈릭 언어로 전통적인 아일랜드의 건배 인사이다. 그것은 격려와 관대함의 정신을 나타내는 것으로, 베니건이 Bennigan's Grill & Tavern을 처음 만들었을 때 마음속에 새겼던 아일랜드의 관대함의 표시이다.

베니건스를 아무리 작은 것이라 할지라도 축하하기 위한 완벽한 공간으로 만든 것도 바로 이 비할 데 없는 아일랜드의 정신이다. 자, 베니건스에 있는 우리와 당신 모두, 건강을 위하여!!!

2. 작가가 이 글을 쓴 목적을 가장 잘 나타낸 것은?

| 정답 | 이 글은 베니건스가 생겨나게 된 배경에 대해 설명하고 있다. 베니건스가 식당임을 고려할 때, 생겨난 배경에 대해 설명하면서 손님들의 호기심을 자극해 더 많은 손님을 확보하고자 광고하는 글일 가능성이 높다.

| 정답 | (a) To advertise

3. 글의 내용 중 'Sl?nte'의 의미가 설명된 부분은?

| 정답 | Sl?nte is a traditional Irish toast in the ancient Gaelic language meaning 'to your health'.

| 오답 | (c) Lines 6–7

예제 4~5

세인스베리 아프리카 미술전시관은 전 세계에서 수집한 뛰어난 아프리카 예술품과 공예품을 위한 실속 있고 영구적인 박람회를 개최합니다. 수집된 작품들은 20만점이 넘으며, 고대부터 현대까지의 작품을 모두 포함합니다. 또한 뛰어난 예술적 걸작에서부터 일상생활 용품까지를 모두 포함합니다. 전시품 중 흥미 있는 것에는 나이지리아 요루바족 통치자의 놋으로 된 두상도 포함되어 있습니다; 또 가나에서 가져 온 금세공품, 중앙아프리카 지역의 조각과 직물, 무기류도 있습니다. 전시장의 개장은 아프리카의 훌륭한 예술작품을 '인류박물관'에서의 전시 이후 거의 삼십년 만에 다시 전시하는 것으로 주목받고 있습니다. (대영 박물관)

4. 작가가 전시회 중 흥미로운 부분에 관해 기록한 것은 글의 어디쯤인가?

| 정답 | Highlights of the collection include a magnificent brass head ~.

| 오답 | (c) Lines 5–7

5. 작가가 이 글을 쓴 목적을 가장 잘 설명한 것은?

| 정답 | 이 글은 세인스베리 박물관에서 아프리카 예술품 전시전이 열린다는 사실을 독자에게 알리고자 쓰여졌다.

| 오답 | (a) To inform the reader

예제 6

미국의 대통령이 반드시 대통령자문위원회를 가져야 한다는 법은 없다. 헌법은 단지 대통령이 "행정부 각 장들의 상관의 의무와 관련된 주제에 대한 자문을 필요로 할지도 모른다"라고만 명시하고 있다. 대통령은 반드시 자문을 요청할 필요는 없으며, 자문이 들어 올 경우에도 이것을 꼭 따라야 하는 것은 아니다. 그럼에도 불구하고, 대통령은 정보와 자문을 얻기 위해 이런 고문관그룹을 의지하고 있다. 왜냐하면 어떤 사람도 나라 안에서 일어나는 모든 일을 알 수는 없기 때문이다.

각 대통령은 의회의 자문과 동의를 얻어 내각의 구성원을 뽑지만 이러한 자문이 대통령이 좋아하는 방향으로만 들어오는 것은 아니고 때때로 대통령을 화가 나게 할 수도 있다. 내각의 구성원은 지식과 경험과 특별한 재능과 일반적인 지혜에 근거해 선출된다. 그들은 나이가 많고 신뢰할 수 있는 사람일 수도 있지만, 종종 (대통령의) 친척일 수도 있다. 그들은 농부일 수도 있고 외교관, 과학자, 정치가일 수도 있다. 그들은 매주 대통령 관저의 서쪽에 있는 대통령 집무실 옆방에 위치한 내각의 방에서 모인다.

6. 작가가 내각 모임 횟수에 관해 언급한 부분은 글의 어디인가?

| 정답 | They meet weekly in the cabinet room ~.

| 오답 | (d) Lines 14–15

예제 7~8

"나한테는 일어날 수 없는 일이야." 이 말이 많은 사람들로 하여금 간단한 의학 검진을 간과하게 하는 불행한 마음 상태이다. 그 결과 치료될 수 있는 수 천명의 사람들이 매년 질병으로 사망한다. 아래의 수치를 생각해 보라:

만약 50세가 넘은 모든 사람이 공식적인 결장암 검사를 했더라면 결장암으로 인한 사망률은 50% 이하로 감소했을 것이다.

※ 널리 보급된 혈압 검사와 치료는 뇌졸중과 심장발작을 최소한 50%까지 낮추어왔다.

※ 50세 이상의 여성 환자는 매년 유방 X선 사진을 찍어 유방암으로 인한 사망률을 30% 감소시킨다.

※ 1955년과 1992년 사이에 자궁경부암으로 인한 사망률이 74% 감소하였는데 이것은 주로 여성들이 정기적인 자궁암 조기 검사를 받기 시작했기 때문이다.

당신에게 필요한 진단을 알아내는 것을 돕기 위해, 우리는 세 가지 연령대의 남자와 여자의 예들을 수집해 놓았다. 이것들은 평균적인 위험에 놓인 건강한 사람들을 위한 충고이다. 당신에게 필요한 진단을 받기 위해 의사에게 검진을 예약하라.

7. 작가가 이 글을 쓴 목적은 무엇인가?

| 풀이 | 작가는 글 전반에 걸쳐서 각종 질병에 대한 조기 검진이 질병과 나아가서는 사망까지도 막을 수 있다고 서술하면서 독자들로 하여금 검진을 예약하도록 권장하고 있다.

| 정답 | (c) canvass for medical tests(의학검진을 권유)

| 오답 | (a) discuss kinds of the cancer 암의 종류에 관한 직접적인 설명이나 논의는 없다.

8. 이 글의 어조는 어떠한가?

| 풀이 | 어조는 글에 드러나는 작가의 말하는 스타일을 의미한다. 글의 목적과 전체적인 분위기를 살피면 어조는 금방 알아차릴 수 있다.
이 글의 경우, 의학 검진이 질병을 예방할 수 있음을 객관적인 수치를 이용해 독자에게 알려주고 있다.

| 정답 | (d) informative

| 오답 | (a) outraged 격분한 (b) judicial 비판적인 (c) hypnotic 최면성의

예제 9~10

삼성의 공동경영철학은 현재와 미래의 비전이다. 삼성은 1938년에 설립되었고, "국가에 대한 경제적인 공헌", "인간자원의 우선권", "합리주의 추구" 등과 같은 것을 모토로 지난 50년 동안 국제적인 수준으로 사업을 확장해 왔다. 삼성은 급변하는 세계 경제에 뒤떨어지지 않기 위해 경영철학을 더욱 세계화를 지향하는 쪽으로 바꿔야 한다고 인식해왔다. 비록 삼성이 지난 50년 간 전례가 없는 성장을 해오긴 했지만, 국제적으로 설립된 라이벌 회사들과의 치열한 경쟁의 시대에 살아남기 위해서는 그러한 인식이 계속 이어져야 한다. 따라서 삼성은 그룹 전체의 정체성과 경영철학을 "우리는 더 우수한 상품과 서비스를 창출하기 위해 인재와 기술을 제공할 것이고, 그것으로 더 좋은 지구촌 사회를 만들도록 기여할 것이다"로 바꾸었다.

9. 작가의 어조를 가장 잘 나타낸 말은?

| 풀이 | 이 글은 기업의 홈페이지에 있는 기업경영 소개글이다.
글쓴이는 이 글을 통해 기업이 추구하는 경영철학과 이념을 잘 설명하고 있다.

| 정답 | (d) descriptive; 설명적인, 기술적인

10. 이 글을 쓴 목적을 가장 잘 설명한 것은?

| 풀이 | 이 글의 1차적 목적은 기업의 경영이념을 소개하는 것이다. 자신들의 바람직한 이념을 소개함으로써 독자들로 하여금 자기 기업에 대해 좋은 이미지를 갖도록 한다.

| 정답 | (c) To advertise good image of the company

| 오답 | (a), (b), (d)의 내용은 본문에 전혀 언급되지 않았다.

예제 11~12

현재의 대학 신입생선발제도는 개선의 여지가 남아 있으며, 특히 적성과 잠재력, 학생의 경험을 일상화하는 사회력과 관련된 부분에서 더욱 그렇다. 우리는 교육받은 인재들의 능력을 상당히 낭비하는 것을 보게 되는데, 이런 낭비의 대부분은 제대로 교육을 받지 못해 생긴다. 불행히도 우리에게는 교육제도나 입시에 대한 지나친 열중의 폐해를 위한 대책을 마련할 현인이나 전문가가 없다. 그러나 최소한 우리는 좋은 교육이 어떤 것인지에 대해서는 잠시 멈춰 신중히 생각해야 한다.

11. 작가가 이 글을 쓴 목적은 무엇인가?

| 풀이 | 작가는 오늘날 대학의 신입생선발제도에 대해 비판적인 시각을 가지고 있다. 학생들의 적성과는 상관없이 신입생을 받아들이고, 또 그나마 입학한 대학생을 위한 알맞은 교육을 제공하지 못해 우수한 인재마저 낭비하고, 교육 문제를 해결할 전문가가 없는 현실을 비관적으로 바라보고 있다. 그리고 독자가 이 사실을 알고, 진정한 교육에 대해 고민하기를 원하고 있다.

| 정답 | (b) demand the educational world's serious reflection

12. 이 글의 어조는?

| 풀이 | 작가는 현재의 교육 제도에 대해 비판적이고 비관적인 시각을 가지고 있다.

| 정답 | (a) critical

예제 13~14

요즘은 인사를 하고 점심을 함께 하는 것이 대개 우정의 기초가 되기 때문에 누구나 친구를 만들 수 있다; 그러나 적을 만들 대에는 기술이 필요하다. 친구보다 적을 이기는 것이 훨씬 더 어렵고, 적으로서의 관계를 지속하는 것이 더 어렵다. 기억하라: 핵심은 실제의 적이지, 단순히 때때로 멍청하고 지긋지긋하다고 생각되는 성가신 사람이나 아니면 딴 세상을 동경하게 만드는 거슬리는 존재가 아니라는 사실을 말이다. 실제의 적은 완전히 다른 부류이다. 그는 싫은 사람이고, 한 사람의 가장 심술궂은 욕망의 반영이다. 그는 당신이 하지 말았으면 하는 그대로 당신에게 행동하고 싶어한다. 어떤 사람이 귀하고 가치가 있고, 적절한 보호와 보살핌을 받는다면 그들은 평생을 살 것이다. 잘 기른 적 하나는 영원한 기쁨이다. 그가 사람들 앞에서 당신을 헐뜯지 않을 때 그는 개인적으로 당신을 헐뜯을 것이고, 그가 개인적으로 당신을 헐뜯지 않을 때는 그렇게 하려고 생각중일 것이다. 그가 어디에 있든지, 너는 모욕을 당할 것이다. 그가 어디에 있었든지, 너의 뼈가 쌓여있을 것이다. 그는 거대하다. 너의 꿈에서 그의 어깨는 너의 해골을 누를 것이다. 그 자신은 절대로 잠들지 않는다. 해악이 매우 많고, 회피해야 할 중상모략 또한 매우 많을 것이다. 그러면 생각하라: 이런 결과를 가져오게 한 것은 바로 당신이다. 그는 단지 너를 위해 살며 너 때문에 약올라 한다.

13. 이 글의 어조를 가장 잘 설명한 것은?

| 정답 | 글의 내용을 잘 살펴보면, 결국 자신의 적인 자기 내면에 존재하는 또 다른 자신임을 알 수 있게 된다. 글의 마지막에 결국 적에 의한 피해는 모두 자신이 만들어 낸 것이라고 말하면서 인간의 이중적인 면모를 경멸/조소하고 있다.

| 정답 | (d) tongue in cheek; 조롱하는 투로, 비꼬아서, 경멸하며 말하다

| 오답 | (a) bitter 가혹한 (b) cavalier 기사다운, 거만한 (c) ominous 불길한

14. 작가가 이 글을 쓴 목적을 가장 잘 나타낸 것은?

| 풀이 | 글의 내용에서 어떤 새로운 정보를 제공하거나 독자를 설득하려는 의도는 찾아볼 수 없다. 처음에는 적의 존재를 실감나게 묘사하다 나중에는 그 모든 것의 원인이 나에게 있음을 밝힘으로써 소설과도 같은 긴장감을 제공하고 있다.

| 정답 | (b) To entertain the reader

예제 15~16

담배를 끊기로 결심을 한 흡연자들은 대개 마지막으로 담배를 피운 지 한 시간이 지나면 처음으로 고통을 느끼게 됩니다.① 최근 연구자들이 흡연에 대한 열망을 불러일으키는 두뇌 회로를 확인했는데, 이것이 중독을 막는 새로운 길을 제공할 것입니다.② 폐 가득 담배를 피우게 되면 뇌 세포는 니코틴으로 가득 차게 되고, 이것은 화학물질인 도파민(신경전달물질)의 방출을 억제합니다.③ 수 초 내에 같은 세포들이 니코틴에 대해 둔감해 집니다.④ 니코틴은 도파민의 방출을 세밀히 조정하는 다른 두뇌 회로에 영향을 미친다고 일리노이 시카고 대학의 다니엘 멕게히와 그의 연구팀이 밝혔습니다. 특히, 니코틴의 공격은 약 한시간 동안 하나의 회로를 아예 절단합니다. 이 (잘려진) 회로는 대개 세포가 도파민을 방출하는 것을 막습니다.

15. 이 글의 어조는?

| 풀이 | 작가는 글을 통해 흡연이 우리의 신경에 어떠한 영향을 미치는지, 그래서 어떤 식으로 금연을 못하게 하는 지를 보여주고 있다. 그러면서 이러한 흡연의 중독성에 대해 걱정하는 분위기로 글을 쓰고 있다.

| 정답 | (a) concerned

| 오답 | (b) disinterested 무관심한 냉담한 (c) placid 차분한 (d) exaggerated 과장된

16. 아래의 문장이 들어갈 자리로 알맞은 곳은?

So it is unclear why smokers enjoy a whole cigarette.

| 풀이 | 주어진 문장은 왜 흡연자들이 담배 한 개피 전체를 피우는지 모르겠다는 내용이다.
주어진 문장이 결과를 나타내는 'so'로 시작했기 때문에, 바로 앞에는 궁금해 하는 원인문장이 와야 한다.
글의 중간 부분을 보면 흡연을 시작한지 몇 초 내에 세포들이 둔감해진다는 문장이 있다. 둔감해지면 담배를 피워도 아무런 느낌이 없을 텐데, 왜 사람들이 단지 몇 초만 흡연하는 것이 아니라 담배 전체를 태우는지 궁금해 질 것이다.

| 정답 | (d) ④

예제 17

알츠하이머병은 치매의 가장 흔한 원인이지만, 특히 병이 발병했을 때에는, 환자의 신체 내부를 조사하는 기술 외에는 병의 원인을 정확히 밝히는 것이 불가능하다.① 대뇌 측두엽의 해마는 측두엽 기억장치 중의 한 부분이며 노인성 치매의 초기 단계에 영향을 주는 것으로 알려져 왔다. 최근의 영상기술의 발달, 특히 MRI(자기공명영상장치)는 해마와 같이 상상할 수 있는 부분적인 뇌 구조 평가를 했다.② 이 연구의 목적이 민감도와 정확성에 초점을 맞춘 것이고, 만약 MRI를 이용해 해마의 영상에 다르게 접근했다면 노인성 치매의 초기단계를 진단하기 위한 것으로 응용할 수 있었을 것이다. ③ 해마 병리학은 가까운 해마의 영역과 체적을 측정하기 위한 수단으로 평가되었으며 1.5 T(테슬라) 영사기를 사용해서 T2 강조영상을 완성했다. 해마측정의 정확도는 편도선과 전두엽에 비교된다. 머리와 두뇌의 크기에 대한 자료들의 일반성을 위한 다양한 과정이 비교되었다.④

17. 아래의 문장이 들어갈 위치로 알맞은 곳은?

Therefore, a reliable diagnostic method is needed.

| 풀이 | 주어진 문장의 내용은 '그러므로 믿을만한 진단법이 필요하다는 것이다.'
문장의 앞이 '그러므로(therefore)'로 시작하므로 앞쪽에는 믿을만한 진단이 필요한 이유가 제기되어야 한다.

| 정답 | (a) ① ➡ 아직 알츠하이머병이 발병했을 때, 그 증상이나 원인을 밝혀내는 방법이 없음을 말하고, 따라서 믿을만한 진단법이 필요하다는 문장을 제시하면 된다.

CHAPTER 5

글의 추론

Indirectly answered questions

예제 1~2

방문객들이 종종 이렇게 묻습니다; 누가 전형적인 하버드대 학생입니까? 하고... 그에 대한 대답은 전형적인 하버드대생은 없다는 것입니다. 각각의 학생은 모두가 독특한 개인이고, 학생들의 모습은 놀랍도록 다양합니다.

하버드의 남녀 학생은 다양한 인종과 종교적 전통, 그리고 다양한 정치적 신념을 대표합니다. 그들은 미국의 전 지역과 백 개가 넘는 다른 나라에서 왔습니다. 그들은 학부생과 대학원생, 평생 교육생, 그리고 여름(계절) 학교 학생들을 포함합니다. 그들의 연령층 또한 10대 초반에서 80대에 이르기까지 다양합니다. 1997년에는 마리 파자노가 하버드대의 학위를 취득한 최고령의 주인공이 되었는데, 그 때 그녀는 89세에 공개개설학교를 졸업한 것이었습니다.

하버드 대학의 학생들은 성장배경이나 학문적인 혹은 학문 외적인 관심분야도 눈에 띄게 다양합니다. 전체 학생의 삼분의 이 정도가 공립학교 출신이고, 약 삼분의 이의 학생이 몇몇 형태의 재정적인 보조를 받고 있습니다. 학생들의 이와 같은 다양성에도 불구하고, 하버드의 학생들은 하나의 공동체로서 몇 가지의 공통적인 특성을 가지기도 합니다.

1. 주어진 본문을 통해 하버드대 학생들이 어떠하다는 것을 추론(추측)해 낼 수 있는가?

| 풀이 | Each student is unique individual, and the student body is incredibly diverse.

➡ 영어로 말을 하거나 글을 쓸 때, 대부분의 경우 중심 문장은 앞쪽에 위치한다. 이 글에서도 방문객의 질문으로 화제를 도입한 후, 바로 중심 문장인 학생들의 다양한 개성과 모습을 제시하였다. 그 이후에도 인종, 종교, 정치적 신념, 출신 지역, 연령, 관심분야 등의 다양한 범주 내에서 학생들이 다양성을 지니고 있음을 계속적으로 드러내고 있다.

| 정답 | (c) various

2. 밑줄 친 'They'가 나타내는 것은 무엇인가?

| 풀이 | 'it'이나 'they'와 같이 대명사가 지칭하는 대상을 묻는 문제에서는, 바로 앞에 나오는 명사 중에서 수와 인칭이 일치하는 것을 찾으면 된다.

위의 글에서 'they'가 가리키는 것은 다양한 지역에서 온 다양한 과정에 있는 학생들, 즉 다양한 개성을 지닌 하버드대 생들을 의미한다.

| 정답 | (d) Harvard College students

| 오답 | (a)는 이야기를 끌어오기 위한 질문을 제시한 사람이고, (b)와 (c)는 결국 (d)의 한 속성으로 포함되는 것이다.

예제 3~4

원래 몽테뉴가 사용한 바에 의하면, '에세이'는 비교적 짧고, 짜임새 없이 조직된 개인적이고 비공식적인 스타일의 산문을 의미하였다. (그러나) 오늘날에는, 비록 많은 작가들이 여전히 몽테뉴의 전통을 유지하고 있긴 하지만, '에세이'는 그 의미를 확장하여 비공식적이고, 격식 없는 특성 이상의 것을 의미하게 되었고, 사용을 지나치게 제한하지 않는 아주 편한 용어가 되었다. 오늘날 우리는 정보를 제공하거나 독자를 설득하거나 또는 독자를 즐겁게 하기 위해 쓰여진 상대적으로 짧은 소설이 아닌 산문문학을 일컬어 '에세이'라고 한다. 따라서 '에세이'는 쉽게 이해되며, 다양한 주제와 목적, 어조, 그리고 스타일을 허용한다.

3. 위 글에 따르면, 우리는 에세이를 어떻게 말할 수 있는가?

| 풀이 | ~ a relatively short piece of prose nonfiction, with the purpose of informing, persuading, or entertaining its reader.
➡ 독자에게 정보를 제공하고, 때로는 독자를 설득한다고 했으므로 독자를 깨우치거나 계몽하는 역할을 한다고 말할 수 있다.

| 정답 | (c) is enlightening

| 오답 | (a) 운문(verse)이 아닌 산문(prose)이다.
(b) informal(비공식적인, 격식을 차리지 않는) in style이 맞다.
(d) 에세이의 의도 중에는 to entertain its readers도 포함된다.

4. 밑줄 친 'the tradition of Montaigne'는 무엇을 의미하는가?

| 풀이 | '몽테뉴의 전통'이라는 것은 전통적인 몽테뉴식 에세이의 정의방식을 말한다. 그리고 그것은 바로, 앞 부분에 나온 'a rather brief, loosely organised prose work, personal and informal in style'을 의미한다.

| 정답 | (a) essay means a brief and loosely organised prose work

| 오답 | (b), (c), (d)는 모두 오늘날 확장된 의미의 '에세이'에 포함된다.

예제 5

나의 경험은 아무런 색도 볼 수 없고, 아무런 소리도 들을 수 없는 세상에서 살아가는 사람의 제한된 경험입니다. 하지만 나는 학창시절 이후 줄곧, 내 신체적 장애가 내 존재의 어떤 본질적인 부분도 차지할 수 없다는 기쁜 확신을 가지고 있습니다. 왜냐하면, 신체적 장애가 내 정신의 어느 한 부분도 차지하지 않았기 때문입니다. 이러한 믿음은 내가 "나는 생각한다, 고로 나는 존재한다"라는 데카르트의 명언을 접했을 때 확고해졌습니다.

이 힘있는 다섯 마디의 말은 내 안에 잠자고 있던 무언가를 일깨웠고, 다시는 잠들지 않게 했습니다. 나는 내 정신이 행복의 긍정적인 매개체가 되고, 어둠을 건너는 다리가 되고, 활기 넘친 생각으로 가득 찬 아늑한 공간이 되고, 빛이 가득한 행복이 될 줄 압니다. 나는 우리가 바깥 세상에서 어떠한 재난이 닥친다 하더라도 우리 내면에 빛과 소리와 질서를 창조해낼 수 있다는 사실을 압니다.

5. 위 글에 따르면 작가는 어떤 사람임을 알 수 있는가?

| 풀이 | I have had a joyous certainty that my physical handicaps were not an essential part of my being.
➡ 이 글의 작가는 비록 신체적인 장애를 가지고 있지만, 그것으로 인해 좌절하는 것이 아니라, 정신적인 내면세계의 질서를 통한 희망을 가지고 살아가고 있다.

| 정답 | (a) is a physically handicapped person

| 오답 | (b) 정신적인 질환을 앓고 있는 것이 아니라 신체적 장애가 있다.
(c) 장애로 인해 슬퍼하는 것이 아니라 오히려 정신적인 강인함으로 장애를 극복하고 있다.
(d) 확고한 신념을 가지고 있음을 글을 통해 알 수 있다. 남자인지 여자인지는 확실히 알 수 없다.

⊃ 예제 6~7

스미스 양의 하숙집 여주인인 베이커 여사는 전혀 놀라지 않고 찰리를 들여 보내주었다. 그녀는 굉장히 굵은 팔을 가진 체구가 큰 여성이었고, 만약 필요하다면 그 팔을 주저하지 않고 사용할 것처럼 보였다. "그래요", 그녀가 말했다. "스미스 양은 안에 있어요. 곧장 올라가도록 하세요. 12호실은 꼭대기 층에 있어요. 내가 스미스 양에게 (당신이 온 것을) 말해주러 올라가지 않은 걸 변명해야겠죠. 하지만 내가 발을 다쳐서 우리 집 하숙생의 친구를 따라 위 아래로 다닐 수가 없어요." 찰리는 그녀가 발을 다친 것을 동정하고는, 활기차게 위층으로 올라가기 시작했다. 베이커 여사는 복도에 잠깐동안 서 있다가 찰리가 이층에 다다랐을 때 날카롭게 외쳤다. "신사는 열한시 이후에는 남의 집에 찾아가지 않아요. 그건 내가 정한 규칙이니까, 스미스 양은 생각할 필요가 없어요."

6. 위 글에 의하면, 베이커 여사의 성격은 어떠한가?

| 풀이 | 글에 나타나 있는 주인공의 말이나 행동 묘사를 통해 성격을 추론할 수 있다.
베이커 여사는 일단 큰 체구로 상대방을 위압하는 경향이 있다. 그리고 찰리가 처음 집에 찾아갔을 때, 스미스 양이 어디에 사는지, 왜 안내를 못 하게 되었는지를 하나하나 설명해 주고 있다. 결정적인 단서가 되는 것은 마지막 부분에 나온다. 올라가는 찰리를 보면서 신사는 늦은 시간 남의 집에 찾아가는 게 아니라고 날카롭게 지적하고 있다.

| 정답 | (b) strict → 겉모습이나 말을 통해 약간 엄하고 규칙을 중시하는 경향을 엿볼 수 있다.

| 오답 | (a) timid 겁 많은 (c) tender 부드러운 (c) amiable 붙임성 있는

7. 밑줄 친 'them'은 무엇을 가리키는가?

| 풀이 | 주어진 단어가 포함된 문장을 살펴보면, 지금 베이커 여사가 발을 다쳐서 계단을 오르내리면서 발을 wear out(지치게 하다) 할 수 없다고 설명하고 있다.

| 정답 | (d) Mrs. Baker's feet → 계단을 오르내리며 혹사당하는 것은 여사의 다친 발이다.

⊃ 예제 8~9

워싱턴은 역사상 오직 통치만을 목적으로 만들어진 최초의 도시이다. 독립 전쟁 후에 의회의 의원들은 그들 자신과 국무성, 재무성, 특허국과 같은 각 부서를 위한 영구적인 공간에 대해 격렬한 논쟁을 벌였다. 1970년, 의회의 논쟁을 중단시키기 위해 조지 워싱턴은 새로 지정할 연방구를 위한 대지를 선택할 책임을 맡았다. 사람들을 놀라게 하는 대신 오히려 많은 사람들을 실망시키면서 그는 자신의 사랑하는 농장인 마운트 버농에서 몇 마일 위쪽에 있는 포토맥 강변 둑 위의 땅을 선택했다.

콜럼비아 지역은 버지니아의 일부와 머릴랜드의 일부로 이루어졌다. 당시에는 그 지역의 수백 평방 마일의 땅이 완만한 구릉으로 이루어져 있었고, 일부는 포토맥 강가에서 경작되었다. 지금은 그 곳에 흔히 'Foggy Bottom'이라 불리는 워싱턴의 일부가 있다; 그 일부는 180년 전에 그러한 별명을 얻었다.

두 개의 항구 도시, 알렉산드리아와 조지타운은 새로운 도시가 보이는 곳에서 번창했고 신생국의 가장 중요한 도시(워싱턴)와 아득히 먼 영국과 대륙의 항구에 배로 접근했다.

8. 글을 통해 추론할 수 있는 "foggy bottom"의 의미는?

| 풀이 | 경작되어 농사를 짓던 땅이 연방구로 지정되면서 주요 국가의 부서가 설치되었다. 그리고 워싱턴의 일부인 'foggy bottom'(미국 국무성의 속칭)도 바로 그 자리에 세워지게 되었다.

| 정답 | (a) used to be mostly swampland(늪, 습지) → 안개가 자욱한 바닥이라는 것은 포토맥강에 의해 토지가 습하고 늪처럼 되었음을 의미한다.

9. 위 글을 통해서 알 수 있는 알렉산드리아가 18세기에 중요했던 이유는 무엇인가?

| 풀이 | 알렉산드리아는 항구 도시로 미국의 연방구와 영국과 대륙의 주요 대도시를 항만으로 연결했기 때문에 중요성을 띄었다.

| 정답 | (a) linked the federal district with the ocean.

CHAPTER 6

실전 종합 문제

Actual Test

예제 1~5

초컬릿은 카카오라고 불리는 열대지방 나무의 씨로 만든 식품이다. 카카오는 '쓴 쥬스'를 뜻하는 마야 인디언 어에서 유래된 것이고, 초컬릿이라는 단어는 '신 물'을 의미하는 마야어에서 유래되었다.

카카오는 씨앗이나 카카오 열매를 만들어내는데, 그것으로 모든 종류의 초컬릿을 만든다. 이 나무는 따뜻하고 습기가 있는 기후에서 잘 자란다. 나무들은 적도를 기준으로 남·북위 20도 지역 안에서 서식한다. 전 세계에서 생산되는 카카오 열매의 대부분은 가나와 아이보리 해안을 끼고 있는 아프리카 서해안에서 재배되고, 나이지리아가 세계 최고의 카카오 열매 생산국이다. 브라질은 서반구에서 가장 많이 카카오 열매를 생산하는 국가이다.

인공적으로 재배된 카카오나무는 7.6미터나 자란다. 그리고 나무는 일년 내내 잎과 꽃, 열매를 맺는다. 꽃은 작다. 꽃들은 혼자서 피거나 줄기나 가지 위에 무리 지어 핀다. 성숙한 과일(또는 꼬투리)은 빨갛거나, 노랗거나, 금빛이거나, 연한 녹색이거나 아니면 이 색깔들을 섞어놓은 듯 하다. 메론처럼 생긴 꼬투리는 아몬드처럼 생긴 씨앗을 스무 개에서 마흔 아홉 개씩 가지고 있는데, 그 씨앗을 발효시키고 말리면, 바로 시중에 판매하는 카카오 열매가 된다.

아마 오래 전에 영국인 수입업자가 저질렀을 철자상의 실수로 인해서, 이 열매들은 영어권 국가에 (카카오가 아닌) 코코아 열매로 알려지게 되었다. 이것은 많은 사람으로 하여금 ______ 생각하게 했다.

1. 이 글의 주제는 무엇인가?

| 풀이 | 글의 주제는 대개 문단의 앞에 오는 경우가 많다.
그리고 무엇보다 중요한 것은, 주제는 글 전체의 내용을 포함하는 것이어야지, 글의 일부분만을 포함하거나 아니면 글에 나타나지 않은 내용까지 포함해서는 안 된다는 사실이다.
이 글에서는 초컬릿의 재료가 되는 카카오나무와 그 열매에 대해, 그리고 코코아 열매로 잘못 알려지게 된 배경에 대해 이야기하고 있다.

| 정답 | (a) a note on chocolate
➡ 카카오나무와 열매를 포괄하는 것은 결국 그것들로 만든 상품인 초컬릿이 된다. 문단의 첫 머리에 초컬릿을 소개하고 있다.

| 오답 | (b), (c), (d)는 각각 글의 부분적인 내용만을 담고 있으므로 주제로서 부적합하다.

2. 글의 내용에 근거해 알 수 있는 카카오나무의 특성은?

| 풀이 | 각각의 보기를 본문에서 직접 찾아 비교해본다.

| 정답 | (c) produce fruits in all seasons of the year.
➡ 인공 재배된 카카오나무의 특성이 아니냐고 의문을 가지는 사람들도 있겠지만, 주어진

답지 중에서 카카오나무의 특성을 나타내는 것은 이 보기 뿐이다

| 오답 | (a) 카카오의 씨앗으로는 cocoa가 아니라 chocolate을 만든다.
(b) 춥고, 건조한 곳이 아니라 따뜻하고 습한 기후에서 잘 자란다.
(d) 카카오나무의 꽃은 작다.

3. 'in clusters'의 의미와 가장 가까운 것은?

| 풀이 | 꽃이 혼자서도 피지만, 송이(cluster)로 무리 지어서도 핀다고 말하고 있다.
➡ singly와 상응할 수 있는 말을 찾도록 한다.

| 정답 | (a) in groups

| 오답 | (b)는 수가 아니라 방향을 말하고 있고, (c)는 꽃의 굵기를, (d)는 꽃의 밀도를 말하고 있다.

4. 'cultivated'의 의미와 가장 가까운 것은?

| 풀이 | 야생의 카카오나무가 아닌 인공적으로 재배되는 카카오나무이 이야기를 하고 있다.

| 정답 | (b) tilled 경작하다

5. 밑줄 친 부분에 들어갈 말로 가장 어울리는 것은?

| 풀이 | 영국인의 실수로 인해서 카카오 열매가 코코아로 잘못 알려지게 됐음을 소개하면서, 그 결과 사람들이 무엇인가를 오해하게 되었음을 소개하고 있다.

| 정답 | (a) 발음과 철자상의 오해로 인해 사람들이 카카오열매가 카카오나무가 아닌 코코넛 나무에서 온 것으로 알게 되었다.

➲ 예제 6~10

유산소운동이 심장 박동 속도를 빨리 하는 것보다 더 많은 영향을 미친다는 것은 놀랄 일이 아니다. 이 운동은 기운을 돋우고 자신감을 갖게 한다. 그러나 많은 두뇌 연구자들은 또 다른 영향도 있을 것이라고 믿는다. 연구자들은 운동이 뼈와 근육, 심장과 폐를 강하게 하는 것처럼 두뇌의 중요한 어떤 부분도 강화할 것이라고 생각한다.

연구자들은 유산소운동이 여러분으로 하여금 새로운 것을 더 잘 학습하고 이미 알고 있는 정보를 더 잘 기억하도록 돕는다고 주장한다. 유산소운동은 보다 많은 양의 피를 두뇌로 보내고 ______한 물질을 공급한다. 만약에 운동이 춤이나 농구처럼 복잡한 움직임을 포함한다면, 두뇌는 더 많은 신경을 서로 연결시킨다. 그리고 더 많은 연결은, 두뇌가 모든 종류의 정보를 더 잘 조작할 수 있음을 의미한다.

과학자들은 아직 운동과 두뇌 회전력 사이의 관계에 대해 완전히 이해하지는 못한다. 우선, 사람들은 운동이 학습이나 기억에 도움이 된다는 사실을 그냥 신뢰해야 한다. 그러나 과학적인 조사는 일주일에 최소 세 번 이상의 운동이 사람에게 좋음을 알려준다. 한 예로, 미국 의사협회의 학회지에 실린 한 연구에서는 시속 4-5마일 정도의 속도로 한번에 45분씩 일주일에 다섯 번 걷는 것이 장수에 도움이 됨을 보여주었다. 그러므로 couch potato가 되지 말라. 그곳을 벗어나서 무엇인가 하라!!!

6. 이 글의 주제는 무엇인가?

| 풀이 | 유산소운동이 두뇌 회전과 건강에 도움이 됨을 알려주는 글이다.

| 정답 | (c) Profits of aerobic exercise

7. 다음 중 어느 것이 이 글의 요지를 가장 잘 나타내고 있는가?

| 풀이 | 보기의 문장들을 본문 속에서 찾아 하나하나 비교해 보면 된다.

| 정답 | (b) Aerobic exercise is all subtly linked with brain power.

| 오답 | 오답을 바르게 고쳐보자.
(a) Exercise lifts the spirit or builds confidence.
(c) Aerobic exercise can help you learn new things and understand old information better.
(d) If the exercise has complicated movements like basketball moves, the brain produces more nerve connection.

8. 다음 중 운동에 관한 진술로 옳지 않은 것은?

| 풀이 | 역시 본문 속에서 일치되는 문장을 찾아보면 된다.

| 정답 | (b) gives you better eyesight.
➡ 시력에 관한 언급은 어디서도 찾아볼 수 없다.

9. 이 글에서 'a couch potato'는 무엇을 의미하는가?

| 풀이 | 운동의 중요성을 이야기하면서 couch potato가 되지 말고, 밖으로 나가 운동을 하자고 주장하고 있음으로 이를 통해 우리는 couch potato가 운동을 하기 싫어하고 게으른 사람임을 쉽게 짐작할 수 있다.

| 정답 | (b) a underexercised person

TIP 영어권에서 생활하는 사람들은 여가시간을 주로 길다란 쇼파에 앉아 팝콘이나 감자칩(potato chip)을 먹으면서 TV를 보는 것으로 보낸다. 여기에서 유래된 것이 바로 couch(쇼파와 같은 긴 의자)+potato(감자), 즉 쇼파에 앉아 감자를 먹으면서 TV만 보는 사람이다. 게으른 사람을 지칭할 때 이 말을 사용한다.

10. 밑줄 친 부분에 가장 적당한 표현은?

| 풀이 | 밑줄 친 부분의 앞 뒤 내용을 살펴보자. 먼저 유산소운동이 학습과 기억을 돕는다고 했고, 운동을 하면 많은 피가 두뇌로 흐른다고 했다. 그리고 빈칸의 뒷부분에서는 운동이 복잡하면 할수록 더 많은 신경 연결이 생긴다고 했다.
따라서 운동을 통해 두뇌로 흐르는 피가 신경 연결에 도움이 됨을 짐작할 수 있다.

| 정답 | (a) develop new nerve connections

예제 11~15

미국의 가족 단위가 변화의 과정에 있다. 20세기 초반에는 대개 대가족과 핵가족의 두 유형의 가족이 있었다. 대가족은 부모님과 자녀들, 그리고 조부모님이나 삼촌, 숙모 같은 다른 친척들이 모두 한 집에 사는 가족이다. 핵가족은 단지 한 지붕 아래에 사는 부모와 자녀만으로 구성된다.

미국의 경제가 농업에서 산업중심으로 진보함에 따라 사람들은 좋은 직장을 얻기 위해 나라안의 여러 지역으로 옮겨가야만 했다. 이러한 직장들은 주로 대도시에만 있었다. 그래서 이제, 미국인의 4분의 3이 전국토의 겨우 2.5%에 해당하는 도시 지역에서 생활한다. 일반 국민 근로자 1억 1,800만 명중에서 겨우 300만명 만이 아직도 농촌에서 일을 한다.

더 나은 직장을 얻기 위한 이동이 대가족을 분열시켰기 때문에, 핵가족이 더욱 널리 퍼지게 되었다. 현재는 미국 가족의 55%가 핵가족이다. 하지만 이와 같은 전통적인 두 가지 가족 유형 외에도 이제 '가족'이라는 단어는 다양한 삶의 모습들을 포함하기 위해 그 의미가 확장되었다.

오늘날 미국의 가정은 많은 ____ 결합으로 구성된다. 두 부부 중 한 쌍은 이혼하게 되면서, 부모 중 한쪽만 있는 가정의 수가 늘었다. 즉 아빠나 엄마 중 한 명이 아이들을 데리고 사는 것이다. 거의 열 가정 중 한 가정은 편부모 가정으로 가고 있다. 이혼은 또한 더 많은 '혼합된 가족'을 양산한다. 혼합 가족은 남성이나 여성이 재혼을 해서 전 배우자의 자녀와 현 배우자의 자녀를 새로운 가족 안에 함께 받아들이게 될 때 발생된다. 어떤 부부들은 자녀를 갖지 않기로 결정하기 때문에, 부부 단독 가구도 증가한다. 또한 많은 커플들이 합법적으로 결혼하지 않기로 결정함으로써, 동거만 하는 커플들도 증가한다. 또한 독신이거나 배우자와 사별을 했거나 이혼을 한 등의 이유로 혼자 사는 사람도 늘어나고 있다. 미국인의 다섯 명 중 한 명은 혼자 산다.

11. 이 글의 주제는 무엇인가?

| 풀이 | 이 글은 미국의 사회상이 변화하면서 그에 따라 가족제도도 점차 변화하고 있음을 설명하는 글이다.

| 정답 | (d) The changing American family

| 오답 | (a) Increase of divorce rate는 글 내용이 극히 일부만을 담고 있고,
(b) a problem of single parent home은 전혀 언급된 바 없다.

12. 'prevalent'의 의미로 가장 적당한 것은?

| 풀이 | 주어진 단어 앞뒤의 내용을 살펴보면, 농업 중심 사회에서 산업 중심의 사회로 변화하면서 많은 사람들이 도시로 옮겨왔고, 그에 따라 대가족이 해체되고 대신 핵가족의 수가 급격히 늘어났음을 말하고 있다.
즉 핵가족이 하나의 시대 흐름을 형성하면서, 유행한 것이다.

| 정답 | (a) current

13. 빈칸에 가장 어울리지 않은 단어는?

| 풀이 | 오늘날 미국의 가족은 다양한 형태의 결합을 통해 이루어진다.
'다양한'의 의미를 지닌 단어가 빈칸에 적합하다.

| 정답 | (c) varied

14. 위 글의 내용을 통해 알 수 있는 핵가족의 특징은?

| 풀이 | 핵가족을 설명한 부분과 보기의 내용을 하나하나 비교해 본다.

| 정답 | (b) became more prevalent by industrialization.

| 오답 | (a)는 대가족에 관한 설명이다.

15. 'blended family'가 발생하는 원인은?

| 풀이 | 본문에서는 이혼했다가 다시 재혼하는 사람들이 각자 데리고 있던 자녀를 같은 집에서 함께 양육하게 됨으로써 'blended family'가 생겨난다고 설명하고 있다.

| 정답 | (c) Digamy(재혼)

| 오답 | (a) Industrialization와 (b) Breaking of the extended family는 핵가족이 유행하게 된 원인에 해당된다.

예제 16~20

웃음의 근원을 조사하기 위해서, 과학자들은 인간의 영장류 사촌에게로 눈을 돌렸다. 만약 당신이 침팬지를 간지럽힌다면(주의하여야 하고, 가급적이면 아기가 더 낫다), 침팬지는 웃을 것이다. 그러나 그 소리는 숨을 내쉬거나 들이쉴 때마다 한 번씩 헐떡이는 소리일 뿐, 인간의 웃음소리와 그다지 비슷하지 않다. 신경과학자인 머릴랜드대학의 로버트 프로바인은 침팬지가 연결된 웃음소리를 내지 못하는 이유가 그들이 호흡할 때 단음 이상의 소리는 만들어낼 수 없기 때문이라는 것을 알아냈다. 인간은, ___1___, 한번의 호흡을 여러 번의 웃음소리나 단어들로 쪼갤 수가 있다(결국 우리가 말하는 것도 한번의 호흡을 여러 소리로 쪼개는 것에서부터 비롯된 것이다). "웃음이란 ___2___지만 침팬지는 할 수 없는가와 같은 기본적인 질문에 대한 시험이다."라고 프로바인은 말한다.

인간처럼 웃을 수 없다면, 인간처럼 말할 수 없다.

16. 이 글은 무엇에 관한 것인가?

| 풀이 | 침팬지와 인간의 웃음을 비교하고, 그것을 언어와 관련시키고 있다.

| 정답 | (a) Laughter

| 오답 | (b) Breathing과 (d) Sound는 역시 글의 일부분만을 포함하고 있다.

17. 이 글의 중심 생각은 무엇인가?

| 풀이 | 글의 중심 생각은 대부분 글의 제일 첫 문장과 마지막 문장에서 찾아볼 수 있다.

| 정답 | (c) No humanlike laughing, no speaking.

| 오답 | (a) Chimps' laughter doesn't resemble human laughter.
(b) Other apes can't speak.가 바른 내용이고,
(d) Laughter can help you to get good health. 는 본문에 전혀 언급된 바 없다.

18. 이 글에서 'our primate cousins'은 무엇을 의미하는가?

| 풀이 | 여기서 우리는 인간을 의미하고, 영장류 사촌이란, 인간과 가장 가까운 동물인 침팬지를 의미한다. 주어진 용어 다음 문장을 살펴봐도, 침팬지를 간지럽힌다는 내용이 나오므로 쉽게 유추해 낼 수 있다.

| 정답 | (b) Chimps

19. part 1에 들어갈 가장 적당한 접속어는?

| 풀이 | 접속어 앞뒤의 내용을 살펴보면, 침팬지는 한 번 호흡시 한 단어 이상의 발화가 불가능한 반면,

인간은 한 호흡을 여러 번으로 나눌 수 있다는 상반된 내용이 나타나 있다. 따라서 반대되는 내용을 끌어오는 접속어가 필요하다.

| 정답 | (c) In contrast

20. blank 2에 들어갈 내용으로 알맞은 것은?

| 풀이 | 내용상으로 봤을 때, 빈칸의 앞 부분에는 침팬지와 인간의 웃음을 비교하면서 호흡과 단어 발화와의 관계를 설명하고 있다.
따라서, 웃음이 언어생활을 증명하는 한 시도가 될 수 있다고 추측해 볼 수 있다.
문장 구조상으로 보면, but other apes can't와 대응할 수 있는 구조는 S can + V 의 구조이다. 이런 구조를 가진 문장을 찾는 것도 한 방법이 될 수 있다.

| 정답 | (a) Why human can speak

예제 21~25

고등학교에서 시행되는 의무 자원봉사는 좋은 생각이 아니다. 첫째로, 많은 학생들이 자원봉사를 하긴 하지만, 그들의 대부분은 억지로 한다. 자원봉사를 하는 학생이 3학년이 될 때까지, 그 학생은 총 천시간 이상의 봉사 시간을 얻을 수 있다. 만약 갓 입학한 신입생이 미리 몇 시간의 자원봉사를 반드시 해야 한다는 이야기를 듣는다면, 그 학생은 화를 내고, 주어진 시간을 다 채우긴 하지만 다시는 자원봉사를 하지 않을 것이다. 그리고 자원봉사를 하는 시간은 지금보다 더 줄어들 것이다.

많은 학생들이 자원봉사를 할 시간이 없다. 학교는 시작부터 끝까지 정해진 시간에 따라 움직인다. 숙제 외에는, 학생들이 방과 후에 해야 할 일은 없다.

_______, 의무 자원봉사는 모순적이다. 만약 학생들이 자원봉사를 강요당한다면, 그것은 더 이상 자원봉사가 아니다. 수행평가(자원봉사)는 고등학교를 졸업하기 위한 또 하나의 과제일 뿐인 것이다. (자원봉사)활동의 질이 크게 훼손될 수 있다. 만약 학생들이 자원봉사를 원한다면, 그들은 말하지 않아도 자원봉사를 할 것이다.

21. 이 글의 중심 생각은 무엇인가?

| 풀이 | 이 글은 의무적으로 시행되고 있는 자원봉사 수행평가가 여러 가지 이유에서 부적합함을 지적하고 있다. 자원봉사가 오히려 학생들의 도덕적 활동을 장려하는 것이 아니라 지속적이고 자발적인 봉사를 방해하는 결과를 초래할 수 있다고 경고하고 있는 것이다.

| 정답 | (a) Mandatory volunteering has reverse effects.

| 오답 | (b) 고등학생을 위한 자원봉사제도는 좋지 않은 생각이라고 글의 전반부에 밝히고 있다.

22. 학생들이 강제적으로 자원봉사를 강요당했을 때 일어나지 않는 일은?

| 풀이 | 본문의 5-6줄에 잘 나타나 있다.

| 정답 | (d) enjoy volunteering seriously

23. 글의 내용에 비추어 볼 때, 'mandatory'는 무엇을 뜻하는가?

| 풀이 | 이 글은 처음부터 끝까지 의무적인 봉사활동에 대해 비판하는 내용을 담고 있다.
따라서 의무나 강요를 나타내는 단어를 찾으면 된다.

| 정답 | (a) obligatory

24. 밑줄 친 부분에 들어갈 접속어로 알맞은 것은?

| 풀이 | 처음에 의무적으로 시행되는 자원봉사활동이 좋지 않음을 제시하고 그에 따른 이유를 제시하고 있다. 첫번째는 많은 학생들이 억지로 해서 결국 자원봉사를 하지 않게 될 것이라는 것. 두 번째는 두번째 단락에 나오듯이 학생들이 봉사활동을 할 시간이 충분치 못하다는 것. 그리고 나서 셋째 단락에서 결국 이러한 제도가 모순적임을 다시 한 번 결론내리고 있다.
따라서 결론을 제시하는 접속어가 필요하다.

| 정답 | (b) Finally

25. 'Mandatory volunteering is an oxymoron.'을 잘 풀어서 설명한 문장은?

| 풀이 | 'oxymoron'은 모순어법이란 뜻을 지니고 있다.
의무적인 봉사활동이 모순되고 실제적인 가치가 없음을 표현한 문장을 찾으면 된다.

| 정답 | (a) Required volunteering is a thing of no worth as sincere volunteering.

예제 26~30

금성, 지구, 그리고 화성은 (처음에는) 비록 동일하게 탄소와 물을 가지고 있었지만, 크기나 태양으로부터의 거리가 달라 서로 다른 방향으로 진화하였습니다.

태양에서 가장 가까운 금성은 가장 많은 태양 에너지를 받았습니다. 금성 역사 초기에는 그 곳에 대양이 있었습니다. 그 당시에는 태양 광선도 지금처럼 밝지 않았습니다. 하지만 태양광선의 방출이 증가하면서 물이 끓어 증발해버렸습니다. 반면에 화산은 대기 중에 이산화탄소를 방출했습니다. 금성은 탄소를 탄소바위와 같이 단단한 물질로 바꿀 물이 부족했고, 이산화탄소량은 무한대로 증가했습니다. 이러한 상황이 "온실"을 만들어냈고, 태양에너지가 금성 대기 중에 침투하기는 하지만, 그 열기가 다시 빠져나가는 것은 막았습니다. 지금 금성의 온도는 너무 높아서 원시생물조차도 살 수 없게 되었습니다.

지구는 물을 보유할 수 있을 만큼 태양에서 충분히 멀리 떨어져 있습니다. 지구는 판구조학을 통해 탄소를 재생합니다(단단한 탄소물질의 구조를 변화시킴). 물의 장기 보존은 해양생물의 진화를 가능하게 했고, 그들이 이제는 대기에서 이산화탄소를 제거하는 역할을 합니다. 판구조학은 화산활동과 함께 계속적으로 이산화탄소를 대기 중으로 되돌립니다. 따라서 (제거와 방출의) 평형으로, 지구의 기후는 적당합니다.

한 때는 화성도 역시 적당한 기후와 물이 흐르는 표면을 가졌었지만, 구조적으로 덜 발달하였습니다. 그 결과, 이산화탄소가 대기에서 제거되고 다시 돌아오지 않았습니다. 따라서 '온실효과'가 약화되었고, 물이 얼어 지대가 높고 건조한 행성으로 남겨졌습니다.

26. 이 글의 중심 생각은 무엇인가?

| 풀이 | 이 글은 금성, 지구, 화성이 어떤 과정을 거쳐 지금의 모습을 갖게 되었는지를 대조해서 보여주고 있다.

| 정답 | (b) The different development of three planets

| 오답 | (a)는 세 화성의 초기 모습을 설명하는 부분에서 잠깐 언급되었다.

27. 세 화성의 생성 초기에 가졌던 공통점은 다음 중 무엇인가?

| 풀이 | 글의 첫 부분에서 언급된다. 세 화성 모두 초기에는 물과 탄소를 보유하고 있었다.

| 정답 | (b) Water and carbon resources

28. 여기서 'greenhouse'이 의미하는 바는?

| 풀이 | 대기 중의 이산화탄소 농도가 증가하고, 그래서 태양에너지를 받아들이기는 하지만, 다시 빠져나가는 것을 막아 행성의 온도가 높아지는 현상이 바로 '온실효과'이다.

| 정답 | (d) an entrapment of heat from the Sun(태양열을 가두어 나가지 못하게 함)

| 오답 | (b) a removal of carbon dioxide from the atmosphere
➡ 이산화탄소가 제거되는 것이 아니라 대기 중 이산화탄소 농도가 증가해야 한다.

29. 'it'이 가리키는 것은?

| 풀이 | 주어진 단어가 포함되어 있는 문장을 살펴보면, 대기 중의 이산화탄소가 제거는 되었지만, 대기 중에 다시 생성되지는 않았다는 내용을 담고 있다.

| 정답 | (d) the atmosphere

30. 위 글을 통해 현재 화성의 기후가 어떻다는 것을 알 수 있는가?

| 풀이 | 화성에 관한 이야기는 제일 마지막 문단에서 찾을 수 있다. 이산화탄소가 다 빠져나가 버린 화성은 '온실효과'의 약화로 물이 얼고, 건조한 행성이 되었다.

| 정답 | (c) cold

예제 31~34

어떤 사람들은 스포츠로 심해 다이빙을 즐긴다. 하지만 대부분의 다이버들에게 심해 다이빙은 물 속에서 이뤄져야 하는 그들의 작업에 이르는 한 방법일 뿐이다. 예를 들어, 심해 다이버들은 침몰한 배를 끌어올린다. 그들은 다리와 방파제를 위한 물 속 기초를 세우는 것을 돕는다. 때때로 다이버들은 가라앉은 배의 화물칸에서 금과 은, 또는 다른 귀한 화물 같은 굉장한 보물을 찾기도 한다. 다이버들은 물에 들어가는 매 순간마다 위험에 직면한다.

다이버의 생명은 수면에서 호스를 통해 주어지는 규칙적인 산소의 공급에 달려있다. 다이버들은 대개 무거운 잠수복과 금속 헬멧을 쓰는데, 그것들은 움직이기가 불편하다. 다이버들은 종종 진흙과 가는 모래로 가득 찬 앞이 제대로 보이지도 않는 얼음처럼 차가운 물을 손으로 더듬으며 가야만 한다. 급류가 다이버를 장애물을 향해 내던지고, 산소 호스를 엉키게 할 수도 있다. 만약 다이버가 수면으로 너무 급하게 상승하면, 그는 'bends'라 불리는 질병으로 고통을 겪을 수도 있다.

네 가지 대표적인 부류의 심해 다이버가 있다. 직업적인 다이버들은 침몰선이나 화물, 침몰한 항공기 등을 인양하고, 둑과 방파제, 부두 다리와 파이프라인을 만들거나 수리하는 것을 돕는다. 공해 다이버들은 해면동물, 진주조개, 해초와 그 밖의 다른 해산물을 거두어들인다. 탐사 다이버들은 원유를 찾아 대양의 바닥을 조사하고, 해양생활, 지질학, 해양학과 관련된 과학적인 조사를 지휘한다. 군사다이버들은 항구 방위를 철저히 하고, 항구의 지뢰를 없애고, 해안을 정찰하고, 또한 침몰한 배와 항공기를 인양한다.

31. 심해 다이버들이 호흡하는 공기는 무엇을 통해 공급되는가?

| 풀이 | 심해 다이버들은 호스를 통해 수면 위에서 제공해 주는 산소로 호흡한다.

| 정답 | (d) an aqualung (잠수용 수중 호흡기)

32. 이 글을 가장 잘 묘사하는 제목으로 적당한 것은?

| 풀이 | 이 글은 심해 다이버들의 잠수를 이야기하면서 네 종류의 각기 다른 분야에서 종사하는 다이버들의 일을 소개하고 있다.

| 정답 | (d) deep-sea diving

| 오답 | (b) diving for sunken ship → 본문에 침몰선을 인양하는 다이버의 활동이 묘사되어 있어 (b)를 답으로 고르기 쉽다.
하지만, 계속해서 강조해 오고 있듯이 주제와 제목은 글의 내용을 포괄적으로 포함해야 한다. 네 종류의 다이버를 모두 포함하는 것은 바로 deep-sea diver이다.

33. 다이버는 bends라고 불리는 병으로 고통을 당할 수도 있다고 한다. “bends”가 의미하는 것은?

| 풀이 | 다이버가 갑자기 수면으로 상승할 때 걸리는 병으로 묘사되고 있다. 따라서 잠수나 다이빙과 관련되는 병이어야 한다.

| 정답 | (c) caisson disease 케이슨병, 잠함병

| 오답 | (a) yellow fever 황열병, (b) poliomyelitis 소아마비, (d) rheumatic fever 류머티스열

34. 양식 진주를 기르는 사람이 될 수 있는 심해 다이버의 종류는?

| 풀이 | 심해 다이버 중 진주 및 해산물을 채취하는 사람은 공해 다이버(open-sea diver)이다.

| 정답 | (b) open sea diver

예제 35~40

1952년 이후 미국의 경제는 풍요했고, 거의 대부분의 사람이 일자리를 가지고 있었다. 1950년대를 나타내는 전형적인 해인 1955년도 경제 조사는 50년대의 상황을 잘 나타내준다. 국가 전체의 생산은 1954년보다 10%가량 증가했다. 제조업계의 생산은 제2차 세계대전 직후 몇 해 동안의 평균 생산량보다 40%나 증가했다. 국가사업에서는 약 3,000만 달러를 새로운 계획과 기계류에 투자했다. 지출이 가능한 국가 수입은 1950년도에 비해 거의 3배가 증가했다. 소비자들은 2,560억 달러를 소비했는데, 그것은 매일 약 7억 달러, 시간당 약 2,500만 달러에 해당한다. 6,500만 명의 사람들이 직업을 가졌고, 단지 2백만이 약간 넘는 사람들만이 원하는 직업을 구하지 못했다. 오직 농업만이 이러한 붐에 합류하지 못했다. 농민들이 생산을 덜 할수록, 시장가격은 상승했다. 그러나 국가 경제를 비관적으로 보는 사람은 거의 없었다. 비관론자들은 이러한 번영이 정부에 의한 거대한 규모의 갑작스런 추진에 의한 것이라고 걱정하는 듯하다.

35. 이 글은 무엇에 관한 내용인가?

| 풀이 | 이 글은 1950년대 미국의 경제상황을 전반적으로 소개하면서 당시 미국의 경제가 농업이 아닌 제조업을 중심으로 급성장했음을 보여주고 있다.

| 정답 | (d) the general economic situation in the 1950s.

| 오답 | (a), (b), (c)는 모두 본문 중 일부의 내용만을 담고 있어서 주제로는 부적당하다.

36. 본문에 따르면, 1955년 미국의 지출 가능한 국가수입이 1950년에 비해 얼마나 증가했는가?

| 풀이 | National income available for spending was nearly a third greater than it had been in 1950. 거의 세 배가 증가했다고 말해준다.

| 정답 | (b) 33%

37. 약 몇 명의 사람들이 1955년에 직업을 가지지 못했는가?

| 풀이 | a little more than two million wanted jobs but could not find them.

| 정답 | (b) Two million

38. 본문의 글은 1955년 대부분의 미국인들이 그들의 국가 경제를 어떠한 관점에서 바라보았다는 것을 나타내는가?

| 풀이 | 1950년대 미국의 경제성장을 비판적으로 바라본 사람은 거의 없다고 했다. 따라서 대부분의 미국인들은 국가의 경제성장에 대해 낙관적이고 긍정적인 생각을 지녔다고 쉽게 추측할 수가 있다.

| 정답 | (d) optimism → 주어진 보기 중 d만이 긍정적인 의미를 담고 있다.

| 오답 | (a) distrust 불신하는 (b) cynicism 냉소 (c) confusion 혼란

39. 다음 중 어떤 부류의 사람들이 1950년대 국가 경제를 덜 만족스럽게 여기는가?

| 풀이 | 오직 농업만이 경제성장의 흐름에 합류하지 못했다고 말했다.

| 정답 | (a) Farmers

40. "boom"을 대체할 수 있는 가장 좋은 단어는?

| 풀이 | 글의 전반부에 미국의 경제가 급속히 성장했음을 보여주고 있고, 뒤이어 농업만이 이러한 '붐'에 끼이지 못한다고 했으므로, '붐'이란 바로 경제가 빠르게 성장하는 양상을 나타내는 말임을 추측할 수 있다.

| 정답 | (d) rapid economic growth

⊃ 예제 41~45

그러나 과학의 성공은 과학의 '자기 수정'이라는 특성에 근거한 것이다. 이 과정에는 유효한 아이디어를 점검하는 과정이 있어야 한다. 어떤 유효한 실험도 재수행하는 것이 가능해야 한다. 과학자들의 신념이나 성격은 관련이 없다; 문제는 증거가 그들의 주장을 뒷받침하느냐 마느냐이다. 권위에 근거한 논쟁은 아무런 소용이 없다; 너무나도 많은 수의 권위 있는 사람들이 자주 실수를 저지른다. 나는 다양한 학파와 언론 매체에 의해 의사소통되는 매우 효율적인 과학적 사고의 방법을 보기 원한다. 그렇게 도출된 결론을 대중 앞에 소개하는 것을 보는 일은 굉장한 놀라움과 기쁨이 될 것이다. 과학자들은 새로운 증거나 새로운 논쟁이 제시될 때, 그들의 생각을 완전히 그리고 공식적으로 바꿔버린다. 나는 정치인이 (마음을) 바꾸는 개방성과 흔쾌함을 보여주었던 지난날을 다시 생각할 수가 없다.

41. 이 글의 중심 생각은 무엇인가?

| 풀이 | 이 글은 과학자들이 자신의 소견과는 다른 증거나 논쟁이 제기되었을 때, 무조건 자신의 의견을 포기하고 바꿔버리는 것은 정치인의 태도와 비슷한 것이라고 비판하고, 다양한 학술토론이나 언론 매체를 통한 효율적인 의사소통을 통해 효과적인 과학적 결론에 도달하기를 희망하는 내용을 담고 있다.
즉 문단의 첫 문장에 나와 있듯이 과학만이 가지는 고유한 특성인 '자기 수정/정정'의 과정이 과학 성공의 바탕임을 알리고 있다.

| 정답 | (c) An important characteristic of science

42. 이 글 바로 앞 문단의 내용으로 적당한 것은?

| 풀이 | 주어진 글의 첫 문장이 '그러나 과학적 성공은 '자기 수정'을 통해 달성된다'로 과학적 성공의 원인을 분석하면서 문단이 시작되고 있으므로, 그 이전에 나오는 문단의 내용은 과학적 성공이나 과학을 통해서 얻은 성취 그 자체에 관한 내용이 될 것이다.

| 정답 | (a) the achievements of science.

| 오답 | (b), (d)의 내용은 본문 자체에 언급되어 있다.

43. 만약 과학자가 여러 번 실험을 반복했는데, 매번 비슷한 결과를 얻지 못했다면, 그 실험은 어떠한 것인가?

| 풀이 | 주어진 글에서는 타당성이 있는 실험이나 생각을 valid(근거가 타당한)라는 단어를 써서 표현하고 있다. 실험을 할 때마다 서로 다른 결과가 나온다면, 그것은 제대로 된 근거가 마련되지 못한 비타당한 실험이 된다.

| 정답 | (c) invalid

44. 과학자의 수행 중에서 가장 본질적인 것을 다음에서 고르시오.

| 풀이 | 과학자의 주장이나 실험이 타당한 것인지를 분명히 하기 위해서는 그것을 뒷받침할 만한 유효한 증거가 있어야 한다.

| 정답 | (c) Evidence

45. 이 글의 작가는 사고의 과학적 양식이 무엇에 의해 보급되어야 한다고 주장하는가?

| 풀이 | 이 글의 작가는 다양한 학파와 언론 매체를 통한 활발한 논의를 통해 유효한 결론이 도출되며, 과학적 사고 이루어져야 한다고 본문에서 주장하고 있다.

| 정답 | a) newspapers ; media의 한 종류임으로 정답이 된다.

예제 46~50

비버들은 사냥꾼이 관찰한 바에 따르면 '비버들은 10계명에 가까이 따른다'는 전형적인 삶을 사는 것 같다. 10계명은 댐, 조그만 집, 인공수로를 건설하는 것에 대한 언급이 아니다. 그러나 비버의 이러한 성향은 마침내 그들을 곤경에 빠지게 했다. 중서부와 뉴잉글랜드 지방의 낚시광들은 비버의 댐이 송어의 흐름을 망친다고 불평하고 있다. 그리고 동남부지방의 목재회사들은 동물들이 상업적으로 가치가 있는 목재들을 물에 잠기게 할 때마다 항의한다. 그러나 몇몇 비버전문가들은 더 관대한 관점을 옹호한다. 그들이 말하기를, 역사적으로, 환경에서 이 생물의 영향은 굉장히 중요했다고 한다. '어떤 사람들은 비버를 매미나방과 같이 생각한다'고 과학자가 말했다. 그들은 비버를 단지 지나가고 먹고 파괴하는 동물로 생각한다. 그들이 이해하지 못한 것은 수 세기동안 이 동물이 그들이 점령하고 있는 숲과 시내의 특성을 조절해왔다는 사실이다.

46. 이 글에 가장 잘 어울리는 제목은?

| 풀이 | 이 글은 댐 짓기 선수인 비버에 대한 상반된 관점을 비교하고 있다.
낚시광들과 목재회사에서는 비버를 나쁘게 보지만, 과학자들은 비버가 환경에 긍정적인 영향을 미치고 있다고 하며 좋은 평가를 내린다.

| 정답 | (c) The Controversy over Beavers and the Environment

| 오답 | (b) The Influence of Beavers on Lumbering은 본문 내용의 한 부분일 뿐이다.

47. "has got it into a lot of hot water"의 의미를 가장 잘 표현한 것은?

| 풀이 | 일단 문자 그대로의 의미를 살펴보면, 뜨거운 물에 빠진다는 것은 좋지 않은 의미임을 쉽게 알 수 있다. 주어진 글의 문맥 속에서 살펴봐도, 낚시 광들과 목재회사 측에서 비버에 대해 불평하는 내용이 나오므로 아마 그들이 어려움에 처하는 내용을 포함하고 있을 것이라고 추측할 수 있다.

| 정답 | (c) are in trouble

48. 위 글에서 알 수 있는 매미나방의 특성은?

| 풀이 | ~ the gypsy moth.' said in scientist. They think it just comes through and eats and destroys.

| 정답 | (d) have a bad reputation.

49. 왜 목재 회사 측에서 비버에 대해 불평하는가?

| 풀이 | ~ lumber companies object whenever the animals flood out valuable stands of commercial timber.

| 정답 | (c) Because they create floods in forests. → 비버들이 댐이나 수로를 만들면서 숲으로 물이 흐르게 해서 목재들을 다 잠기게 한 것이다.

| 오답 | (b) Because they spoil trout streams.는 낚시 광들의 불평이다.

50. "it"이 지칭하는 것은 무엇인가?

| 정답 | (a) the beaver

| 오답 | (b)의 매미나방으로 착각할 친구들도 많을 듯싶다.
그러나 주어진 문장은 매미나방의 생태에 비유해서 '비버'의 생활을 묘사한 것이다.

예제 51~59

→[1] 정신 기능의 손실이 노인들과 관련 질병을 염려하는 가족들로 하여금 불안감을 느끼게 하는 가장 큰 원인입니다. 사람이 나이를 먹으면서, 이따금씩 건망증이 생기는 것은 건강한 사람들이 경험하는 유일한 변화일 것입니다. 그러나 노인 인구가 가지고 있는 건망증의 약 10%가 적당한 혼란을

초래하고, 다른 15%는 알츠하이머 타입의 노인성치매(SDAT)와 파킨슨병으로 불리는 노인성 질환으로 발전됩니다. SDAT(노인성치매)는 대뇌 출혈 또는 뇌의 특정 부분으로의 혈액 공급이 방해받아서 생기는 뇌세포의 손상이 있을 때 발병합니다. 심한 치매로 인한 일시적인 정신착란은 나트륨과 칼슘 수치의 변화, 갑상선 기능장애, 두뇌로의 산소 공급을 감소시키는 질병 치료를 위한 약품의 독성 등을 포함하는 심한 전해질의 방해로 인해 발생할 수 있습니다. 뇌세포의 심각한 손실로 인한 SDAT에서 기인한 인지 기능의 변화는 되돌릴 수가 없습니다.

→² 약 백만명의 미국인이 파킨슨병을 앓습니다. 비록 이 질병이 50세 이하의 사람들에게는 흔하지 않지만, 연령이 높아질수록 질병은 증가하고, 약 75세가 되면 최고조에 달합니다. 파킨슨병은 신경전달물질인 도파민을 생산하는 역할을 담당하는 두뇌의 일부분이 신경을 손실함으로써 발병합니다. 도파민이 더 이상 충분한 양만큼 생산되지 않을 때, 근육경직과 경련, 다리를 저는 걸음걸이와 같은 파킨슨병의 주요 증상이 증거로 나타납니다. 파킨슨병을 치료하기 위해서 체내의 자연적인 도파민 공급을 원활히 하는 엘도파(levodopa; L-dopa)가 사용됩니다. 더 많은 신경을 잃을수록, 환자는 증상을 완화시키기 위해 더욱 많은 양의 약품을 공급받게 됩니다.

최근의 연구는 신경 손실 속도를 늦춰서 치료에 사용되는 엘도파의 양을 줄일 수 있는 약품에 초점이 맞춰져 있습니다.

51. 이 글의 main topic은 무엇인가?

| 풀이 | 글쓴이는 정신 기능과 관련된 노인성 질환의 예로 두 가지-SDAT와 파킨슨병-를 들면서 발병 원인, 증상, 치료방법 등을 소개하고 있다.

| 정답 | (b) Age related disorders of the nervous System.

| 오답 | (a)를 답으로 선택하는 사람이 많은 줄 안다. 그러나 SDAT와 파킨슨병은 topic을 부연하는 예에 해당된다.

52. 1문단에 나와 있는 anxiety라는 단어와 의미상 유사한 단어나 표현을 역시 1문단에서 찾아보라.

| 풀이 | 정신 기능의 손실에 대한 노인들의 '걱정(anxiety)'을 언급하면서 관련 질병을 걱정(concerning)하는 가족에 대해서도 소개하고 있다.

| 정답 | concerning

53. 노인 인구의 첫번째 근심은 다음 중 무엇인가?

| 풀이 | Loss of mental function is the number one cause of anxiety in older individuals ~.

| 정답 | (b) Loss of mental function

54. 노인 인구의 몇 퍼센트가 SDAT와 파킨슨병을 앓는가?

| 풀이 | Another 15% of the older population develops two age-related disorders ~.

| 정답 | (c) 15%

55. 치매로 인한 정신착란의 요인으로 글에서 언급되지 않은 것은?

| 풀이 | ~ can arise from acute electrolyte disturbances, (중략) thyroid dysfunction, drug toxicity, of illnesses that decreases the oxygen supply to the brain.

| 정답 | (d) Cerebral hemorrhage → 뇌세포가 손실되는 요인에 해당된다.

56. 이 글에 따르면, SDAT의 주요 원인은 무엇인가?

| 풀이 | SDAT develops when there is a loss of brain cells ~.

| 정답 | (a) Loss of brain cells

| 오답 | (b), (c)는 뇌세포의 손실을 가져오는 요인에 해당된다. 다시 말해, SDAT 발병의 간접적인 요인이 되는 것이다.

57. 위 글에 따르면, 몇 살에서 파킨슨병이 최고조에 달하는가?

| 풀이 | ~ the incidence increase with age and peaks about age 75.

| 정답 | (a) 75 years

58. 위 글에서 파킨슨병의 증상으로 언급되지 않은 것은?

| 풀이 | ~ the characteristic symptoms of Parkinson's disease which is muscular rigidity tremors, difficulty with balance, and a shuffling gait become evident.

| 정답 | (d) Loss of muscle

59. 위 글에 따르면 엘도바(levodopa)는 무엇을 보충해줍니까?

| 풀이 | ~ the drug levodopa is used to supplement the body's natural supply of dopamine.

| 정답 | (b) Dopamine

예제 60~70

→[1] 1880년대 중반동안 시카고건축공학학회는 철근콘크리트와 금속의 원리에 관해 성공적으로 연구하고 실험을 했다. 그들의 이러한 노력은 당시에는 높이 솟은 건물로 알려졌던 건물의 설계에서 두 가지 재료의 엄청난 발전을 가지고 왔다. 그 후에, Sullivan, Burnham, Root, Holabird, Roche 등의 공학자가 초고층건물의 개념을 발전시켰다. 이 원리는 단단한 무쇠대신 금속으로 만든 골격구조에 바탕을 두고 있었다. 금속 골격은 건물에 엄청난 수직상태를 제공하였다.

다음에 철근 콘크리트(1인치 짜리 금속 막대를 안에 박아 넣은 콘크리트 판)는 금속 골격에 볼트로 죄어지고 용접된다. 초고층 빌딩이 건축학적인 디자인뿐만 아니라 역사적인 디자인을 가지고 건축되기 시작한 것은 1990년대 초부터였다. 예를 들어, 1911년에서 1913년 사이에 Cass Gillbert에 의해 설계된 Woolworth Buildings은 신 고딕 장식의 형태에 초점을 맞추었다. 이러한 디자인 흐름은 1925년까지 계속된다. McKenzie, Voorhies, Gemlinlab라는 건축가들이 건축 디자인을 표현 쪽으로 강화한 것은 1920년대 중반 동안의 일이었다.

→[3] 이러한 설계 원리는 'International Style Design'으로 알려졌다. Shreve, Lamb, Harmon라는 건축가들은 이러한 건물 디자인을 1931년 엠파이어스테이트빌딩을 건축하는 데 이용했다. 엠파이어스테이트빌딩은 1250피트의 엄청난 높이와 30만 톤이 넘는 무게를 가지고 있다. 끝으로 Raymond Hood라는 건축가는 1931년에서 1939년 사이에 편편한 원반 모양의 고층 건물을 여러 개 설계했다. 이 설계 구조의 한 예가 뉴욕에 있는 거대한 록펠러 센터로 그것은 아름다운 아말감을 이용해 실용적으로 건물의 틀 작업을 했었다.

요약해보면, 금속과 강화 콘크리트의 관계가 오늘날에도 여전히 이용되는 역사적인 주요 빌딩의 건축에 있어서 기술과 건축의 이용을 잘 결합시켰음을 알 수 있다.

60. 이 글에 가장 잘 어울리는 제목은?

| 풀이 | 제목은 topic을 포함해야 한다. 위 글에서 글쓴이는 철근 콘크리트와 금속이 어떻게 해서 건축에 사용되게 되었고, 이것의 사용으로 고층 건물이 발달하기 시작했음을 주요 빌딩들을 예로 들면서 설명하고 있다.

| 정답 | (b) The background of skyscraper construction

| 오답 | a, c, d는 topic을 이야기하기 위한 부연 설명들이다.(too specific)

61. 첫 문단에 나와 있는 concept의 의미를 잘 살펴보고 이것과 가장 유사한 의미를 지니는 단어를 세 번째 문단에서 찾아보아라.

| 풀이 | 대개 'concept'을 개념으로 이해하기 쉽지만, 여기서는 철근 콘크리트와 금속을 건축에 이용하기까지 그 원리를 연구하고 검증하는 과정을 말하고 있다.

| 정답 | principle

62. 첫 분단에 나와있는 Their를 살펴보고 그것이 지칭하는 다른 단어나 구를 같은 문단에서 찾아보아라.

| 풀이 | 그들의 노력이 건축 발전에 있어서 철근 콘크리트와 금속의 발전을 가져왔다고 말하고 있으므로, 여기서 그들이란 이 원리를 밝혀 낸 시카고건축공학학회를 의미한다.

| 정답 | the Chicago School of Architectures and Engineers

63. 위 글에 의해서 추론할 때, 19세기 초에는 건물의 건축을 위해 어떤 재료를 사용했나?

| 풀이 | 19세기 초는 1800년대 초를 의미한다. 본문에 따르면 1800년대 중반에 들어서 철근 콘크리트와 금속의 원리가 밝혀졌고, 이후에 건축에 사용되었다고 하고 있다.
This concept was based on skeletal structures made of steel instead of cast iron.
결국, 금속을 이용해서 건물을 짓기 이전에는 cast iron이 쓰였음을 알 수 있다.

| 정답 | (d) Concrete and cast iron

64. 위 글에 따르면 고층 건물을 짓는 재료가 어떻게 바뀌었음을 알 수 있나?

| 풀이 | concrete → reinforced concrete로, iron → steel로 바뀌었다.

| 정답 | (a) Iron → Steel

65. 위 글에 따르면 누가 신 고딕 스타일을 초고층 건물을 짓는 데 이용하였나?

| 풀이 | ~ designed by Cass Gillbert (중략) focused around neo-gothic ornamental form.

| 정답 | (b) Gillbert

66. 'International style design'의 주요 초점은 무엇인가?

| 풀이 | ~ intensified construction design towards expression. This construction principle became known as International Style Design.

| 정답 | (a) Expression

67. 엠파이어스테이트빌딩을 건축한 사람에 해당되지 않는 인물은?

| 풀이 | Architects Shreve, Lamb and Harmon further developed this design in building the Empire State Building

| 정답 | (d) Raymond

68. 첫 문단에 있는 lead와 가장 의미가 유사한 단어나 표현을 세번째 문단에서 찾아라.

| 풀이 | 시카고 학회원들의 노력이 건축에 있어서 엄청난 발전을 '이끌었다, 성취했다'로 해석될 수 있다.

| 정답 | achieved

69. 셋째 문단에 나와있는 this design이 지칭하는 다른 낱말이나 표현을 같은 문단에서 찾아 써라.

| 풀이 | 지금 International Style Design을 설명하면서 몇몇의 건축가들이 엠파이어스테이트빌딩을 설계하는 데 그 디자인을 사용했다고 말하고 있다.

| 정답 | International Style (Design)

70. 이 글에 따르면, 어떤 건물이 편편한 원반 모양으로 설계되었는가?

| 풀이 | ~ designed several disk-shaped skyscrapers during the period of 1931 to 1939. An example of this design structure is the immense Rockefeller Center ~.

| 정답 | (b) Rockefeller center

예제 71~81

→[1] 중국의 야생지대에서만 태어나고 서식하는 자이언트팬더는 때때로 팬더곰이라고도 불리지만, 이 때 사용되는 곰의 개념은 과학계에서 특히 동물학계에서는 전적으로 받아들여지지 않는다. 이 문제의 일부는 또 다른 팬더류, 즉 붉은팬더가 존재한다는 사실에서 비롯된다. 붉은팬더는 자이언트팬더보다 작은데, 약 170센티미터에 달하는 자이언트팬더에 비해서 붉은팬더는 길이가 약 60센티미터밖에 안 된다. 그들의 무게도 또한 다양해서 자이언트팬더는 무게가 약 90에서 140킬로미터인데 비해, 붉은팬더는 거의 50킬로미터가 최고이다. 크기와 관련한 차이와 연관지어서 이 두 포유류는 모습에서도 또한 차이를 보인다. 붉은팬더는 당신이 쉽게 추측할 수 있듯이 색깔이 붉고 털은 길고 부드럽다. 이 동물은 꼬리 근처에 고리가 있다는 이유로 종종 너구리와 비교된다. 반면에 자이언트팬더는 색깔이 희고 붉으며, 꼬리는 매우 짧고 색깔은 완전히 검다.

→[2] 이 두 동물은 모두 대나무를 먹는 다는 점에서 공통점이 있긴 하지만, 자이언트팬더가 오로지 대나무만 먹는데 반해서 붉은팬더는 오히려 영양분을 보충하기 위해 부분적으로만 대나무를 섭취하고 과일이나 열매 등도 먹는다. ■a 이 두 동물이 하루에 먹는 먹이의 양은 여러 가지 원인에 의해 다양하다. ■b 첫 번째, 그리고 아마도 가장 명백한 이유는 두 동물의 엄청난 크기의 차이일 것이다. ■c 다른 이유는 너무나도 비효율적인 소화 체계와 관련이 있는데, 이러한 사실 때문에 자이언트팬더는 하루에 40킬로그램의 대나무를 먹는다. ■d 이러한 사실에 근거해서 우리는 우리의 초점을 이 두 동물의 생활습관으로 돌릴 때에도 겉으로 드러난 차이점에 대한 근거에 기초를 둘 수 있다. 붉은팬더는 하루 중 대부분의 시간을 나무에서 자는 데 쓰고, 새벽녘이든 황혼이든 아님 둘 다든 오직 먹기 위해서만 땅 위로 내려온다. 반대로 자이언트팬더는 하루 중 대부분의 시간을 먹이를 찾는 데에 소비해야만 한다.

→[3] 이러한 전제 위에 이 글의 앞에서 제기되었던 의문은 이제 이해될 것이지만, 그러나 아직 대답은 몇 가지 의문을 남긴다. 초보자로서 몇몇 동물학자들은 자이언트팬더가 덩치가 크고, 그들의 유전자(DNA)가 곰의 것과 비슷하다는 인식 속에서 곰과 닮았기 때문에 곰과에 위치시켜야 한다고 생각한다. 붉은팬더의 DNA는 곰보다는 너구리의 유전자와 더 잘 맞고, 또 붉은팬더는 너구리처럼 앞발로 물건을 잡을 수 있는 능력이 있다. 이것 외에 세 번째 가능성은 곰과 이면서 자이언트팬더 뿐만 아니라 붉은팬더도 포함할 수 있는 새로운 동물과를 하나 만드는 것이다.

71. 글쓴이의 main purpose는 무엇인가?

| 풀이 | 글쓴이는 '팬더'의 개념이 명확하지 않음을 처음에 지적하면서, 자이언트팬더와 붉은팬더의 크기, 식성, 생활습관 등의 차이점을 보여주고, 따라서 새로운 팬더의 분류 체계가 필요하다고 주장하고 있다.

| 정답 | (c) To compare the habit of two pandas

| 오답 | a, d는 두 팬더를 비교하는 데 있어 사용한 부연 설명에 해당된다.(too specific)

72. 첫 번째 문단에서 글쓴이가 자이언트팬더와 붉은 팬더를 처음으로 비교하는 문장을 찾아라.

| 풀이 | 첫 번째 비교는 크기에서 시작된다.

| 정답 | The red panda is smaller than the giant panda, – (Line 4–5)

73. 첫 문단에 있는 approximately와 가장 가까운 의미를 지니는 단어나 표현을 같은 문단에서 찾아라.(2개)

| 풀이 | 'approximately'는 '대략 약'이라는 뜻이다.

| 정답 | about/around

74. 첫 문단에 있는 scales와 가장 의미가 가까운 단어나 표현을 같은 문단에서 찾아라.

| 풀이 | 사전적인 의미는 '규모'로 여기서는 두 가지 팬더의 몸집을 비교하고 있으므로, 몸의 크기라고 보면 된다.

| 정답 | size

75. 위 글에 언급된 자이언트팬더와 붉은팬더를 비교한 예가 아닌 것은?

| 풀이 | 위 글에서는 두 팬더의 크기와 색깔, 식성, 생활습관, 그들의 유전자 구조를 차례로 비교하고 있다.

| 정답 | (d) Their inhabitation
➡ 자이언트팬더와 붉은 팬더는 모두 중국의 야생지대에 서식한다.

76. 첫 문단에 있는 밑줄 친 it이 지칭하는 것은?

| 풀이 | 붉은 팬더에 대해 묘사하고 있는 부분이다. 너구리와 비슷하게 꼬리 근처에 둥근 고리모양의 무늬가 있는 것은 바로 붉은 팬더이다.

| 정답 | red panda

77. 위 글에 따라, 붉은 팬더는 자이언트팬더 외에 무엇과 비교되고 있는가?

| 풀이 | This animal is often compared to the raccoon ~.

| 정답 | (a) Raccoon

78. 위 글에 따르면, 자이언트팬더는 하루 중 대부분의 시간을 어떻게 보내는가?

| 풀이 | The giant panda ~ spend a vast majority of its day in search of or eating food.

| 정답 | (b) Eating food

79. 두 번째 문단에 있는 reason과 뜻이 가장 가까운 단어나 표현을 같은 문단에서 찾아라.

| 풀이 | 두 팬더가 하루 동안 섭취하는 먹이의 양이 다르다고 소개하면서 그 '이유'를 설명하고 있다.

| 정답 | impetus ▶ 먹이의 양이 다름을 설명하고 나서, 이제 생활습관의 차이를 설명하면서 앞에서 예로 든 그러한 '근거'에 기본을 둘 수 있다고 말하고 있다.

80. 다음의 문장은 어디에 들어가야 하는가?

| 풀이 | "the bigger your are the more you have to eat."
주어진 문장은 '더 클수록 더 많이 먹는다'이다.
이것은 몸집의 차이에 따라 먹는 먹이의 양이 달라진다는 설명을 보충하는 것이므로 일단 크기가 언급된 문장과 관련이 있다. 따라서 크기의 차이를 general하게 언급한 b 문장 다음에 보다 specific한 주어진 문장이 삽입되면 된다.

| 정답 | ▌c

81. 세 번째 문장에 나와있는 DNA와 가장 가까운 의미를 지닌 단어나 표현을 같은 문단에서 찾아 써라.

| 풀이 | DNA는 'deoxyribonucleic acid'의 약자이다.

⊃ 예제 82~92

→[1] ▌a 이러한 연구과정이 점차 정교해지면서 사회학이나 인간 행동과 관련한 가정들에 대해 더욱 중요한 조사와 검사를 허락했다. ▌b 연구 노력에 대한 특별한 관심은 특히 세 그룹의 연구자들에게 있었다. ▌c 그들은 미네소타대학의 Rogers와 David Johnson, 존스 홉킨스대학의 Robert Slavin 그리고 텔아비브대학의 Shlomo Sharon이다. ▌d

→[2] Slavin과 Johnson 팀은 사회집단의 교수 모형에 대한 가정을 연구하는 데 있어 조금은 다른 전략을 사용했다. 근본적으로 그들의 연구는 협동 과제와 보상 구조가 긍정적인 학습 효과를 일으키는지 아닌지를 분석하는 것이었다. 또한, 그들은 협동 학습 과정에서 향상이 일어나는지를 알아보기 위해서 집단 사이의 관계, 협동 행위, 그리고 응집에 대한 논점들을 연구했다. 거기다 더하여 그들은 학생들이 반드시 완수해야 할 "전통적인 과업"을 수행할 때의 보상 구조와 협동 과업의 효과를 연구했다.

→[3] 협동 그룹이 그룹에서 생겨나는 에너지 덕분에 학습이 증진되는지에 대한 질문에 대답을 한다면 "yes"이다. 이것은 학생들이 큰 그룹을 만들어 집단으로 학습하고, 학생들끼리 서로 가르치고, 긍정적인 보상을 나눈 교실에서 증명되었다. 학생들을 개인적으로 학습시킨 반대 접근은 과제 수행에서 훨씬 더 좋지 않은 결과를 가져왔다. 또한, 협동 학습 모델은 그룹 사이의 관계를 증진시키고, 낮은 성취감을 가졌던 사람들에 대해서 자기 이미지를 강화하고, 과업에 대해 보다 긍정적인 느낌을

갖도록 한다.

→[4] Shlomo sharon의 연구 노력은 모델의 원동력에 더욱 초점을 맞추었다. 그와 그의 동료들은 그룹간 관계와 지시의 강약에 따른 성취의 효과에 대해 분석했다. 여기에 더하여, Joyce, Showers 그리고 Baveja라는 연구자들은 협동 학습 모델을 다른 모델과 연합하여 연구했다. 그들의 연구는 구체적으로 협동 그룹의 개념과 협동 그룹 안에서의 귀납적 절차를 조사하는 것이었다. 연구 결과는 강화된 정보처리 대 집중적인 개인학습을 받은 학생들을 비교함으로써 증명되었다.

82. 이 글에 가장 잘 맞는 제목은 무엇인가?

| 풀이 | 위 글은 협동 학습 모델에 대한 여러 연구자들의 연구를 소개하고 있다.

| 정답 | (c) Cooperative learning model

| 오답 | (d)와 비교해 봤을 때, 연구자들이 단순히 협동학습의 효과만을 연구하진 않았다.(too specific) 그들이 협동학습의 원리, 방법, 과정을 전반적으로 연구했음을 글의 내용을 통해 알 수 있다.

83. 첫 번째 문단에 있는 research와 가장 가까운 의미를 지닌 단어를 네 번째 문단에서 찾아 써라.

| 풀이 | 보통 research는 조사라고 말하지만, 여기서는 보다 학술적이고 넓은 의미에서 연구라고 해석하는 것이 좋다. 연구에는 조사(investigation)하고, 분석(analysis)하는 모든 과정이 포함된다.

| 정답 | study

TIP 보통 비슷한 의미를 가진 낱말을 찾아 쓰라고 했을 때, 특별한 경우를 제외하고는 품사까지 동일한 단어를 찾는 것이 좋다.

84. 첫 번째 문단에 있는 investigators와 가장 가까운 의미를 지닌 단어나 표현을 넷째 문단에서 찾아 써라.

| 정답 | investigators는 조사자, 연구자를 의미한다.

| 오답 | researchers

85. 아래에 주어진 문장은 1문단 중 어디에 들어가는 것이 좋은가?

| 풀이 | "Cooperative learning models have recently generated renewed research efforts."
"협동학습모델은 최근 새로운 연구 노력에 의해 파생되었다"라는 문장이다.
1문단의 첫 번째 문장을 보면, 'these research'가 나온다. theses는 알다시피 앞에서 나온 명사를 다시 한 번 지칭할 때 사용하는 지시대명사이다. 따라서 앞에 research에 관한 내용이 나오고 그것의 반복을 피하려고 했음을 알 수 있다. 따라서 주어진 문장은 첫 번째 문단의 맨 앞에 와야 하는 것이다.

| 정답 | a

86. 두 번째 문단의 밑줄 친 they가 지칭하는 바를 찾아 써라.

| 풀이 | 두 번째 문단에서는 Slavin과 Johnson 팀의 연구를 소개하고 있다.

| 정답 | the teams of Slavin and Johnson

87. 세 번째 문단에 있는 improved와 가장 뜻이 비슷한 단어나 표현을 같은 문단에서 찾아 써라.

| 풀이 | 협동그룹이 학습을 '증진시켰는지'에 대해서 연구한 것을 소개하고 있다.
➡ improved는 학습이 더 나아지고 좋아진 상태를 설명하는 말이다.

| 정답 | enhanced 증진시키다, 강화하다

88. 세 번째 문단에 있는 lower과 뜻이 가장 가까운 단어나 표현을 같은 문단에서 찾아 써라.

| 풀이 | 여기서 사용된 lower는 가장 보편적인 의미인 '더 낮은' 이 아닌, 연구 결과가 '더 부정적으로, 좋지 않게' 나왔다는 의미로 쓰는 것이 자연스럽다.

| 정답 | poor

89. 누구의 연구가 학습모델의 원동력에 초점을 맞추었는가?

| 풀이 | Shlomo sharon's research efforts have focused more on the dynamics of the model.

| 정답 | (a) Shlomo Sharon

90. 위 글에 따르면 누가 협동그룹의 개념에 대해 연구했는가?

| 풀이 | Joyce, Showers and Baveja ~. Their study specifically investigated the concept and inductive procedures in cooperative groups.

| 정답 | (a) Baveja

91. 위 글에 따라, Joyce의 연구에 근거하면, 어떤 그룹의 정보처리기능이 강화되는가?

| 풀이 | The study result demonstrated enhanced information processing versus a group of students that received intensive individual study.
➡ 개인적으로 강도 높은 학습을 한 학생들과 비교해서 정보처리 기능이 강화된 그룹이므로 개인이 아닌 협동 학습 그룹이 된다.

| 정답 | (a) Cooperative study group

92. 위 글에 이어질 문단의 내용으로 가장 적합한 것은?

| 풀이 | 계속해서 협동그룹의 학습효과를 긍정하다가 위 글의 마지막에서 역시 강도 높은 학습을 하는 개인과 그룹을 비교했을 때 그룹학습을 한 학생들의 정보처리기능이 강화되었다고 설명하고 있다. 따라서 이어질 글에서는 그러면 왜 위험을 무릅쓰고 강도 높은 학습을 한 학생이 그룹에 비해 학습을 실패하게 되는지를 설명할 것이다.

| 정답 | (c) risk student's disruptive behavior

예제 93~102

→[1] 뼈의 움직임이 일어나는 곳은 신체의 관절입니다. 그 움직임 자체는 근육이라고 불리는 매우 단단한 조직의 시트와 인대의 당김에 의해서 일어납니다. 근육조직은 스스로 수축되는 특별한 능력을 지니고 있기 때문에 뼈 위에 붙어있는 근육을 당기면 뼈는 움직여야만 합니다. 근육조직이 수축되면 주름도 생깁니다. 근육조직은 피부와 뼈대 사이에 있는 근막과 힘줄로 신체를 덮습니다. 뼈는 신체의 틀이지만, 근육은 우리 몸을 모양이 나게 채웁니다. 대부분의 근육은 뼈와 뼈로 이어집니다. 뼈 사이에

있는 근육이 수축되면, 한쪽 뼈는 움직여야만 합니다. 움직이지 않는 뼈 쪽에 근육이 붙어있는 지점을 근육의 수점이라고 하고, 반대로 움직이는 뼈 쪽에 근육이 붙어있는 지점을 삽입점이라 부릅니다. 때때로 근육은 뼈에 바로 붙어있지 않고, 강하고 펴지지 않는 인대 또는 뼈에 붙어있는 건에 붙어있습니다.

→² 근육은 밀지 않습니다. 근육은 오로지 당길 수만 있습니다. 팔꿈치를 굽히기 위해서 위쪽 팔의 앞쪽에 있는 근육은 수축되고 주름져야만 합니다. 팔을 펴기 위해서는, 팔의 뒤쪽에 있는 다른 근육이 수축되어야 합니다. 이와 같은 앞쪽과 뒤쪽의 근육 세트는 서로 반대로 움직입니다. 한쪽이 일을 하면, 다른 쪽은 대개 쉬고 있습니다. 하지만 양쪽이 다 일을 할 때도 있습니다. 때때로 근육은 한 방향으로 당기는 것처럼 단순한 것보다 더 많은 일을 요구받을 때가 있습니다. 근육은 회전운동을 해야 할지도 모릅니다. 그러기 위해서, 근육은 뼈에 한 각도로 붙어야만 합니다. 근육을 당김으로써, 그것을 축으로 하여 뼈가 선회하도록 할 수 있습니다.

→³ 어떤 근육들은 특별한 기능을 합니다. 예를 들어, 횡경막은 폐로 하여금 공기를 받아들이도록 합니다. 이러한 호흡의 일부는 근본적으로 뼈의 움직임과 관련된 작동이 아닙니다.

93. 첫 문단에 나오는 'it'이 가리키는 것은?

| 풀이 | 'the bone on which it pulls has to move.'에서 which는 바로 앞에 나오는 bone을 가리킨다. 뼈 위에서 뼈를 당겨 움직이게 하는 것은 바로 뼈에 붙어있는 근육이다.

| 정답 | (a) muscle

94. 이 글의 main subject는 무엇인가?

| 풀이 | 위 글은 근육의 구조와 종류, 붙어있는 위치에 따른 명칭, 근육의 움직임과 그에 따라 뼈가 움직이는 원리 등을 소개하고 있다.

| 정답 | (d) The anatomy and operation of human muscles

➡ anatomy는 해부학으로 구조, 위치 등이 여기에 해당된다.

95. 위 글에 따르면, 움직임은 근육이 어떻게 될 때 일어나는가?

| 풀이 | When the muscle between the bones shortens, one bone has to move.

| 정답 | (b) shortens

96. 첫 문단에 있는 attached와 가장 가까운 의미를 지니는 것은?

| 풀이 | 근육이 뼈에 바로 '붙어있지' 않은 경우도 있다는 것을 설명하는 부분이다.

| 정답 | (b) fixed in place

| 오답 | (a) detached 떨어진

97. 움직이는 뼈 쪽에 근육이 붙어있는 지점을 무엇이라 하는가?

| 풀이 | ~the point where the muscle is fastened to the bone that is to be moved is called the insertion.

| 정답 | (b) insertion

98. 두 번째 문단의 밑줄 친 unbend와 의미가 가장 가까운 것은?

| 풀이 | unbend는 bend의 반대이다. 따라서 '구부리다'의 반대인 '펴다'의 뜻이 된다.

| 정답 | (c) straighten

| 오답 | (a) upright도 '똑바로 선'의 의미로 해석된다. 하지만, 가능성이 있는 두 개의 단어가 있을 때는 품사까지도 고려하는 것이 좋다고 앞에서 설명하였다.

99. 두 번째 문단에 있는 called upon과 의미가 가장 가까운 것은?

| 풀이 | 때때로 근육은 좀 더 복잡한 운동을 해야 할 때가 있다. 즉 그러한 운동을 요구받을 때가 있는 것이다.

| 정답 | (a) required

100. 위 글을 통해 팔을 구부리기 위해서 서로 반대쪽에 있는 근육과 뼈의 움직임은 어떻게 됨을 추론할 수 있는가?

| 풀이 | These two sets of muscles are said to act in opposition to each other.

| 정답 | (b) the use of different muscles

101. 왜 어떤 근육들은 뼈에 한 각도로 붙어야 하는가?

| 풀이 | ~ have to perform a turning motion. To be able to do this, the muscle must be attached to the bone at an angle.

| 정답 | (d) To perform a turning action

102. 첫 문단에 있는 take in과 의미가 가장 비슷한 것은?

| 풀이 | 폐가 공기를 '받아들인다, 흡수한다'는 말이다.

| 정답 | (a) receive

⊃ 예제 103~113

→1 미국이 담당해야하는 제1차 세계대전의 비용은 부상을 포함한 생명의 손실, 참전용사에 대한 후속급여를 제외하고도 거의 인간의 상상을 초월하는 액수이다. 다른 정부에 빌려준 약 95억 달러를 포함하여 전쟁선포 이후 삼년 동안의 직접적인 비용만 해도 대략 355억 달러였다. 이것은 연방정부 설립 이래 초기 백년 동안의 연방정부 총지출의 세배에 해당되는 것이었고, 전쟁선포 이후 25개월 동안 일년에 백만 달러이상을 소비한 것과 같았다.

→2 전쟁이 경제에 가져다 준 첫 번째 문제는 "비용의 얼마를 세금으로 충당하고, 얼마를 차용해야 할까?'하는 것이었다. 다시 말해, 비용의 얼마만큼을 다음 세대의 등에 짊어지게 해야 할 것인가? 하는 문제였다. 밝혀진 바에 의하면, 약 3분의 1이 세금에 의해서, 그리고 나머지가 차용에 의해서 충당되었다. 전쟁세입법안을 시작했을 때, 의회에서는 소득세, 상속세, 소비세를 올렸고, 초과 이윤과 사치품에 대해 세금을 부과하기 시작했다. 그러나 의회는 낮은 관세 원칙만큼은 고수했다.

→3 정부가 빌린 돈은 네 가지의 "자유공채"와 한 가지의 "승리공채"로 획득되었다. 전쟁 전과는 다르게, 정부는 전에는 한 번도 국채를 보지 못했던 수백만의 사람들에게 50달러 정도의 낮은 액면가

로 국채를 팖으로써 국민들에게 직접 호소했다. 22만 명이 넘는 사람들이 "자유공채"에 서명했다. 모든 공채가 모집액 이상이 신청되었고, 약 215억 달러가 충당되었다. 전쟁기간 동안 정부는 결코 기금이나 신용의 부족으로 고통받지 않았다.

103. 이 글의 main topic은 무엇인가?

| 풀이 | 글쓴이는 글을 통해 미국이 제1차 세계대전 이후 부담해야 했던 전쟁 관련 비용을 국민들의 세금과 각종 공채 등을 통해 부족하지 않게 마련했음을 소개하고 있다.

| 정답 | (d) Paying for the First World War

| 오답 | (a) patriotism(애국심) → 군인이 아닌 국민들의 애국심이 발휘되었다.

104. 첫 번째 문단의 exclusive of와 의미가 가장 가까운 것은?

| 풀이 | '~을 제외하고'의 의미를 나타낸다.

| 정답 | (c) not including 포함하지 않고

| 오답 | (d) unacceptable 받아들이기 어려운

105. 위 글에서 언급된 355억 달러에는 다음 중 무엇이 포함되는가?

| 풀이 | Including nearly $9,500,000,000 lent to foreign governments, the direct cost ~was around $35,500,000,000.

| 정답 | (b) Loans to foreign government

106. 첫 번째 문단에 나오는 expenditures와 의미가 가장 가까운 것은?

| 풀이 | '지출'이라는 뜻을 나타낸다.

| 정답 | (a) expenses 지출, 비용

| 오답 | (b) casualties 불상사 (c) losses 손실 (d) expensive 비싼

107. 첫 번째 문단에 있는 its가 가리키는 것은?

| 풀이 | 전쟁비용이 연방정부 지출의 세 배에 달한다고 설명하면서, 보다 구체적으로 그것(연방정부)이 존재하고 나서 초기 백년 동안의 지출보다 세배가 더 많다고 설명하고 있다.

| 정답 | (d) federal government

108. 첫 번째 문단에서 언급된 백만 달러에 해당되는 것은 다음 중 무엇인가?

| 풀이 | ~over $1,000,000 an hour during the 25 months following the declaration of war.

| 정답 | (a) The hourly cost of the war for approximately two years

109. 전쟁 중에 경제적으로 직면한 첫 번째 문제는?

| 풀이 | The first problem to be settled in financing the war was, "What proportion of the cost was to be borne by taxes, and what proportion by loans?"

| 정답 | (d) What part of the cost of the war should be paid by taxes and what part by borrowing.

110. 두 번째 문단에 있는 subsequent와 의미가 가장 유사한 것은?

| 풀이 | 만약 전쟁자금을 획득하기 위해 개인이나 다른 정부를 상대로 빚을 진다면 그것을 갚는 것은 앞으로 올 세대의 몫이 된다. 'subsequent'는 '앞으로 올', 즉, '다음의, 후의'의 뜻을 지닌다.

| 정답 | (d) following

| 오답 | (a) subordinate 하위의, 종속적인 (b) subsidiary 보조의

111. 두 번째 문단의 principle과 의미가 가장 유사한 것은?

| 풀이 | 의원들이 전쟁자금 마련을 위해 다양한 정책을 폈지만, 낮은 관세와 관련한 '원칙, 방침'만큼은 확고히 했다는 것을 설명하고 있다.

| 정답 | (c) fundamental rule(근본방침)

| 오답 | (a) integrity 성실, 완전 (d) arrangement 정돈, 협정

112. 전쟁을 돕기 위해 조성된 세금의 종류가 아닌 것은?

| 풀이 | ~ raised the income, inheritance, and excise taxes, and inaugurated taxes on excess profits and luxuries.

| 정답 | (c) Tariff

113. 세 번째 문단에 있는 inadequate과 의미가 가장 유사한 것은?

| 풀이 | '부적당한, 불충분한' 등의 뜻으로 쓰이는 단어이다. 여기서는 전쟁자금을 충당하기 위해 여러 방법으로 모아진 돈이 많고 적음을 평가하고 있으므로 '부적당한' 보다는 '불충분한'이 더 어울린다.

| 정답 | (a) insufficient

| 오답 | (b) indefinite 불명확한 (c) impiety 불손한 (d) dissatisfied 불만족스러운

예제 114~123

→1 원룸학교는 미국 유산 중 하나이지만, 원룸학교에 대한 언급은 사람들로 하여금 "사물이 있었던 방식"에 대한 막연한 갈망을 느끼게 한다. 그러나 원룸학교는 소멸될 위기에 처한 종이다. 백년이 넘도록 원룸학교는 제도적으로 금지되었고, 그곳의 학생들은 중앙의 학교로 보내졌다. 1930년까지 미국에는 14만 9,000개의 원룸학교가 있었다. 1970년까지는 1800개가 있었다. 오늘날에는 약 800개의 원룸학교만이 남았고, 그 중 350개 이상이 네브라스카에 있다. 나머지 학교는 몇몇 다른 주에 흩어져 있는데, 대개 지도 위에서 보면 마을 사이의 넓은 공간에 있다.

→2 이제는 (원룸학교의) 개척자를 만족시켰듯이 오늘날에도 또한 교육자를 만족시킬 무엇인가가 거의 남아있지 않지만, 교육자들은 어쩌면 아직도 원룸학교를 통해서 배울 만한 것이 있을지도 모른다고 생각하기 시작했다. 진보적인 교육자들은 교육과정에 있어서 원룸학교에서 자연적으로 발생했던 '동료집단교수'나 '다연령집단'처럼 진보적으로 들리는 이름들을 좇아간다. 원룸학교에서는 교사가 다른 누군가를 가르치느라 늘 바쁘기 때문에 학생들이 서로를 가르친다. 4학년 학생은 유급이나 월반과 관련한 오점 없이 수학은 5학년 수준, 영어는 3학년 수준을 공부할 수 있다. 학습능력이 없는 학생은 다른 소년과 분리되지 않은 상태에서 자기의 수준을 찾을 수 있다. 오늘날의 조금 더 큰 도시나 교외 학교에서는 이것을 "차별교육철폐론"이라고 부른다. 교실이 하나밖에 없는 작은 학교에서 몇

시간을 보내고, 많은 부모들이 네브라스카에 사는 것의 이점 중 하나가 자녀들이 학교에 가야하기 때문인 것이라고 느끼는 이유가 이제는 분명해진다.

114. 첫 번째 문단에 나오는 heritage와 의미가 가장 유사한 것은?

| 풀이 | 원룸학교는 미국에서 1930년 이전부터 전해져 내려오는 '유산' 중 하나이다.

| 정답 | (b) inheritance(상속, 물려받은 것)

| 오답 | (a) fate 운명, (c) emission 발산, (d) hereby 이단, 이교

115. 이 글을 쓴 글쓴이의 main purpose는 무엇인가?

| 풀이 | 글쓴이는 글을 통해 원룸학교가 비록 제도적으로 금지되어 그 수가 현저히 줄어들긴 했지만, 협동학습이나 개인 수준별 학습 등이 가능한 점을 들어서 오늘날 교육에도 적용점이 많으며, 또한 많은 학부모들도 이제는 원룸학교를 선호하고 있다고 소개하고 있다.

| 정답 | (b) To mention some advantages of one-room schools

| 오답 | (a) To discuss present-day education → 실제 내용보다 광범위하다(too general)
(d) To summarize the history of education in the United States → 이것 역시 미국 전체의 교육을 말하고 있으므로 너무 광범위하다(too general)

116. 지은이는 오늘날 많은 교육자들과 학부모들이 원룸학교를 어떻게 느끼고 있다고 말하고 있는가?

| 풀이 | educators are beginning to think that there is something to be learned from ~.
many parents feel that one of the advantages of living in Nebraska ~.
➡ 이제 교육자들과 학부모들은 원룸 학교의 이점을 인정하고 받아들이려고 한다.

| 정답 | (d) provide a good education

117. 첫 번째 문단에 있는 vague와 의미가 가장 유사한 것은?

| 풀이 | 원룸학교가 '사물이 원래 있었던 방법', 즉 여기서는 '교육이 원래 갖췄던 모습, 원래의 교육방법'에 대해 사람들로 하여금 '막연한, 모호한' 동경을 느끼게끔 한다고 하고 있다.

| 정답 | (a) ambiguous

| 오답 | (b) distinct 별개의, 뚜렷한 (c) tenacious 고집하는 (d) abstruse 난해한

118. 위 글에 따르면 왜 원룸스쿨이 사라질 위기에 처했는가?

| 풀이 | ~ and their students sent away to centralized schools.

| 정답 | (c) There is a trend toward centralization

119. 두 번째 문단에 있는 served와 의미가 가장 가까운 것은?

| 풀이 | 전혀 새로운 교육형태였던 원룸학교를 개척하기 위해서는 원룸학교의 선구자들을 '뒷받침할, 도울' 무엇인가가 필요했다.

| 정답 | (c) aided

| 오답 | (a) relieved 구제하다, 긴장을 풀게 하다
(b) legalized 공인하다, 법으로 인정하다
(d) ejected 쫓아내다, 추방하다

120. 위 글에 따르면 오늘날 미국에는 약 몇 개의 원룸학교가 있는가?

| 풀이 | Today, of the nearly 800 remaining one-room schools, ~.

| 정답 | (c) 800

121. 두 번째 문단에 나온 come up with와 의미가 가장 유사한 것은?

| 풀이 | 진보적인 교육자들은 보다 진보적인 교육형태를 '생각하고, 제안'한다.

| 정답 | (a) thought of

| 오답 | (b) made up with -과 화해하다
(c) named 명명하다, 이름을 붙이다
(d) predicted 예언하다, 예보하다

122. 두 번째 문단에서 원룸학교제도의 주요 특징으로 언급된 것은?

| 풀이 | A fourth grader can work at a fifth-grade level in math and a third-grade level in English ~.

| 정답 | (d) It does not limit learning to one grade level at a time

| 오답 | (a) It causes many children to be left back. (Line 17-18)
(b) It must work in conjunction with an urban school (Line 19)
(c) It does not allow teachers to do any individual teaching (Line 14-15)

123. 두 번째 문단에 나오는 stigma와 의미가 가장 가까운 것은?

| 풀이 | '오명, 치욕, 오점'의 뜻을 지닌다. 학생이 진급을 하지 못하고 유급당하거나, 월반을 강요당하는 것은 학생에게 있어서는 오점이 될 수도 있다.

| 정답 | (d) disgrace

| 오답 | (b) bequest 유산, (c) disparity 불균형

예제 124~133

→[1] 알래스카의 파이프라인은 북극의 차가운 끝에서 시작된다. 미국의 가장 크고 가장 북쪽에 있는 주를 거쳐 남쪽으로 이어지고, 시작 지점에서 거의 800마일쯤 떨어진 먼 얼음이 얼지 않는 항구 마을에서 끝난다. 파이프라인은 크기도 엄청나고 다루기도 굉장히 복잡하다.

→[2] 금속파이프는 바람 부는 광야와 언 땅을 덮고 끝없이 펼쳐져 있는 툰드라를 가로지른다. 구불구불한 협곡을 파헤쳐 나가고, 깎아지른 산을 넘고, 험한 바위산을 넘어서 깊은 숲을 지나, 수백 개의 강과 시내를 위로 건너고 아래로 건넌다. 파이프는 지름이 4피트이고, 매일 최고 2백만 베럴(84백만 갤론)의 천연 원유를 끌어올릴 수가 있다.

→[3] 파이프라인의 긴 부분은 "bents"라고 불리는 H자 모양의 금속대로 있으면서 얼어붙은 땅 위의 구불구불한 길을 따른다. 다른 긴 부분은 폭신하거나 또는 바위로 덮여있는 땅 바로 밑으로 들어갔다가 나중에 표면으로 나온다. 파이프라인의 아래위로 움직이는 패턴은 종종 북극과 북극 가까이의 기후와 비비꼬인 지층, 토양과 바위 또는 영구동토층의 다양한 복합 등의 혹독한 요구에 의해 결정된다. 파이프라인의 반 이상은 땅 위로 나와있다. 나머지는 지형의 유형과 토양의 특성에 근거하여 3에서 12피트 사이 아무데나 묻혀있다.

→4 세계에서 가장 큰 파이프라인 중 하나는 대략 80억 달러나 하고 그것은 지금까지 개인 산업체에서 수행한 건설작업 중에서 가장 크고 비용이 많이 드는 것이다. 사실, 어떠한 개인사업체도 그만한 돈을 모을 수는 없었고, 그래서 여덟 개의 거대한 정유회사가 그 비용을 분담하기 위해 협회를 형성했다. 각 회사는 유전에서 특정 지역에 바로 속한 원유를 차지했고 소유 정도에 따라 파이프라인 건설기금에 돈을 냈다. 오늘날, 기후와 공급 부족, 기구 파손, 노동력 부족, 위험한 지형, 수많은 그릇된 처리와 심지어는 도둑까지 많은 문제에도 불구하고, 알래스카 파이프라인은 완성되고 있고, 가동되고 있다.

124. 위 글은 파이프라인의 무엇에 대해 이야기하고 있는가?

| 풀이 | 파이프라인이 건설되는 원리, 세계에서 가장 큰 파이프라인의 건설 과정 등을 소개하고 있다.

| 정답 | (d) construction

125. 위 글에서 글쓴이가 파이프라인의 길을 결정하는 중요한 요인으로 언급하지 않은 것은?

| 풀이 | Line 13–15; route is determined by climate, the tortuous lay of the land, and the varied compositions of soil, rock, or permafrost.

| 정답 | (c) local vegetation

126. 세 번째 문단의 <u>tortuous</u>와 의미가 가장 가까운 것은?

| 풀이 | '구불구불한, 비뚤어진'의 의미를 가진다.

| 정답 | (d) crooked 구부러진, 굴곡

| 오답 | (b) rough 거친, 울퉁불퉁한

127. 세 번째 문단의 <u>permafrost</u>와 의미가 가장 가까운 것은?

| 풀이 | 본문 바로 다음에 설명되어 있다.

➡ ~ <u>permafrost</u> (permanently frozen ground)

| 정답 | (a) permanently frozen ground

128. 몇 개의 회사가 파이프라인 건설비용을 분담했나?

| 풀이 | ~ 8 major oil companies formed a consortium ~.

| 정답 | (c) Eight

129. 네 번째 문단의 <u>particular</u>과 의미가 가장 유사한 것은?

| 풀이 | '특별한, 특정의'란 뜻을 지닌다.

| 정답 | (b) specific

| 오답 | (a) peculiar 특유한, 이상한 (c) exceptional 예외의 (d) equal 동등한

130. 네 번째 문단의 <u>holdings</u>와 의미가 가장 가까운 것은?

| 풀이 | 회사들이 특정 지역의 원유를 개발함으로써 얻게 되는 '이익/이윤'을 의미한다.

| 정답 | (b) property

131. 협회의 각 회원 회사들이 건설비용의 몇 퍼센트를 지불하게 되는지는 다음 중 무엇에 의해 결정되는가?

| 풀이 | Each company controlled oil rights to particular shares of land in the oil fields and paid into the pipeline-construction fund according to the size of its holdings.

| 정답 | (a) How much oil field land each company owned

132. 글쓴이가 언제나 언 상태로 있는 지표면을 언급하는 용어를 제시하고 있는 곳은 어디인가?

| 풀이 | permafrost (permanently frozen ground)

| 정답 | (c) Line 15

133. 두 번째 문단의 treacherous와 의미가 가장 가까운 것은?

| 풀이 | 'treacherous'는 '위험이 뒤에 숨겨져 있는, 음험한'의 뜻을 지닌다. 여기서는 지형의 특성을 설명하고 있으므로 지형이 안전하지 않은, 불안정한의 뜻으로 해석하면 된다.

| 정답 | (c) unstable

| 오답 | (d) abbreviate (말 따위를) 단축하다

예제 134~144

→[1] 많은 무용 분야에 걸쳐있는 Martha Graham의 영역과 자부심 넘치는 무용 기술은 대단하지만 폐쇄되어있는 영역이다. 개인의 경험으로만 예술을 창조한다는 것이 결국에는 스스로를 제한하는 행위이기 때문이다. Graham의 재능과 위업을 가진 다른 안무가가 있었더라면, 그녀의 작품은 미국 무용사에서 좀 더 균형 있는 한 부분으로 여겨졌을지도 모른다. 그러나 그녀가 레파토리를 짤 때, 그녀만의 언어는 다른 종류의 언어를 모두 차단하는 것 같았다. 심지어 청중들이 그녀의 무용이 다른 스타일의 무용에서 영향 받은 흔적을 뚜렷하게 인식하고 있다고 생각할 때에도 Graham의 연극풍 작풍의 전세성과 의상과 조명의 통제, 그리고 무용으로 인한 모든 충격은 작품을 마치 신기루처럼 느끼도록 만들었다. 무용은 그녀의 주요 주제가 아니었다. 그것은 단지 그녀의 도구였다.

→[2] Graham은 1931년에 자율을 획득했다. 그 때까지, 20세기의 새로운 무용을 발명했던 세 명의 위대한 무용가인 Sergei Diaghilev, Anna Pavola, Isadora Duncan이 사망했다. 그들의 시대는 그들과 함께 끝났고, 그들 무용의 가치도 거의 사라졌다. 그들의 동료인 Michel Fokine과 Ruth St. Denis도 직장을 잃고 미국에서 살았다. 20세기 동안 Graham과 그녀의 동료들은 보드빌과 영화, 뮤지컬 코미디, 그리고 미국의 전원적인 방식의 모든 반향으로부터 예술 무용을 건져냈다. 하지만, 그렇게 함으로써 그들은 무용을 통해 다른 이들에게 전달할 수 있는 다양한 생각의 통로를 차단했다. 그리고 이러한 통로는 반세기 동안 닫혀졌다. 현대무용은 깊은 의미에 스스로를 바쳤다. 현대무용은 가벼움을 포기했고, 풍부한 이국적인 색깔을 포기했고, 어떤 종류의 연극적인 재치와 무용수와 무용수의 운율적이고 음악적인 소재사이의 오래된 변덕을 포기했다. 현대무용의 소재는 어떤 것도 중립적이지 않다. 예술의 핵심은 몸으로 표현되는 의미와 비유의 관념이 되었다. 현대무용은 우연한 공연, 이유 없는 명랑함, 자발적인 겉치레와 같은 연극적인 전통을 배척했고, 다양한 장르를 배척했다. 그러나 이 모든 것들이 대중의 영역에서는 생존했고, 그곳에서 언제나 존재했고, 단지 우연에 의해서라도 계속해서 미국무용에 나타났다.

134. 이 글의 main purpose는 무엇인가?

| 풀이 | Graham의 뛰어난 재능과 독창적인 작풍, 그녀의 무용이 현대 미술에 미친 영향 등을 소개하고 있다.

| 정답 | (a) To discuss Martha Graham's influences on modern dance

135. 첫 번째 문단의 innumerable과 의미가 가장 유사한 것은?

| 풀이 | '무수히 많은'이란 뜻을 지닌다.

| 정답 | (a) numerous

136. 위 글에 따르면, Graham의 무용과 기술에 가장 영향을 많이 미친 것은 무엇인가?

| 풀이 | ~to create an art out of one's experience alone is ultimately a self-limiting act.

| 정답 | (a) Her own experiences

137. 두 번째 문단의 achieved와 의미가 가장 유사한 것은?

| 풀이 | '이루다, 성취하다'의 의미를 나타낸다.

| 정답 | (a) attained

138. 두 번째 문단의 colleagues와 의미가 가장 유사한 것은?

| 풀이 | '(직업상의)동료, 친구'를 의미한다.

| 정답 | (a) co-workers

139. 두 번째 문단에서 글쓴이가 like whales on the beach라는 문구를 사용한 것은 Fokine과 St. Denis가 어떠했기 때문인가?

| 풀이 | 20세기의 새로운 무용을 만들어냈던 세 명의 위대한 무용가가 죽고, 그들의 동료는 할 일을 잃고 살아간다.
'해변 위의 돌고래'는 직역하면 원래 물 속에 있어야 할 돌고래가 갈 곳을 잃고, 또는 할 일을 잃고 있는 모습이다.

| 정답 | (c) out of place 제자리에 놓이지 않은, 어울리지 않는, 실직하여

140. 두 번째 문단의 mode와 의미가 가장 유사한 것은?

| 풀이 | '양식, 방식'의 의미를 지닌다.

| 정답 | (a) manner

141. 16-21째 줄에서 글쓴이는 Graham과 동료에 대해 어떤 비판을 제기하고 있는가?

| 풀이 | ~but in so doing they closed the channel through which different kinds of dance could speak to one another.

| 정답 | (d) They prevented modern dance from expanding beyond their personal interpretation.

142. 두 번째 문단의 these가 가리키는 것은?

| 풀이 | 반세기 동안 막힌 채로 있었던 주체가 되는 것이 'these'이고, 이것은 결국, 앞에 나오는 'the channel'을 가리킨다.

| 정답 | (d) channels

143. 두 번째 문단의 dedicated와 의미가 가장 유사한 것은?

| 풀이 | '바치다, 헌납하다, 드리다'의 뜻을 가진다.

| 정답 | (a) devoted

144. 두 번째 문단에 나오는 surface와 의미가 가장 유사한 것은?

| 풀이 | '표면'이라는 중심 의미와 함께 '나타나다, 겉으로 드러나다'의 뜻을 지닌다.

| 정답 | (a) emerge

예제 145~155

→[1] 1879년 토마스 애디슨에 의한 백열전구의 발명은 많은 양의 전기를 발생시키기 위한 값싸고, 쉽게 이용할 수 있는 연료의 수요를 창출했다. 석탄이 가격도 적당한 것 같았고, 최초의 발전소에 연료를 공급했다(발전소는 19세기 말 에디슨 자신에 의해 세워졌다). 전국에 걸쳐서 더 많은 발전소가 건설될수록, 석탄 의존도도 증가했다. 제1차 세계대전 이후로 화력 발전소는 매년 미국에서 생산되는 전기의 거의 반을 생산했다. 1986년에는 이러한 발전소들의 총 발전량이 28만 9천 메가와트였고, 그 해에 전국에서 캔 약 9억 톤에 달하는 석탄의 83%를 소비했다. 앞으로의 핵 발전소의 성장과 석유와 천연가스의 공급을 예측하지 못한 채로, 화력 발전소는 그 세기의 마지막까지 미국 전기의 70%를 공급할 수 있었다.

→[2] 그러나, 석탄이 오랫동안 전기의 원천이 되었고, 오랫동안 가장 큰 비율을 차지할 것(석탄은 미국 화석연료의 80%를 담당한다)이라는 사실에도 불구하고, 실제로 석탄은 발전소를 위한 가장 매력적인 화석연료는 결코 아니었다. 석탄은 천연가스나 석유보다 단위 발열량이 적고, 운반하기도 힘들고, 환경문제 중에서 산성비의 주범과 관련이 있다. 1980년대 이후에 배출 규제와 폐기물 처리 문제가 화력발전소의 등장을 급격히 감소시켰다. 화력발전소처럼 거대한 공장단지와 같은 시설을 짓는 비용도 증가하고 이와 함께 환경문제를 개선하기 위한 비용은 또한 순수한 경제적 관점에서도 그런 발전소를 덜 매력적으로 보이도록 만들었다.

→[3] 그러나 과학기술을 바탕으로 한 화력발전소의 변화는 그들의 매력을 회복시켰다. 이러한 변화의 일부는 진화론적이고 대부분이 현존하는 발전소의 생산력을 향상시키려는 것이었던 반면에, 석탄을 깨끗하게 연소시키기 위한 완전히 새로운 기술도 또한 발전하고 있다.

145. 위 글의 main idea는 무엇인가?

| 풀이 | 위 글을 통해 글쓴이가 말하고자 하는 것은 석탄을 원료로 하는 화력발전에 대한 것이다. 화력발전이 전력 생산에서 중요한 역할을 담당하다가 중간에 다른 연료의 등장과 환경문제로 인해 어려움을 겪기도 하지만, 그러나 기술발전을 바탕으로 한 진보로 보완을 거듭하면서 계속 발전의 중요한 역할을 담당할 것을 소개하고 있다.

| 정답 | (a) Coal-fired plants are an important source of electricity in the United States and are likely to remain so.

146. 첫 문단에 나오는 available과 의미가 가장 유사한 것은?

| 풀이 | 석탄이 값싸고 쉽게 '이용할 수 있는' 원료임을 설명하고 있다.

| 정답 | (d) attainable ➡ 이용하기 쉽다는 것은 그 원료로 접근/도달하기가 쉽다는 말로 이해할

수 있다.

| 오답 | (a) peaceable 평온한 (b) disposable 처분할 수 있는 (c) affable 상냥한

147. 첫 문단의 generate와 의미가 가장 유사한 것은?

| 풀이 | 전기를 '생산'하는 것이다.

| 정답 | (a) produce

148. 에디슨의 전구가 위 글에서 언급된 이유는?

| 풀이 | The invention by Edison created a demand for a cheap, readily available fuel with which to generate large amounts of electric power.

| 정답 | (b) increased the need for electrical power

149. 첫 번째 문단의 reliance와 의미가 가장 유사한 것은?

| 풀이 | 석탄을 이용한 화력발전소가 많아지면서 석탄에 대한 '의존도'가 높아졌다.

| 정답 | (d) dependence

| 오답 | (a) relocation 재배치 (b) barrier 장벽 (c) reluctance 싫음

150. 미국에서 석탄이 전력의 주원료가 된 이유 중 위 글에서 추론할 수 있는 것은?

| 풀이 | a demand for a cheap, readily available fuel; Coal seemed to fit the bill, ~.
➡ 첫째 문단 전반부의 내용을 통해서 석탄이 값싸고 쉽게 구할 수 있기 때문에 발전 원료로 가장 많이 사용되었음을 추론할 수 있다.

| 정답 | (b) was comparatively plentiful and inexpensive

| 오답 | (a) required no complicated machinery (Line 23–24)
(c) was easy to transport (Line 19)
(d) burned efficiently (Line 18–19)

151. 글쓴이의 견해에 따르면, 석탄을 원료로 한 전기의 중요성이 왜 증대될 수 있었다고 하는가?

| 풀이 | Line 11–14

| 정답 | (c) The future availability of other fuels is uncertain.

152. 산성비는 다음 중 어떤 이유로 위 글에서 언급되었는가?

| 풀이 | it(coal) is associated with a host of environmental issues, among them acid rain.
➡ 석탄과 관련한 환경문제 중 산성비가 지적되었기 때문에 점차 석탄을 원료로 한 화력발전의 수요가 줄었음을 설명하고 있다.

| 정답 | (c) It is an environmental problem associated with coal use.

153. 두 번째 문단의 complex와 의미가 가장 유사한 것은?

| 풀이 | 화력발전소는 상당히 '복잡한' 건물이다.

| 정답 | (c) complicated

154. 위 글에 따르면 화력발전소와 관련한 신기술의 목표 중 다음에 있는 것은 무엇인가?

| 풀이 | to increase the productivity of existing plant & for burning coal cleanly

| 정답 | (d) To increase the productivity of existing plants

155. 두 번째 문단의 mainly와 의미가 가장 가까운 것은?

'주로, 대부분'의 의미를 지닌다.

| 정답 | (a) largely

저자소개

■ 신 규 철

고려대학교 영어교육과 졸업
한국외국어대학교 대학원 영어과 졸업(영어학석사)
고려대학교 대학원 영어영문과 박사과정 졸업(Ph.D) (영어교육학박사)
고려대학교 · 한국외국어대학교 · 서울시립대학교 강사
동덕여자대학교대학원 강사
한국영어학학회/ 현대영어교육학회/ 한국영어어문교육학회 이사
미국 하와이대학교(University of Hawaii at Manoa) 언어학과 연구교수
극동대학교 영어학과 교수(언어교육연구소 소장)

[저 서]

주니어 토플
90단계 기초영문법
60단계 핵심영문법
차세대 One-Stop 영작문
Power Vocabulary in Reading
English Idioms 800
영어교육학
한국인을 위한 자동화영어학습법外 多數

핵심 영문 독해

1판 1쇄 찍음 • 2008년 2월 20일
1판 1쇄 펴냄 • 2008년 3월 3일

저 자 • 신 규 철
발행인 • 정 현 걸
발 행 • 신 아 사
인 쇄 • 남양인쇄

출판등록 • 1956년 1월 5일 (제9-52호)
서울특별시 은평구 녹번동 28-36 2F
전화 (02)382-6411 • 팩스 (02)382-6401
홈페이지 • www.shinasa.co.kr
E-mail • shinasa@chol.com

* 저자와의 협의로 인지를 생략함.

ISBN 978-89-8396-595-0

정가 **12,000**원